Multiparty Politics in Mississippi, 1877–1902

Multiparty Politics in Mississippi, 1877–1902

STEPHEN CRESSWELL

University Press of Mississippi
JACKSON

Copyright © 1995 by the University Press of Mississippi
All rights reserved
Manufactured in the United States of America

98 97 96 95   4 3 2 1

The paper in this book meets the guidelines for permanence and durability of
the Committee on Production Guidelines for Book Longevity of the Council
on Library Resources.

Library of Congress Cataloging-in-Publication Data

Cresswell, Stephen Edward.
  Multiparty politics in Mississippi, 1877–1902 / Stephen Cresswell.
    p.   cm.
  Includes bibliographical references and index.
  ISBN 0-87805-770-6 (alk. paper)
    1. Political parties—Mississippi—History. 2. Mississippi—
  Politics and government—1865–1950. I. Title.
  JK2295.M72C74 1995
  320.9762'09'034—dc20   94-44902
                                                             CIP

British Library Cataloging-in-Publication data available

To
TERESA,
the one who seems to make all things possible—
all of the important ones, anyway

Contents

Maps

Acknowledgments

I am glad to finally have a chance to publicly thank the hundreds of people who have helped me with the research for this book. The administration at West Virginia Wesleyan College did everything possible to aid me; a sabbatical leave in the spring of 1993 allowed me to write the final two chapters. I especially want to thank Academic Dean Thomas Mann, who provided abundant encouragement and help.

Also at West Virginia Wesleyan College, I want to thank the librarians, who went out of their way to help me find the materials I needed. It was not easy to research Mississippi history from West Virginia, but the staff of the Annie Merner Pfeiffer Library was not easily discouraged, and was able to provide me with a great number of books and microfilms. I especially want to thank interlibrary loan librarian Sue Dawson for her endless help.

The writing of this book gave me a welcome chance to return twice a year to my native state of Mississippi. While in the state, my home away from home was the Department of Archives and History in Jackson. The staff there cheerfully met a very large number of researchers every day and still provided a high quality of service. I owe a special debt to the staff of the Mitchell Memorial Library at Mississippi State University. They were kind enough to loan me hundreds of reels of microfilm newspapers on interlibrary loan, and to help me through the personal papers of a number of Mississippi politicians. The archivists at the McCain Library and Archives at the University of Southern Mississippi and at the John Davis Williams Library at the University of Mississippi provided invaluable help.

The early part of the research for this book came prior to the National Newspaper Project of microfilming and cataloging. Accordingly, I had the enjoyable experience of visiting a number of county courthouses and poring over the huge volumes of bound newspapers there. In particular I want to thank the clerks at the Pontotoc, Lafayette, Covington, and Benton County courthouses for their kind hospitality.

Outside Mississippi, I am indebted to the librarians and archivists at the Library of Congress; the United States Senate Library; the National Archives; the Federal Records Center at East Point, Georgia; the Southern Historical Collection at the University of North Carolina; and at the libraries of the University of Virginia, the University of Kentucky, and West Virginia University.

Among the archivists and librarians who have been especially helpful, in West Virginia, Mississippi, and elsewhere, are: Janne Abreo, Michael Ballard, Margaret Balli, Nancy Bass, Kathy Baxa, Carol Bowman, Sandra E. Boyd, Althena Church, Robert W. Coren, Benjamin Crutchfield, Dale Foster, Gene DeGruson, Dwight Harris, Michael Hennen, H. T. Holmes, Martha Irby, Terry S. Latour, Anne Lipscomb, Judith Martin, Carolyn Merrill, Madel Morgan, Lynn Mueller, Walter L. Newsome, David Nowak, Kathleen Parker, D. M. Pilcher, Murella Hebert Powell, Vera Richardson, Richard A. Shrader, and Mattie Sink.

I have benefited from the comments of a number of colleagues when I presented portions of this research at colloquia at West Virginia Wesleyan College, the University of Southern Mississippi, and the University of Virginia. Several faculty members were kind enough to evaluate parts of this work or prospectuses for it and write evaluations for grant-making bodies. These colleagues included Charles W. Eagles, John F. Marszalek, Robert Rupp, and John R. Skates, and I thank them for giving most generously of their time when all of them were deeply involved in their own research.

I want to acknowledge gratefully the support of a number of institutions and foundations that helped make this research possible by providing monetary support. These groups include the National Endowment for the Humanities Travel to Collections Program, the West Virginia Humanities Council Fellowships Program, and the Faculty Innovation Grants of West Virginia Wesleyan College. A one-semester leave funded by the Mellon Appalachian Fellowships program allowed me to do considerable research on Mississippi in 1876 and 1877, allowing me to understand more clearly the background of the period I am addressing here. Without the travel and research materials provided by these grants, this research would have been literally impossible.

For her energy, encouragement, and insights, I thank Seetha A-Srinivasan, the editor-in-chief at the University Press of Mississippi. Copy editor Anders Lars Thompson was a pleasure to work with, and I want to express my gratitude to him for the improvements he brought to the

manuscript. I also want to salute cartographer James Bier of Champaign, Illinois; photographer Deana Smith of Rock Cave, West Virginia; and photo curator Elaine Owens of the Mississippi Department of Archives and History at Jackson. These individuals were of immense help in preparing this volume for final production.

Finally, I want to pay tribute to my parents, William Ephraim Cresswell and Catherine Moore Cresswell. Although they raised me in Alexandria, Virginia, they sought to make me—in some degree—a Mississippian. Even in Virginia, their conversation was full of references to their childhood home of Durant and to the elusive Samuel Cresswell, who in the 1850s was hunting wild boars and selling wood to the steamboats from his farm near Belzoni. Even in our Virginia exile, they kept me current on the political careers of James P. Coleman, Sonny Montgomery, Ross Barnett, and a host of others. When I began to be interested in writing history, it seemed natural that I should write about Mississippi politics, and I thank my parents for fostering this interest. I also thank them for giving me nearly forty years of unbroken encouragement, support, and love.

Multiparty Politics in Mississippi, 1877–1902

ONE

Introduction

MISSISSIPPI HAS LONG BEEN DOMINATED BY THE DEMOCRATIC party. During the period from 1836 to 1960, the state's electoral votes went to the Whig or Republican presidential candidate in only two of the thirty-two campaigns. In only four elections out of forty-four did Mississippi choose a non-Democrat for governor in the long span of years from 1833 to 1987. At the level of the congressional district the non-Democrats did a little better, winning a handful of the seats before the Civil War and after 1875, and a majority of the seats during the brief period of congressional Reconstruction. Yet Mississippi elected only Democrats to Congress during the eight decades beginning in 1884. No other state showed this degree of devotion to the Democratic party.[1]

One-party politics, however, was not unique to Mississippi, nor to the southern states. Consider this comparison of Mississippi's vote in the 1888 presidential election with that of the great plains state of Kansas:

Mississippi: 7 counties Republican, 67 counties Democratic
Kansas: 80 counties Republican, 2 counties Democratic[2]

Vermont elected only Republican governors between 1854 and 1962. Iowa did not give a majority of its votes to a Democratic presidential candidate from 1856 to 1932. In Mississippi, South Carolina, Iowa, Vermont, Kan-

sas, and Minnesota, the second place presidential candidates regularly received an embarrassing 25 to 30 percent of the vote, or even less.[3]

None of these states, however, was a "one party state" in the most literal sense of the term. Mississippi and South Carolina did feature Republican state and local candidates, while Iowa, Vermont, Kansas, and Minnesota did have active Democratic parties. All these states also saw the rise of third-party movements, and because one of the major parties in the state was especially weak, these third-party movements often filled a vacuum and proved surprisingly strong. Yet if these states were not one-party states in the most literal sense of the term, certainly they qualified as one-party states in the way the term is usually used. A one-party state may be defined as a state that gives its overwhelming support to one party in virtually all statewide races. The term *opposition parties* will be used regularly in these pages; this phrase refers to the one major national party and all third parties that challenged the dominant party of a state's one-party system.

This book traces the history of opposition parties in the state of Mississippi in the last quarter of the nineteenth century. It will describe who joined these dissident movements, what they believed in, and what they accomplished. It will define the geographic area where each of the opposition parties wielded power, and will probe similarities and connections between the various dissident groups. The book will also assess why the opposition parties were not able to win statewide elections, even as Democratic incumbents were failing to solve the many problems the state faced.

Mississippi's inter-party political history divides logically into two parts. The first, comprising the twenty-five years after the end of Reconstruction, may be called the period of locally strong opposition parties. Although the Democratic party was dominant and invariably won the statewide races in this period, Mississippi did see the flourishing of a number of opposition movements, including the Republican, Greenback, Populist, Gold Democrat, and Prohibition parties, as well as a variety of Independent political groups. None of these organizations was able to carry the Magnolia State for its presidential or gubernatorial standard-bearer, but they sometimes demonstrated surprising strength at the level of the congressional district, the county, and the town.

The period of the locally strong opposition parties came to an end in 1902. In that year, for the first time in Mississippi history, no opposition

candidates challenged the Democrats for the state's congressional seats, and all eight Democrats were elected with 100 percent of the vote. Also in 1902 the legislature passed a primary election law making the Democratic primary—not the general election—Mississippi's most important political event.[4]

The second era of Mississippi's two-party politics may be briefly noted. Spanning the years 1902 through 1964, this was a period of skeleton opposition. Democratic candidates for statewide office usually went unchallenged in this era, as did most Democratic congressional candidates. When Republican, Socialist, or Independent candidates did run, they certainly could not be called locally strong. These opposition party candidates typically won 5 to 10 percent of the vote and almost never carried a county. By the early 1960s Republicans began to win a few offices in Mississippi, and the party elected a congressman by a large majority in 1964.

In studying Mississippi's opposition candidates, it is useful to change the rules of political analysis somewhat. In speaking of the nation as a whole, a presidential candidate who won less than 45 percent of the vote would be considered a weak candidate by historical standards. In Mississippi, a Republican or third-party candidate who won 45 percent would be doing very well indeed. Nationwide, the success of a political party may be measured by asking, "How many governors and U.S. senators have they elected, and how many state legislatures do they control?" But in Mississippi, meaningful comparisons of the strength of the various opposition movements are possible only if we do change the rules of comparison. In Mississippi's one-party system, a dissident party's winning a statewide election was a near impossibility. The carrying of one congressional district in one election was a signal achievement. The carrying of one or more counties became an important indication of success for a given party, even if success was confined to the local level.

By using these revised measures, comparisons of the influence of the several opposition parties are possible, as well as studies of change over time. The opposition parties did win some surprising successes. Republicans elected two members of Congress in the period 1877–1902, while Greenback-Republican fusionists elected one. Republican mayors presided over two of the largest cities, Vicksburg and Jackson, until the late 1880s. Important blocs of non-Democrats sat in the state legislature, too. In 1879 the non-Democrat members of the legislature numbered twenty-

seven, while in the 1894 special session they numbered twenty-five. By 1902, however, no group opposing the Democrats could even hope to carry a county. All cities and counties had Democratic governments, and inter-party competition for statewide offices, congressional seats, and even county offices became a rarity.

Politics was the most important spectator sport of the late nineteenth century in Mississippi as well as the rest of the United States. Most literate persons subscribed to a local newspaper affiliated with a political party, while many also belonged to neighborhood political clubs. Voter participation was high in Mississippi in 1877, reflecting keen interest in the activities of the various political parties and movements. Elections were an annual event in the state, with national elections (presidential and congressional) coming in even-numbered years and state elections (gubernatorial, legislative, and county) in odd-numbered years. Presidents and governors served four years, while congressmen, state legislators, and county officers served two. In 1890, the new constitution lengthened the terms for legislators and county officers to four years, bringing a modest reduction in the number of elections held. Mississippians found elections exciting. They attended great political barbecues where they heard string band music, enjoyed food provided by the candidates, and listened to speeches lasting three hours apiece.

An 1898 issue of the *Lawrence County Press* provided a portrait of the generic county candidate. As the election approached, the *Press* reported, "He goes to church oftener," and "takes more interest in the affairs of his neighbor." According to the Lawrence County editor, the face of the would-be candidate "broadens more regularly [into] a benignant smile as he approaches the good old friend whom he wishes to cultivate, and lengthens with the shadow of sadness that beclouds it when all is not well with the old codger." Some of the keenest interest was reserved for county politics, since the county officers had such important duties as law enforcement, upkeep of the roads, imposition of quarantines, recovery of stray livestock, foreclosure of mortgages, and assessment for state and local taxation.[5]

Interest in county races was also high because so many residents knew the candidates personally, which was not true at the district or state level. The county candidate who could call everyone by his or her first name was in a good position; even stronger was the nominee who could also ask about bird dogs and coon dogs by name. Some candidates benefited from

their ability to play the fiddle or to lead a singing school. Having a sizeable family was also an asset for the county candidate, and frequently two large families would form an alliance, agreeing to support each others' candidates. In rural areas, farmer candidates often would show their hands to voters they didn't know to prove that they were working men and not dandies who hoped to avoid work by getting a political office. A Webster County political observer recalled that typically the people "would reserve at least one office for a crippled person."[6]

At the county, district, and state levels, the candidates would travel together, making joint appearances before the voters. In presidential races, the presidential electors traveled and met the voters. Feelings often ran high and the language used at political rallies could be rough. Only a minority of the announcements of political meetings stated that the women of the community were invited to be present. Dozens of campaigns in the late nineteenth century featured dueling candidates or editors, the ambush of candidates or voters, and even riots in towns ranging from Coffeeville to Marion to Lexington.

On election day, political workers were at the polls distributing the ballots, which had been printed up by each party. To aid voters who were illiterate or nearly so, the two parties' ballots were often printed in different colors; the Republican ballot featured a picture of Lincoln, while the Democratic one had the traditional rooster. The secret ballot did not come to Mississippi until the early 1890s; prior to this voters had to live with the knowledge that their neighbors would know how they had voted. Influencing the votes of others by threats or by bribes was always possible, since the person doing the influencing could watch as the ballots were deposited.

Every county was divided into five districts, called *beats*. Each beat elected one member to the board of supervisors, which formed the legislative branch of county government. Each beat also elected minor judicial officers, usually two justices of the peace and one constable. The beats were divided into precincts, or voting places, for the convenience of voters, but there were no officers elected at the precinct level. The county's chief executive was the sheriff, and this generally was the most highly prized county office. Other important county offices were those of the treasurer, assessor, chancery clerk, and circuit clerk. All told, each county elected seven or eight officers, while the five beats elected four officers apiece. Each county also elected one or more members of the state house

of representatives. State senators usually were elected in conjunction with other counties, although the largest counties had senators wholly their own.

Mississippi in 1877 was an overwhelmingly rural and agricultural state. The 1870 census reported only one city with more than 10,000 persons (Vicksburg), while the state capital of Jackson had only 4,200 inhabitants. Incredibly, even under the Census Bureau's lenient definition of a "city" as any municipality with 2,500 residents, Mississippi had only five such places in 1870: Vicksburg, Natchez, Jackson, Meridian, and Columbus. Yet if Mississippi was not experiencing the wrenching pangs of urbanization, it *was* suffering from acute agricultural distress and going through a period of great social and economic change.[7]

This change was most distressing to the state's yeoman farmers. Prior to the Civil War, Mississippi's small farmers pursued an ideal of self-sufficiency, raising food crops and livestock to feed their families, and some cotton to earn cash to pay taxes and buy a few store-bought necessities. Outside the plantation counties, farmers had little trouble controlling local politics in these antebellum years. In the small towns lived a few merchants and professionals, but in numbers so low that the farmers' dominance of county politics was rarely threatened. In the Delta and black belt counties, a powerful slaveholding class exercised control on their vast plantations and also dominated county governments and enjoyed a strong voice in the state legislature. In the state capitol, farmers and planters were often at odds over such matters as tax policies.[8]

Immediately after the war, cotton prices were very high, and small farmers began to plant large amounts of the staple in order to take advantage of these prices. Farmers also felt the need to raise a cash crop to pay for improvements on their farms after the devastation and disruption of war and to pay the newly high taxes imposed by the Reconstruction state governments. New railroad lines brought food into the hinterlands as farmers deemphasized subsistence crops; railroads also brought guano, a fertilizer that could help compensate for declining soil quality. As farmers purchased food and fertilizer, they brought themselves ever deeper into the cash economy, and became increasingly tied to cotton. Because they received their income only once a year, when they sold the crop, farmers typically made purchases on credit, which also tied them into the commercial world, while furthering their movement away from self-sufficiency. Now in many counties, and in the state as a whole, there was a newly

strong political bloc: merchants and creditors. The merchants and their allies soon became great boosters of their localities, and often sought to use tax dollars to entice railroads and factories, or to build better roads and a more impressive courthouse. For their part, farmers wished above all else to keep taxes low, and they often found themselves locked in political battles with merchants and their allies.[9]

Indeed, farmers began any recitation of their ills by focusing on the general stores, located in small towns and in crossroads communities. In a cash poor state where relatively few banks were operating, farmers typically bought goods on credit from a local merchant. The merchant charged his credit customers considerably more for a given item than he charged his other patrons. In addition, he charged a flat 10 percent interest at the end of each year. This meant, for example, that purchases made just before settling time were assessed at an annualized rate of more than 100 percent. There were other fees as well, in many cases, making the farmers' cost of credit astronomical. To secure his loan, the merchant obtained a lien on the farmer's crop. At settlement time, the farmer was obligated to sell his crop directly to the merchant, and more often than not found that he had not earned enough from sale of the crop to pay for the purchases made during the year. In that case, the farmer would begin the new year already in the red.[10]

Thomas Jefferson once said that what made America great was its sturdy, independent farmers. Yet Mississippi's farmers no longer felt independent. They were badly in debt, did not really own their crops, and were in constant danger of losing their farms. Moreover, the storekeeper would often tell the farmers what to plant or even how to plant it as a condition of granting credit. Farmers who rented land often had to obtain a permission slip from their landlord before the merchant would sell them a hat or shoes (for example) on credit. While farmers' organizations such as the Grange denounced the reliance on one crop, merchants insisted on cotton because it was a cash crop that could readily be applied to the customers' debt.[11]

Matt Brown was a typical Mississippi farmer who lived at a community called Black Hawk, just northwest of the state's geographic center. He owned his own farm, but had to rely on credit at Ike Jones's store to make purchases of supplies. Brown began trading at Jones's establishment in 1884, but he never finished out the year in the black. The year 1892 in many ways was typical for Brown. Jones's ledgers for that year show Brown spending $35 on food, $29 on clothing, $10 on chewing tobacco, $.55 for

medicine, and $181 for supplies for the farm. Brown began 1892 indebted
to Jones in the amount of $227; by the end of the year this debt had grown
to $452, as his cotton crop did not bring nearly enough money to cover his
purchases. Evidence suggests that Brown eventually lost his farm to the
merchant, although he did continue to work the land. Ike Jones's record of
the life of Matt Brown ended in 1905 with charges for a coffin. In death,
Brown found economic release, as Jones simply wrote off the remaining
indebtedness. Many farmers like Matt Brown felt helpless anger as they
looked at the local merchant. The storekeeper was not, however, the only
villain farmers saw in their world.[12]

The farmer felt trapped in dealing with the local merchant, because the
actual cotton markets were so far away. If he could break out of the cycle
of perpetual indebtedness to the local merchant, the farmer could take
charge of his destiny by marketing his own crop and selling it to the
highest bidder. Here, though, transportation was a problem. Mississippi's
roads, built and maintained by each county's board of supervisors, were
abysmal. The railroad seemed to offer great promise, but farmers faced
what they saw as an outrageous price structure. It was not simply that
prices were high. The prices seemed blatantly unfair, as they favored the
person shipping goods over large distances, while charging far more to the
local shipper. It proved cheaper to ship goods from Meridian to Baltimore
than to send something from the little farm town of DeKalb to Meridian.
The former distance was one thousand miles, while the later was less than
thirty.[13]

It irked Mississippi's farmers that the railroads were present but not
useful. The situation was all the more maddening when farmers remembered that these railroads had been built with aid from the state government; in other words, their tax dollars had been used to help build a hated
system. While agrarians did call for railroad regulation, the railroads had a
strong influence in the Mississippi legislature. Railroads had placed a
number of key legislators on a general retainer, while free passes were
distributed to other members. In these days before good roads, when
railroads were the chief means of travel between towns, distributing a free
pass on the railroads was arguably analogous to giving a legislator a free
automobile in modern times.

Agrarian discontent was heightened by farmers having few options
other than continuing to farm under an oppressive system. Economist
Gavin Wright, in his 1986 book *Old South, New South*, has enumerated
some of the South's most pressing economic problems after the Civil War.

First, there were very few industrial jobs to offer an alternative to farming, even as agriculture was stagnant and the South's population growing. Second, agricultural wages were very low; the South was a "low wage region in a high wage country." Third, the South formed a closed labor market, where tradition, racism, ignorance, and legislation discouraged movement of workers to northern states. Wright points out that a worker from Italy was much more likely to take a factory job in New England than was a citizen from Mississippi. With few alternatives to farming, Mississippi's small freeholders and tenant farmers aimed to make the best of things, and to seek solutions to the immediate problems they faced.[14]

In order to battle the enemies they saw in their world, farmers vowed to elect state and county officers who would look out for their interests. More than anything else, this would mean keeping taxes low. Also, farmers called for railroad regulation and new laws to protect them from the most hurtful aspects of the crop lien system. Increasingly, agrarians found themselves involved in bitter political struggles with merchants, lenders, lawyers, and town boosters. Small farmers vowed they would use their overwhelming strength in numbers to protect themselves from the frightening change they saw as they looked out on their world. If the Democratic party would help them achieve and wield power, they would vote for Democratic candidates. If the Democratic party seemed to cater to the new commercial class and to planters, then the small farmers would be willing to turn to protest parties, or to Independent movements.

Farmers did enjoy some legislative success in slashing state expenses, even though it required gutting institutions such as the state-supported colleges. In a cash poor economy, taxes were one of the few things that absolutely required cash, and farmers watched any rise in state or county taxation with horror. On other matters, farmers were not able to get strong legislation passed. In this period, they never succeeded in abolishing the lien system or in genuinely regulating the railroads, although the legislature did pass some laws with these goals.[15]

While small farmers had a clear set of goals for their state lawmakers, they did not have enough influence in the legislature to secure enactment of strong statutes to meet their goals. Although one writer has claimed that farmers always had a majority in the state house of representatives in the late nineteenth century, this assertion was based on the belief that planters should be counted as farmers.[16] Actually, planters and farmers had a number of very different goals. Planters were very large landholders, large-scale landlords and employers, and often credit-granting merchants.

They were unlikely to favor abolition of the crop lien law, for example, or reapportionment of the legislature to reduce the influence of the conservative Delta.

It is difficult to say with precision how many Mississippi legislators were primarily farmers, since many had more than one occupation. The legislative rosters included some members who described themselves as "merchant and farmer" and others who were listed as "lawyer and farmer." Yet even if we accept as farmers everyone who claimed farming as a first or second occupation, only two of the twelve legislatures elected between 1877 and 1902 had farmer majorities, despite the overwhelming farmer majority in the general population. The legislatures of 1890 and 1892, under this lenient method of counting, had farmer majorities of 57 and 54 percent respectively. On the other hand, the 1884 legislature had only 41 percent farmers, and the figure for 1900 was only 38 percent. Despairing of gaining the reforms they sought in the state legislature, many agrarians called for national reforms as the best solution to the major problems the nation faced.[17]

Indeed, one of the most striking things about agrarians in the late nineteenth century is that while praising Jacksonian ideals of small government, they simultaneously called for strong government action, especially at the national level. This was true whether the farmers in question were Greenbackers, Independents, Populists, or radical agrarian Democrats. One way to help indebted farmers would be a nationwide inflation of the money supply, by the printing of greenback dollars (unbacked by precious metals), or by supplementing gold-based currency with money based on silver. Inflation would drive up the price of farm goods like cotton, while the farmers' previously contracted indebtedness would stay the same. Farmers also called for tough national regulation or even national ownership of railroads. Moreover, they believed that the near-monopolies in farm machinery and in cotton bagging were contributing to their problems and they asked Congress to abolish trusts and restore free enterprise. On the national level only modest progress was made toward these goals by the turn of the century.

Where farmers at one time had had to worry "only" about bugs, birds, rain, hail, cold, rust, gullies, and poor soil, now they faced these enemies and a host of others. Farmers used politics to do battle with merchants, lenders, railroads, near-monopolistic trusts, commodities speculators, rising taxes, and a tight national money supply. If the leaders of the state

Democratic party proved uninterested in agrarians' concerns, then farmers were willing to organize third-party and Independent movements.

For Mississippi's vast numbers of black farmers, one political issue was more important than crop liens or railroad rate regulation. For black Mississippians the most important political issue was their desire for "free ballot and a fair count." Black voting rights were under constant attack in the 1870s and thereafter, as Democrats used threats, violence, fraud, and legislation to reduce sharply the number of blacks who voted. Blacks often had to make the uncomfortable choice of whether to give up their beloved Republican party to support white dissidents who promised to work for a free ballot, or to renew their uphill battle to restore the strength of the state GOP. A number of white Mississippians joined with blacks in supporting the Republican party. Many of these were former Whigs who had long battled Democrats, while others were northerners who had settled in the state after the war, and who were already wholehearted Republicans when they arrived. For a number of state residents, prohibition was the most important issue. They believed that liquor ruined individual lives and polluted the morals of the entire community. Many of these people joined the Prohibition party in the 1880s and 1890s, adding additional political diversity to the state.[18]

To understand Mississippi's overwhelming support of the Democratic party in the late nineteenth century, it is necessary to know something about the events of Reconstruction. The postwar period of military government ended in February of 1870, as Congress readmitted Mississippi to the Union. The new state government was overwhelmingly Republican, headed by the moderate governor, James Lusk Alcorn, who was a former Whig. The Republican party seemed invincible, since the newly enfranchised black citizens were almost unanimous in their support of the GOP and since the state had a black majority of about 57 percent. Yet the Republican party was very badly split into radical and moderate factions, while the Democrats were carefully rebuilding their party after a long period of disorganization. The elections of 1873 left a majority of counties back under the control of Democratic-Conservative governments, while at the state level the government remained Republican.[19]

The 1875 election featured races for county offices, legislative seats, and the vacant state treasurer's office. Congressional elections, too, were held in 1875, the last time that such elections would be held in an odd-

numbered year. Historian David G. Sansing has noted that in 1875, white Mississippians felt a unanimity of purpose "rarely known in any state." In their efforts to make sure black voters no longer held the balance of power, Democrats later admitted they intended to use whatever techniques might prove necessary to carry the election. As it turned out, these techniques included threats, violence, ballot box stuffing, and the fraudulent counting of votes. Democrats also used "color line" arguments, telling white Mississippians that it was the duty of every white voter to vote Democratic. Of course, Democrats charged that it was Republicans who had first used color line politics, as black leaders had stressed the need for unanimous Republican voting by the freedmen.[20]

Democrats warned of an impending race war unless the government were returned to conservative white control. A Democratic speaker in Monroe County warned that black Republicans "had resolved to burn down the town of Aberdeen," and "to kill the women and children." Radical Republican Governor Adelbert Ames (a native of Maine) was in an awkward position. If he called out the largely black state militia to protect Republican voters, he would give credence to the charge that a race war was brewing. If he did not, Republican defeat seemed certain. At a well-publicized meeting with Democratic campaign leader James Z. George, Ames promised not to use the militia, while George promised a free and fair campaign. The violence and intimidation toward Republicans continued, however, and Ames finally asked President Ulysses S. Grant to provide U.S. troops to stop Democratic threats and acts of violence. Grant's attorney general prepared a proclamation for the president, calling on violent persons to disperse, and threatening martial law. Grant never issued the proclamation, though. He feared the effect on northern elections if the army were called out, and he also believed Ames should first attempt to use state forces. Ames continued to resist employing the militia, fearing that its use would make the Democrats' prediction of race warfare a reality.[21]

After one of the most turbulent election campaigns in U.S. history, the Mississippi Republicans were routed. The legislature elected in 1875 had a large Democratic majority, while only a few county governments remained in Republican hands. Of the six congressional seats, only one went to a straight Republican: John R. Lynch was elected in the heavily black Delta district. One other Republican, U.S. Attorney G. Wiley Wells of Oxford, won election as an Independent Republican with the support of the Democrats. The new Democratic legislature impeached or bullied

into resignation all remaining Republican officers in the executive branch, thus leaving two branches of the state government in Democratic hands. By 1876, the judicial branch was also securely Democratic, and Reconstruction in Mississippi was at an end.[22]

The Reconstruction story would be recounted by Democratic candidates as late as 1963 as a reason for the state's white voters to remain loyal to the Democratic party. In one sense this seems amazing, given that Reconstruction lasted such a short period. Republican electoral victories resulted in GOP control of local governments that lasted less than four years in most counties, while the party controlled the state government only about six years. Any fair appraisal of the state's Republican officials show that they were no more dishonest or wasteful with the taxpayers' money than were Democrats from the later period. In 1874, the average county tax rate for persons living in Republican counties was thirteen mills; for persons in Democratic counties the rate was twelve mills. Yet the Democratic legends would later stress that Republican rule had meant astronomical taxes, as well as corrupt government and black domination.[23]

It is true that the *state* tax rate reached an all time high under the Republicans. It is also true, however, that the Republicans faced a vast number of expenses made necessary by the war's destruction and by the large increase in the number of citizens because of emancipation. The greatest increase in expenses came from the new system of publicly supported schools. White Democrats often attacked the public schools, arguing that black children were receiving a large percentage of the school funds, while black adults often paid relatively little in taxes. Clearly, racially charged issues were the ones that most upset white Mississippians, and led them to vow to carry the election of 1875 at any cost. In one sense Mississippi never had the "black domination" the Democrats charged was present—there never was a black governor, or a black majority in either house of the legislature, or in the constitutional convention of 1868. In another sense, though, the state did experience black domination, since black voters made up a large majority of the electorate in the Reconstruction era.[24]

By modern standards of democracy, if blacks were in the majority in the adult citizenry, then they *should* have constituted a majority of the electorate. But white Democrats complained first of all that blacks abused the ballot by not really studying candidates or issues, but by voting almost automatically for the Republican candidates. (This charge of automatic voting could later be applied with equal validity to white voters' loyalty to

the Democratic party.) Democratic leaders also refused to concede the balance of power to the state's black electorate because of their low opinion of the black race as a whole. Democrats were horrified to see former slaves now serving as justices of the peace and winning seats on boards of supervisors. Democrats noted, too, that the illiteracy rate among the black population was very high. Even as late as 1900, 49 percent of blacks were illiterate; the comparable number for the white population was 8 percent. Democrats rebelled at the idea that a group of largely illiterate former slaves should hold the balance of power in Mississippi elections.[25]

Modern historians can explain that blacks who held important offices tended to be former free blacks, not former slaves, and were not illiterate. Historians can also explain that charges of corruption and extravagance in the Republican governments were usually unsupported. But those Mississippians who had recently owned slaves felt cold fury as they were carried before a black justice of the peace for trial of a minor violation of the law or had to approach a black county tax assessor to plead for a reduction in assessment. The anger at black-majority voting and at black office-holding led Democrats to overthrow the Republicans, and the state was left by 1877 with only one strong party. Republicans were in such disarray that political observers were not surprised when very few Republican tickets appeared in the county and legislative elections of 1877. No opposition group nominated a candidate for the gubernatorial election of that same year.[26]

Yet small farmers across the state were not content with the political status quo, seeing that the local Democratic leaders were often the very same men who advanced them credit at ruinous rates of interest, charged them outrageous prices at the local stores, and proved willing to foreclose if they fell behind in paying the debt. Farmers believed their prized independence was disappearing, and in many counties in 1877 they began to organize to challenge the local, commercially oriented Democratic party. One of the strongest Independent movements arose in Clay County, where a number of farmers had seen their farm mortgages foreclosed and their land sold at auction. W. W. Graham lost his farm to a local banker; he believed it went for far less than its actual value because of the hard times prevalent in the community and because the auction was controlled by members of the local political ring for their own enrichment. Graham joined the Independent movement in Clay County and became one of its most vocal leaders. "We have a class and always have had," Graham asserted, "that is domineering over and plundering the farmers, and it has been

growing worse." Graham urged local farmers to unite politically to preserve what was left of their independence and to fight "class legislation,"
or else abandon politics and consent to allow themselves to become
"slaves" of the commercial interests.[27]

The election of 1877 coincided with a new birth of agrarian anger as
cotton prices fell to eleven cents per pound from nineteen cents four years
earlier. In the southwestern part of the state some farmers spoke of going
on strike, while others threatened to refuse to pay their bills at the local
store unless the storekeepers would substantially increase the price they
paid for cotton. Hinds, Copiah, and Lincoln counties (among others)
featured agrarian Independent tickets, although the Jackson *Weekly Clarion*
claimed that some of the Hinds Independents were really Republicans at
heart. In a number of black majority counties, including Bolivar, Hinds,
Holmes, Madison, and Panola, Democrats aimed to entice blacks to vote
their ticket by offering a small number of offices to black candidates who
agreed to cooperate. At the same time, Democrats used demagogic tactics
to appeal to the fears of white voters. The *Weekly Clarion* editor claimed
that one mulatto Independent campaigner had once said he would like to
see every white man in his county killed so that each black Republican
"could have a white wife."[28]

Democrats also appealed to voters' common sense, saying that any
county that sent Independents to the legislature, "might as well send
nobody." The new legislature almost certainly would be firmly in Democratic hands, and the Democratic leaders of the two houses would "not pay
much attention" to members who were not Democrats. Voters apparently
heeded these Democratic arguments. The results of 1877 were keenly
disappointing to those who hoped to see a flourishing of Independent
movements in the state. The Independents won all the county offices only
in Marshall County, while they also elected a sheriff in Rankin County
and a treasurer in Lincoln County. The new legislature would have seven
Independent members and four Republicans. It would include six black
members, of whom three were Democrats, two Republicans, and one an
Independent from Marshall County.[29]

In some areas, such as the northeastern county of Clay (where W. W.
Graham had lost his farm), it seems clear that the Democrats won by using
intimidation and fraudulent counting of the ballots. In Hinds, where the
capital of Jackson was located, Independents were hurt by lack of organization. For the four Hinds County seats in the state house of representatives, there were four Democratic nominees and fourteen Independents.

Still, judging from the election returns it seems unlikely that the Independents would have won more than one of the four Hinds County seats even had they not been divided. Scattered and amorphous county Independent movements were not likely to offer serious opposition to the state's dominant Democratic party. Yet political agrarianism did not subside after 1877, and farmers began to ponder what vehicle they would use in coming elections.[30]

Few recent historians have written about Mississippi politics of the late nineteenth century. The basic treatment of the subject, Albert D. Kirwan's *Revolt of the Rednecks: Mississippi Politics, 1876–1925*, was published in 1951. Kirwan's work emphasized the Democratic party almost exclusively; he devoted two paragraphs to the Greenbackers, while the Independent and Populist movements received less than nine pages apiece. To Kirwan, Independent movements grew out of "the impossibility of rewarding everyone [within the Democratic party] to the degree that his self-valuation merited." Kirwan admitted that the Greenbackers and Populists were motivated by genuine ideological difference with the Democrats, but still he saw them as largely irrelevant in a one-party state. To Kirwan, the Populists were important only as a training ground for future agrarian leaders of the Democratic party.[31] Archivist Willie D. Halsell, writing in the 1940s, devoted a series of articles to Mississippi's post-Reconstruction politics. For her, however, the chief point of interest in the Independent candidates of the 1880s was their link to national Republican party leaders.[32] In these pages, I will argue that this link was not very important, while at the same time challenging Kirwan's assertion that the Independent movements were built up by mere disappointed office-seekers. I believe the Greenbackers, Independents, and Populists played an important role in shaping Mississippi politics in the late nineteenth century.

One recent book did an excellent job of demonstrating the importance of dissident politicians in the lower South. In *The Anti-Redeemers: Hill Country Political Dissenters in the Lower South* (1990), Michael R. Hyman looked at Independents and Greenbackers in the hill counties of Georgia, Alabama, and Mississippi. He chose the hill counties because this was where he believed white agrarian dissent was the strongest. In Mississippi, Hyman examined ten hill counties in the state's northeast corner.[33] Although Hyman did a fine job of examining the ideology of the agrarian dissenters in the Deep South, and of proving the importance of the movements they led, his choice of counties for Mississippi was unfortunate.

Across the state, fourteen counties elected one or more Greenback or Independent legislators, between 1877 and 1890; of these fourteen counties, only two were among those in Hyman's study area.

Hyman said the Greenback party tended to attract white dissidents living in black counties, while in white counties the dissidents supported Independent movements. Yet the strongest Independent movements in Mississippi arose in black majority counties, mostly in the southern part of the state. The Greenback party in Mississippi, moreover, experienced success in both white and black counties and in counties that were racially balanced. Hyman notes that as Independents did not flourish in his Mississippi study area, Populism also failed to take root. While this is largely true for his ten counties, it can be misleading as one broadens one's focus to include the entire state—especially since Hyman argued that his hill counties were such important centers of white dissent. As with the Greenbackers and Independents, the Populists in Mississippi tended to flourish outside Hyman's hill counties. Of the ten counties strongest in their support of the 1895 Populist gubernatorial nominee, only two were in Hyman's hill counties. Of the four Populist victories in elections for the legislature, none occurred in the ten hill counties examined by Hyman.[34]

Indeed, despite the Democratic regularity of Hyman's ten hill counties, Mississippi featured some of the strongest dissident movements in the South. When James B. Weaver sought the presidency on the Greenback ticket in 1880, Texas was the only southern state to give him a higher percentage of the vote than did Mississippi. When Weaver ran again twelve years later as the Populist nominee, only two southern states gave him a higher percentage. Of the three states Michael Hyman examined, Mississippi had easily the strongest of the non-Democratic gubernatorial candidates of the 1880s. This study, then, aims to supplement Hyman's by making it clearer just where the dissidents displayed their strength and why, and to emphasize the vitality of dissent that is apparent in Mississippi when compared with other southern states.

Two masterworks of southern political history focus on the South as a whole. V. O. Key's *Southern Politics in State and Nation* (1949) dealt largely with the twentieth century but included an important chapter on the disfranchising laws and state constitutions that were framed in southern capitals beginning in the late nineteenth century. Key played down the importance of the disfranchising laws, saying that they really reflected a fait accompli. Disfranchisement had already taken place by means that included threats, ostracism, actual physical attacks, and even murder. The

new constitutions could be passed only because the southern electorate was already much reduced. Key also added that the whites-only Democratic primary instituted in the early twentieth century was arguably more important in denying blacks a meaningful voice in politics than were the new state statutes and constitutions.[35]

Taking issue with Key was J. Morgan Kousser who, in *The Shaping of Southern Politics: Suffrage Restriction and the Establishment of the One-Party South* (1974), argued that Key's fait accompli thesis should be modified or abandoned. Kousser proved that the disfranchising laws and constitutions did serve to reduce markedly the southern electorate, and so did not merely formalize an already existing condition. In looking for the motivation of the disfranchisers, Kousser did not discount their desire to lessen blacks' ability to play key roles in southern elections. He did, however, place great emphasis upon partisanship as a motivating force of the framers of disfranchisement. In other words, the framers expected their enactments would end the threat of a resurgent Republican party or of a rebirth of agrarian dissident movements. While Kousser is correct in saying that the fait accompli thesis has serious flaws, his stressing of partisanship as a motivating force of the disfranchisers does not work for Mississippi, as I will argue in chapter 4. Nor did the new constitution always work to the detriment of the Democratic party's rivals. In at least one sense—though not in others—the new constitution benefited the Populist party, and this was reflected in the party's vote totals.[36]

The pages that follow trace the history of political dissent in Mississippi during the final quarter of the nineteenth century. Chapter 2 explores the history of the state's Greenback party, which flourished as it supported agrarian politics and benefited from the absence of any credible Republican opposition. The chapter will assess who the Greenbackers were, what they accomplished, and why they were not able to win statewide elections. Chapter 3 examines the response of the Greenback party to a Republican resurgence. The chapter examines the startling strength the opposition parties developed in the 1882 elections, but once again appraises the failure of Greenbackers, Republicans, and Independents by the end of the 1880s.

Chapter 4 addresses that watershed event in Mississippi's political history, the framing of the 1890 state constitution. This chapter will evaluate the impact of the constitution on the state's opposition parties. Chapter 4 also assesses the rise of agrarianism in the state at about the same time

delegates were framing the constitution and examines the decision of many farmers to form a new political party rather than support the Democrats.

Chapters 5 and 6 probe the history of Mississippi's Populist party. These chapters appraise the differences between Democratic and Populist individuals, and between Democratic and Populist counties. This part of the book describes the Populists' basic ideology as conservative. The two chapters gauge the accomplishments of the party, evaluate the obstacles it encountered, and assess the effect of the new constitution on Populist vote totals. The book's final chapter offers comparisons of the various dissident movements in the state, looking especially for common ideology, shared geographic areas of strength, and shared personnel. Finally, the chapter describes Mississippi in 1902 and evaluates the role of twenty-five years of politics in shaping the state as it was in that year. The concluding chapter ends by looking to the future, and enumerates the events that finally led to a renewal of two party politics in the state, some six decades after opposition parties all but disappeared in Mississippi.

What follows then, is the story of several hardy bands of dissidents who took on the formidable task of challenging Mississippi's powerful Democratic party. Despite their great efforts, they never succeeded in dominating the Legislature or electing a governor. Nevertheless, they did win some surprising successes, sometimes securing control of their own county governments and other times helping to push an alarmed Democratic party in an agrarian direction.

TWO

Birth of the Greenback Party

IN THE SUMMER AND FALL OF 1878, DISASTERS STRUCK MISSISSIP-
pi repeatedly. The most terrifying was yellow fever, which attacked the
lower Mississippi valley in one of the worst outbreaks of this disease in
recorded history. Yellow fever was especially terrifying because no one
really knew what caused it or how it should be treated. Citizens debated
endlessly over whether the disease was caused by contaminated water,
contagion in the soil, or "bad vapours." The single fact that was clearly
understood was that only a hard frost would bring the epidemic to an end.[1]

In the space of only a few months more than 1,100 people died in
Vicksburg and 327 in the little town of Grenada. Among the towns hard-
est hit was Holly Springs, ironically one of Mississippi's popular health
resorts. With a population of about 2,300, Holly Springs sustained 314
deaths. News dispatches from the town reported that no banking was
going on because the banker was dead, while the post office too was
deserted, its employees having either died or fled the town. In the western
half of the state, only two newspapers (one in Jackson and one in
Vicksburg) continued to publish. Stretching from Memphis to Vicksburg
to New Orleans, the epidemic finally left more than fifteen thousand
people dead.[2]

While trying to deal with the devastation of the epidemic, farmers also
had to cope with the economic devastation of an ongoing depression. The

state's farmers were hard hit by low cotton prices in 1878, while prices for goods they purchased remained constant. The farmers' poor economic situation was aggravated by the crop lien system, under which they obtained credit by giving the merchant a lien on their crop. Under this notorious system, farmers purchased goods at prices 25 percent higher than those paid by cash customers; they were forced to sell their crop to the lending merchant at his price; and they were forced to sell at harvest rather than holding the crop for a propitious time to sell. The entire national economy was depressed in the mid to late 1870s, but Mississippi farmers believed that railroads, banks, and merchants fared better than tillers of the soil. As they moved into a commercial, cash crop economy, they often felt they were losing the independence they had once enjoyed as subsistence farmers.[3]

Tax policies enacted by the state government seemed to make matters worse. Prior to the Civil War, small farmers in Mississippi had paid very little in taxes. The most significant antebellum taxes had included luxury taxes, taxes on professionals, and most importantly, the slave tax. With the demise of slavery in 1865, the state and counties began to depend upon a land tax instead. The land tax took relatively less wealth away from the large planters and more wealth from small farmers. Although planters were affected by the land tax, they were now relieved of the burdensome slave tax. Personal property taxes soon began to weigh more heavily on small farmers, too. Before the war many items were exempt from personal property tax, typically including furniture and a certain number of horses and mules. In the postbellum years many of these popular exemptions were eliminated, adding to the tax burden of the small farmer. Although the Democrats who took control of the state government in 1875 had promised to reduce the high taxes imposed by the Republican legislature, in fact the Democrats had lowered state taxes largely by transferring certain kinds of expenses from the state to the counties—including, most notably, the cost of schools. Soon no other southern state had county taxes as high, relative to state taxes, as did Mississippi. Depending on the county, small farmers saw their local tax bills increase sixfold, or even eightfold.[4]

Mississippi's Democratic officeholders, already on the defensive in trying to deal with the yellow fever and an economic depression, soon were alarmed at a third threat. Only three years after wresting the state government away from the Republicans, Mississippi's Democrats began to hear alarming reports of a substantial new political movement, strongest in

northern Mississippi. In July 1878 the Jackson *Weekly Clarion* reported that the *Batesville Blade*, an established and respected Democratic newspaper, had become "the organ of the Nationals in Panola County." The *DeSoto Press and Times*, publishing at the northern edge of the Mississippi Delta, also reported the rise of the new organization, and complained that just as the state Democratic party was assuming a position of strength, its growth "is to be retarded, if not checked . . . by this new departure—Nationalism."[5]

The National Greenback party, soon called the Greenback Labor party, organized north Mississippi quickly. Scores of towns and rural neighborhoods organized "Greenback clubs," where "tillers of the soil and laboring men" could "discuss, read, and exchange views on the current issues of the day." A Greenbacker reported from the town of Aberdeen in northeastern Mississippi that the club there had 102 active members; he linked the organization of clubs to the fight against commercial agriculture's worst effects. "Thus bravely goes on the work of promised emancipation from impending dependency and ultimate enslavement," the Aberdeen Greenbacker concluded.[6] Week after week, the state's Democratic press counted defections to the new party. Under the headline "Sorry to Hear It," the *Weekly Clarion* reported in August 1878 that former congressman Daniel B. Wright of Tippah County had gone over to the National Greenbackers. Under the headline "It Must Be A Mistake," the *Clarion* published a report that an incumbent state senator, Jackson Taylor Griffin, had defected and was organizing a Greenback party club in his home county of Chickasaw. The *Clarion*'s report proved accurate. Next, reports reached Jackson that Absalom M. West, another incumbent senator, had deserted the Democrats, and the *Clarion* was quick to doubt the accuracy of these reports. But West, a curious combination of agrarian activist and railroad entrepreneur, had indeed wholeheartedly joined the Greenback cause.[7]

The Greenback party was a nationwide organization founded in 1875, dedicated to supplying relief from the effects of a depressed economy by increasing the supply of paper money. It was true that the nation's money supply had shrunk from more than $1 billion to $773 million in the brief period from 1865 to 1878 as the government withdrew from circulation the greenback bills used to finance the civil war. Greenbackers knew that as the money supply grew smaller, the income of farmers and mechanics fell, while their indebtedness remained constant. Alternatively, if the money supply were made to grow through a new issue of greenbacks, farmers'

income would rise with inflation, while their indebtedness would remain the same. The Greenback platform was a popular one with small farmers and was viewed with horror by the commercial interests in the towns and cities.[8]

Although at its peak the party would poll more than a million votes nationwide, nearly all of its victories were won by fusion with one of the two major parties. In 1878, for example, fourteen Greenbackers won seats in the U.S. Congress. Of these, seven were elected in fusion with the Democrats and three in Republican fusion.[9] Mississippi's early Greenbackers are notable for the successes they enjoyed while avoiding fusion. In many parts of Mississippi—especially in the north-central counties— Mississippi's new two-party system was Democrats versus Greenbackers. Mississippi, Texas, and Alabama were home to some of the strongest Greenback parties in the United States.

In Mississippi the strongest counties for the new party were in the northern part of the state, beginning with DeSoto County near Memphis and stretching due south to Holmes County and east to Benton and Sumner (later called Webster) counties. The party was also strong in Hinds County, where the capital city of Jackson was located, and adjoining Rankin County. These two counties are southwest of the state's center. The party was weak or nonexistent in the Mississippi River counties south of DeSoto, in the southern counties, and in east-central Mississippi.

Mississippi members of this new agrarian party tended to fall into three categories. Most white Greenbackers were former Confederates and former Democrats. Typical in many ways was John B. Yellowly of Madison County. Yellowly had been elected to the legislature as a Democrat in 1875, but was defeated for renomination by a less agrarian Democrat. He then attempted to organize a statewide Independent agrarian movement for the 1877 legislative races, but the movement won few successes. As late as June 1878, Yellowly was a member of the Democratic Executive Committee for the fourth congressional district, but he soon joined the Greenback movement and became an active campaigner and occasional candidate.[10]

A smaller group numerically were former Whigs. Despite their small numbers, these Greenbackers were important because of the leadership they exerted. Prior to the Civil War, Mississippi Whigs devoted their entire political careers to battling the Democrats. After the war, they often felt as if they had no viable political choices; they did not want to join their former enemies, the Democrats, but they often chose not to join

what they saw as a party of blacks and carpetbaggers, the Republicans. The Greenback party now provided a new vehicle for these politicians to continue opposing the Democrats. Although the Whig party and the later Greenback party differed on some matters, both believed as a cardinal tenet that the federal government should play a large and active role in the economy. That Whig sentiment was far from dead in Mississippi can be seen by the fact that even as late as 1879 a Copiah County tailor announced his candidacy as a Whig for a county office. This Whig candidate won over 42 percent of the vote—a good showing for a member of a long-extinct political party. Among the Whigs-turned-Greenbackers were two state senators, Absalom M. West and Jackson Taylor Griffin. The latter declared on the official roster of the 1880 legislature that his politics were "Whig and Greenbacker."[11]

An example of the Whig-Greenback connection is found in the career of M. D. L. Stephens. In antebellum Calhoun County, Stephens was a physician who supported the Whig party. In 1860 he was elected as a Union Cooperationist to Mississippi's secession convention, where he opposed secession until the last ballot. During the war Stephens served as a state legislator, also as a second lieutenant and later lieutenant colonel who fought at First Manassas, Ball's Bluff, and Vicksburg. Stephens was so severely injured during the war that he was unable to resume his medical practice (he could not ride horseback to attend his patients) and instead he became a merchant at Water Valley in Yalobusha County. His biographer noted that Stephens' store prospered until contraction of the money supply "brought ruin to the country, culminating in 1878 in suspension and the surrender of everything to his creditors." Stephens was forced to become a clerk to support his family. Thus, ironically, the failed merchant joined an agrarian party that had many objections to merchants and the credit system they sponsored. In 1879 Stephens was elected representative from Yalobusha County on the Greenback ticket; like Jackson Taylor Griffin, Stephens listed himself in the legislative directory as "Old line Whig and Greenbacker."[12]

The third group of Greenbackers was at once the largest and the least represented on the party tickets. Black Mississippians flocked to join the new political movement primarily because the Greenbackers worked assiduously to assure free and honest elections. Or, as one white Greenbacker put it, "The colored men will vote for any man or any ticket in opposition to the Democratic party." Many Democrats feared that blacks

would support the Greenbackers until free elections were restored to the state, then would reorganize the Republican party.[13]

A well-known black Greenback partisan was Murdock M. McLeod of Hinds County. A former Republican, McLeod joined the Greenbackers in 1879 and was regularly a candidate for county offices. McLeod also served in positions of honor and leadership within the party: as vice-chair of the 1880 state convention, delegate to the national convention of 1880, and presidential elector that same year. McLeod returned to the Republican fold in 1883. Although disgruntled Greenbackers called him a "Go-backer," McLeod remained in the party longer than did most black members.[14]

White and black Greenbackers often endured a very uneasy relationship. One white Greenbacker, thinking he was making a generous statement, testified before a congressional committee that in Mississippi, "some colored citizens are good neighbors and good citizens; the great majority, however, are illiterate, improvident, dishonest, drunken, and worthless." For their part, blacks resented the fact that in most counties they provided over half of the Greenback votes but were rarely given places on the tickets. White Greenbackers told them that the party's only hope was to avoid the appearance of "Negro rule," but the resentment remained. In most strong Greenback counties, blacks provided the margin of victory, as white voters divided between the Democratic and Greenback parties. Still, Michael R. Hyman's assertion that white dissenters in black counties tended to support the Greenback party while white dissenters in white counties tended to support Independent movements is only sometimes true in Mississippi. The state's Greenback party strongholds ranged from counties that were overwhelmingly white (Calhoun and Sumner), to counties balanced racially (Benton and Tate), to counties that were predominantly black (Holmes and Hinds). The great majority of the Greenbackers who were elected to office were elected in counties outside Hyman's study area. Independent candidates, as we will see, were usually elected in black majority counties.[15]

Historians have linked the Greenback Party to the Patrons of Husbandry, also called the Grange. The Grange was a farmers' organization that encouraged cooperation among farmers (including cooperative stores), helped disseminate new agricultural information, and served as a social club for farmers. One historian has gone so far as to say that the Greenback party was the political arm of the Grangers.[16] In Mississippi, when

lists of prominent Grange leaders are compared with lists of state Greenback leaders, there are few matches. On the other hand, the Granges did
give aid to the Greenback movement. As the state Grange newspaper
Patron of Husbandry put it in 1879, "The great question of the day is that of
the currency. It is the only question in politics that interests the masses."
While the editor of this Grange organ voted Democratic, "We believe
that the Greenback movement will accomplish immense good, and we
look upon its steady increase in strength and numbers with deep interest
and pleasure."[17]

Throughout 1879 and 1880, the *Patron of Husbandry* urged Grangers to
form Greenback clubs in their neighborhoods. If the Democrats nominated town politicians who were uninterested in monetary policy and lien
law reform, then the clubs should bring out Greenback party candidates to
oppose the Democrats. The *Patron* warned farmers that Democrats would
pretend the major issue of the day was "the Southern question," when
clearly the currency issue was much more important to farmers. While
many Democratic candidates supported currency inflation, many did not,
and "if the Greenbacks nominate men who can be relied upon to represent
the public interests, vote for them." On a few occasions the *Patron of
Husbandry* named specific Greenback candidates whom farmers should
support over the Democratic nominees.[18]

Although the Greenback party's name implies that monetary policy was
its chief concern, actually the state party offered a broad platform. One of
the chief planks, given Mississippi's troubled recent past, was that all
citizens must be protected in the right "to vote without molestation, and
to have that vote counted." Surprisingly, for a group led largely by former
Jacksonian Democrats, the Greenbackers called for an active government
at the state and national level. They justified this position by arguing that
while a large government *might* pose a danger to the liberty of citizens, a
greater danger was posed by the new combinations of power wielded by
corporations, bankers, investors, and merchants. Greenbackers argued
that the state and national governments must end the special privileges
extended to these groups, thus helping all the people. At the national level,
Greenback partisans called not only for federal action to inflate the money
supply and an end to the power of privately controlled national banks but
also for railroad regulation. They sought laws that would preserve the
public lands for actual settlers (not speculators), and an end to the Chinese
immigration that was limiting the opportunities of railroad laborers, agricultural laborers, and others.[19]

At the state level, Greenbackers first took aim at those who had the privilege of being state employees, advocating a reduction in the number of offices and more severe penalties for corruption in office. The Greenback party members opposed Mississippi's convict leasing system, because it provided a special privilege for a select group of investors, while at the same time competing with "our mechanics and artisans." The party also had the vision to call on the government to institute a fair, graduated income tax system, under which each person would pay taxes according to his or her ability to pay.[20]

A number of planks in the various platforms adopted by Mississippi Greenbackers did focus on currency matters. The party sought inflation by free and unlimited government coinage of silver and by government issue of greenback dollars that would be equal to a gold dollar for all purposes, even though not backed by gold or silver. To foster a careful government regulation of the money supply, only the U.S. government would be permitted to issue paper money—banks would be required to stop their issue of banknotes. The government was to keep the money supply steady at a certain number of dollars per capita. Finally, the federal government should buy back all outstanding bonds and issue no new ones. In other words, the federal government should not be in debt.[21]

The Greenback party nominated its first candidates in Mississippi in the summer of 1878. The party tapped Reuben Davis to run for Congress in the first (northeast) congressional district and James H. Amacker to be the candidate in the second (northwest) district. Reuben Davis was a sixty-five-year-old resident of Aberdeen. He had practiced both medicine and law, and had also served as a Democratic congressman from 1857 to 1861. Early in the war Davis was a Confederate brigadier general; later he was Jefferson Davis's gadfly in the Confederate Congress, opposing, for example, conscription. In the early 1870s Davis was again a Democratic politician, urging that the "color line" be used to destroy the Republican party and black political power. Ironically, as an 1878 Greenback candidate, Davis sought and received black support.[22]

Nominated by the Greenback party at Okolona in August 1878, Davis was a reluctant candidate and agreed to the use of his name only if he were not asked to campaign. Later, however, the yellow fever epidemic closed the courts in Davis's county, and he found himself with leisure time to campaign. The Jackson *Weekly Clarion* warned that Davis's nomination "is not to be treated lightly," since he was an able politician, personally popular, and an effective speaker. At first the campaign went smoothly;

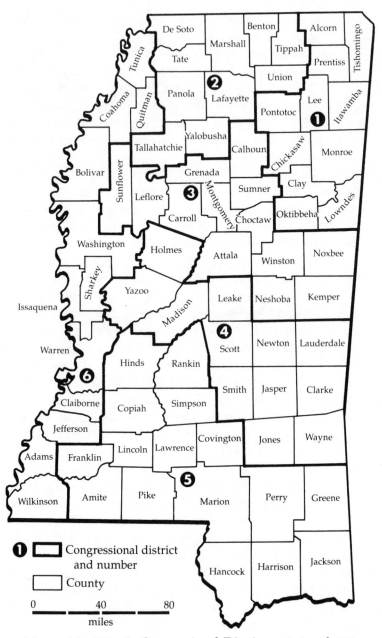

Map 1. Mississippi's Congressional Districts, 1878 and 1880

Davis traveled with his Democratic opponent Henry L. Muldrow. At the joint speakings between the two men audiences were small at first, probably owing to the epidemic.[23]

The unpleasantness began late in the campaign. We get a hint of Davis's problems in an article from a Democratic paper, reporting a joint speaking in Pontotoc County: "The Democrats cheered lustily for Muldrow during [Davis's] speech." Davis himself, summoned later by a congressional investigating committee, reported that ten minutes into a speech, Democrats typically would begin cheering for his opponent, and the din was "deafening and terrific." Davis added that soon "it was only an effort at making a speech," because he was "so confused" by the racket that he could not proceed. On many occasions Davis was interrupted repeatedly by hostile questions; at the village of Mayhew the meeting disbanded after terrific yelling and the firing of guns outside the school where the meeting was being held. Davis was repeatedly warned that either he or his campaign manager was about to be killed; over and over he was informed that he would not be permitted to speak at various towns and villages. At West Point Davis did not speak because "a singing noise and demonstrations of a riot commenced." The campaign was capped by Davis being hung in effigy on election eve in Columbus, and burned in effigy on election morning.[24]

In this 1878 first district congressional race, Democrats also turned to a variety of devices to neutralize the black vote, since it was believed that nearly all blacks favored the Greenback candidate. In predominantly black Lowndes County, Democrats borrowed a trick from 1875 and fired a cannon every half hour on election day. To blacks the cannon was a potent symbol that whites were willing to use force of arms to carry an election. In Clay County Democrats circulated a last-minute report that popular Republican politician William D. Frazee was running for Congress and that Davis had withdrawn in Frazee's favor. Democrats even printed up a Frazee ballot that was distributed to many black voters. Frazee was not a candidate and in fact was supporting Davis, but because Democrats cut telegraph wires into Clay County the Greenbackers were not able to squelch the rumor. At many precincts in many counties Democrats threw out Greenback ballots for alleged technical violations of the election laws. One such box in Monroe County had more than two hundred votes for Davis and only twenty for Muldrow, but was thrown out because of alleged irregularities. From Jackson, the secretary of state finally declared

Muldrow elected, with 59 percent of the district vote, while official returns gave only Monroe County to the Greenback candidate.[25]

Davis firmly believed that he would have been elected in a fair count of the ballots cast and he began to gather evidence to contest Muldrow's election. Yet he could find no man to help him take down the testimony. One man began, but by nightfall he refused to continue; local citizens were making it too "disagreeable." White Democratic leaders criticized Davis severely for having sought black votes. Davis told the congressional committee investigating this 1878 race, "I have been about as severely abused as any candidate ever was," in both the press and in public conversation. In a masterful understatement, Davis concluded: "It is a little odious."[26]

Unable to gather the testimony, Davis never officially contested his seat. His campaign manager, William H. Vasser, was made foreman of the federal grand jury at Oxford; the grand jury consisted of thirteen Greenback voters and six Democrats. A lack of court funds cut short the grand jury's investigation, but the panel did indict several men for crimes committed in the farcical election. Three of those indicted pleaded guilty; one pleaded innocent but was found guilty in a jury trial.[27]

Little is known about the second congressional district race in 1878. Congress did not investigate this campaign, and no relevant 1878 newspapers from this district have survived. Greenback candidate James H. Amacker of Marshall County was a minister of the gospel; although elected to the legislature as a Democrat in 1875 he was an early convert to the Greenback party. Amacker campaigned actively in 1878; the official returns showed him winning 44 percent of the vote, carrying a number of counties. As in Davis's district, Greenbackers felt certain that Democrats had deprived them of victory by a fraudulent counting of the ballots.[28]

Still, the 1878 election was not a bad beginning for the new party. Even if we trust the election returns reported by Mississippi's secretary of state, the Greenbackers won over 40 percent of the vote in both districts—a respectable showing for a brand new party. If the party could continue to attract white membership, especially respected white leaders, and if it could hold on to its black supporters, it could make a strong showing in the 1879 elections for the legislature and for county offices. Discontent in Mississippi was fed by continued low prices for cotton, and a partial failure of the crop in 1879.[29]

One of the first counties to organize for the 1879 election was Hinds, a county near the state's center and site of the state capitol. The county's

population was 73 percent black; its Republican leaders, however, were nervous about their future. They had watched with dismay the rout of their party in numerous black majority counties, including Hinds. In the city of Jackson lived a number of white men who were interested in the new Greenback party, and they were quick to perfect their organization and invite blacks to their meetings. By late August the party had nominated a full slate for county offices in Hinds, including two blacks. State senate nominee John T. Hull, a white Jacksonian, began editing a Greenback campaign organ, the *Weekly Independent*.[30]

The Jackson *Weekly Clarion* tried a variety of tactics to defuse the Greenback threat in Hinds County. More than anything else, the paper appealed for white unity, and it rekindled fears of "Negro domination." For example, the *Clarion* was quick to report that many of the Greenback meetings featured "fife and drum" music played by black members of the party. Not to be confused with the military music played by whites, Mississippi fife and drum music was played by blacks upon homemade cane flutes and drums, and was decidedly African in sound. To many whites, this black fife and drum music reminded them of the sounds of Reconstruction and rule by Governor Adelbert Ames. As the *Clarion* put it in October 1879: "The rub-a-dub-dub, and the pee-wee-wee of the Radical fife and drum on the streets Monday night was a forcible reminder of Ames and his gang." In another article the paper asked white Greenbackers, "How did you like the sound of the Radical fife and drum on last Monday night? If it was not sweet to your ears, charge it to your leaders, who have aroused the Radical tiger."[31]

Late in the campaign, a small group of Hinds County Republicans nominated a ticket. Although the Greenbackers laughed at the weakness of the Republican slate, the *Clarion* at least made a pretense of being alarmed, warning white Greenbackers that if the "Radical" ticket won, it would be their fault for encouraging black political participation. The Greenbackers strongly suspected that the Democrats had encouraged the Republicans' nomination of a ticket in order to divide the black vote between Republicans and Greenbackers. Democrats denied the charge.[32] The *Clarion* did give substantial coverage to the Republicans' campaign in the county. The paper quoted one black Republican speaker as warning blacks that "the Greenbackers were Democrats in disguise." Another black Republican speaker was quoted as criticizing the Greenbackers for their anti-bond policy: "Greenbackers wanted to repudiate the debt that had been contracted to make the negroes free."[33]

In this 1879 Hinds county election, the Greenbackers were about half-victorious. They won three of the four seats in the legislature, and also the office of county treasurer. The Democrats won the remaining countywide offices, but the Greenbackers gained control of the governing board of supervisors in beat elections. The Greenbackers, claiming fraud, contested several of the lost offices, including sheriff and circuit clerk. The Republican ticket did very poorly; the legislative slate, for example, won only about 8 percent of the vote.[34]

Another county that featured a vigorous Greenback campaign was Benton, in the rolling hills along the Tennessee line. Benton County was populated almost entirely by small farmers; its population was about 53 percent white. The county was "evangelized" for the Greenbackers in the summer of 1879 by two prominent Marshall Countians: Absalom M. West and Thomas W. Harris. Soon Benton County was home to a number of popular Greenback clubs, and the county's only newspaper, the Democratic *Benton County Argus*, went over to the Greenback side. Democrats had to scurry to catch up, hurriedly founding a new Democratic paper they called the *Ashland Register*.

At the county Greenback convention, competition was keen for the various nominations, but schisms were avoided. As in Hinds County, Republican candidates appeared midway through the campaign; as in Hinds County the Greenbackers accused Democrats of encouraging the Republicans to run. The Democratic *Register* was complimentary to black politician L. F. Parham, Republican candidate for the legislature, and repeatedly reminded blacks that the Greenback ticket was made up of white candidates only. But the Republican candidates did not win very many votes. Instead, Greenbackers won a majority of the offices, while Democrats salvaged several victories. Greenback winners included farmer Reuben E. Taylor, who captured Benton County's seat in the legislature, and the candidates for circuit clerk, treasurer, surveyor, and coroner and ranger. Democrats took the sheriff's office, the chancery clerkship, and the assessor's office. Greenbackers won two of the five seats on the county board of supervisors in beat elections.[35]

In Marshall County, reputed to be a Greenback stronghold, the election campaign was a nightmare for the party from the beginning. Marshall County had a large majority of black voters, as well many prominent black and white Republican leaders. White Republican George M. Buchanan, a longtime county resident and a former Confederate officer, organized a Greenback-Republican fusion ticket. Most white Greenbackers were hor-

rified when the ticket that emerged was Republican-dominated, with a number of blacks among the nominees. James H. Amacker announced that he was a Greenbacker "but not a Republican," and said he would not support the ticket. Absalom M. West worked quietly to change the ticket without publicly airing the controversy. Blacks in Marshall became less and less enthusiastic about Greenbackism as they watched that movement's leaders recoil from the black candidates on the ticket.[36]

Finally, just days before the election, the Greenbackers took steps to bring out a new, strictly Greenback ticket. It is not clear whether such a ticket was finally perfected by election day. Black voters, though, remained loyal to the original ticket, and to complicate matters the Democrats gave blacks a few places on their ticket. On election day, the Democrats nearly swept the field. A black Republican was elected to one of Marshall County's four seats in the legislature, and another to the post of assessor. Several "straight Greenbackers" received 7 to 8 percent of the vote; whether they actually considered themselves candidates is not known. The debacle in Marshall County was a great embarrassment to the party, since Marshall was home to well-known Greenback leaders including West, Harris, and Amacker.[37]

In Panola County, at the Delta's edge in north Mississippi, Democratic leaders followed Marshall County's example and gave blacks representation on their ticket. Blacks also won places on the Greenback ticket. Most Panola County blacks maintained a deep distrust of the Democratic party, and in November the county went Greenback with well over 60 percent of the vote. In nearby Tate County the Greenbackers brought out a full ticket, targeting especially the two incumbent Democratic legislators. When the race seemed to be going badly for the Democrats the two incumbents promised "that through no act of theirs will taxes ever be increased," but Greenbackers swept Tate County in November.[38]

Controversial elections in Holmes and Yalobusha counties will be considered later. Taken as a whole, though, the 1879 election was a remarkable achievement for a new political party. The party won legislative races in Benton, Calhoun, Hinds, Holmes, Panola, Sumner, Tate, and Yalobusha counties. The party also won some county offices in all of these counties except Calhoun, and also in DeSoto. The 1879 election provides an excellent example of a locally strong opposition party. While the Greenbackers fell far short of winning a majority in the legislature, they did win the offices in a cluster of counties in north-central Mississippi and in Hinds County to the south. In Benton, Holmes, Panola, Tate, and

The Panola County courthouse, from which Greenbackers governed the county
for a number of years. Voters chose a Greenback county government in three
successive elections. (Photo courtesy of the Mississippi Department of Archives
and History)

Yalobusha counties the party had shown itself to be especially strong. The
legislature elected two years earlier had included eleven Independent
or Republican members. The new legislature would have twenty-seven
non-Democrats, including seventeen Greenbackers, seven Republicans,
and three Independents.[39] The Democrats' opponents were growing in
strength, as the Republicans held their own and the new Greenback party
won some important first victories.[40]

The new Greenback legislators could hope to play an important role in
the 1880 session. Since the 130 Democratic members of the legislature

ranged from radical agrarians to conservative merchants and railroad lawyers, Greenbackers conceivably could play an important role by using
their seventeen votes to "decide" votes when the Democrats were badly
divided. Democrats, however, took some early steps to prevent such a
scenario. One of the first tasks of the 1880 legislature was to choose a
United States senator to replace the Republican Blanche K. Bruce, whose
term had expired. Democrats were divided in their sentiments as to which
member of their party would make the best senator; they decided, however, to select someone in caucus, then vote unanimously on the house
floor for their nominee. It took nine days and forty-nine ballots for the
caucus to settle upon James Z. George, but by selecting George in caucus,
the Democrats allowed the opposition party members to play no role. On
the floor of the house chamber the Greenback legislators cast their votes
for their fellow-partisan, state senator Absalom M. West, while the Republicans voted to reelect Bruce.[41]

The issue that most interested Greenback legislators was Campbell's
Code of 1880. The previous legislature had hired Judge J. A. P. Campbell
to codify the state's laws; Campbell occasionally went beyond mere codification and made material changes in the laws. The legislature was now
asked to ratify the code as Campbell had drafted it. The most controversial feature of the code was its crop lien provision. This provision made a
farmer's crop subject to seizure to satisfy indebtedness to his landlord or
to a merchant. Greenbackers and other agrarians opposed this provision
of the code, arguing that the farmer should be permitted to sell his own
crops and settle his own debts. Conservative Democrats argued, disin-
genuously, that the provision was actually designed to protect small farmers, since without this kind of provision landlords and merchants would be
reluctant to advance credit. Despite vocal Greenbacker opposition to the
crop lien provisions, the legislature passed them, giving the third-party
candidates a new issue to take to the voters in the next legislative election,
in 1881.[42]

Greenback legislators voted consistently to keep state expenses low.
They voted to limit the amount of stationery available to each member, to
keep the session short, and against preparing a published digest of state
supreme court cases. In some instances the votes of Greenback lawmakers
were decisive on the outcome of a given roll call. For example, many
agrarians objected to a senate bill calling for county superintendents of
education to be paid fifty dollars per 1,000 pupils per annum. On a house

motion to cut this amount to thirty dollars, all but one Greenbacker present voted aye, and the Greenbackers' votes were decisive in securing passage of the amendment.[43]

At the end of the legislative session the Greenbackers nearly, but not quite, played a decisive role on a crucial vote. A bill to provide for state regulation of railroad rates passed the house of representatives forty-four to thirty-one, with all Greenbackers present voting for the bill. This was a very important bill for Mississippi farmers, and without Greenback support it would not have passed. But although a version of the bill passed both houses, on the last day of the session the final version failed to reach a vote in the house, and the bill did not become law.[44]

The Greenback legislators were in some ways a diverse group, including former Whigs, former Democrats, and a former Republican. A party that openly distrusted lawyers and merchants had in its delegation one lawyer (Louis K. Atwood) and one man recently a merchant (M. D. L. Stephens). Some Greenback members represented counties that were overwhelmingly white, while some represented counties with large black majorities. These differences raise the question of whether the Greenback delegation acted in concert, or whether their diverse background led to actions that were not at all unified.

One way to assess the internal unity of a group like the Greenback legislators is the statistical measure called the index of relative cohesion. If a group of legislators all vote the same way in a legislative session, their index of relative cohesion for that session is one hundred, while if they are perfectly divided in their voting, their score for that session is zero. Other voting patterns will lie between zero and one hundred on this scale. When we compare the index of relative cohesion of Democratic members of the house of representatives with that of the Greenbackers on the ninety-three recorded roll call votes in 1880, we find that the Greenback delegation demonstrated a substantially stronger cohesion than the Democrats.

> Index of relative cohesion, Greenbackers: 43
> Index of relative cohesion, Democrats: 30

The index of relative cohesion for the Greenback legislators is at a respectable level, while the Democratic delegation shows much less cohesion. Of course, the difference in cohesion of the two groups may not be surprising, since the overwhelming dominance of the Democratic party in Mississippi meant that Democratic legislators represented a wide range of opinions, while Greenbackers—a new party that elected legislators from a

well-defined band of counties—were more likely to adhere to a clearly defined party line. Still, this is one measure that makes the Greenbackers seem more like an ideologically unified movement, while the Democrats held a motley assortment of views on the important issues of the day.[45]

By comparing biographical data of Democratic and Greenback partisans in the legislature, we can probe differences between the two groups. Both groups were predominantly white, although the Greenback delegation had three blacks in a group of seventeen (senators and representatives), while the Democrats had only one black legislator out of 130. With both groups, the average member was in his forties. In the area of religion, as reported in the legislative directory, some differences do emerge. Eighty-two percent of the Greenbackers were either Methodist or Baptist, while the comparable figure for the Democrats was 51 percent. The Democratic delegation included, in addition to Baptists and Methodists, a number of Episcopalians, Presbyterians, Catholics, and members with "no preference" or "friendly to all." No Democrats and no Greenbackers were born outside the South, but the Greenbackers were almost twice as likely to have been born in a southern state other than Mississippi. Perhaps the Greenbackers, being more recent arrivals, found their chances for political advancement slim in an already-crowded Democratic field and were quick to sign on to the new movement. An alternative explanation is that the more recently arrived Greenbackers were less settled economically, more likely to be hurt by the depression of the 1870s, and thus more likely to join the protest party.[46]

The most striking differences between the two delegations emerge as we look at occupations. Sixty-five percent of the Greenback lawmakers were farmers, while only 41 percent of Democratic legislators were. Democratic legislators were more than six times as likely to be attorneys. Only one of the Greenback legislators was a lawyer (black legislator Louis K. Atwood of Hinds County), while forty-eight of 130 Democratic legislators practiced law. The Grange paper *Patron of Husbandry* had urged farmers in 1879 to avoid "lawyer-politicians" of the "town rings." The paper also warned, "Don't take one of these farming lawyers," either. In Benton County in 1879 the Democratic *Ashland Register* had poked fun at the Greenback convention delegates: "The farmers all got their men nominated in their plain farmer-like way." The voters of Benton County also elected the Greenbackers in a plain farmer-like way.[47]

Further differences between Democrats and Greenbackers emerge as we look at the candidates who comprised the Democratic and Greenback

tickets in for local offices in Benton County in 1879. The average age of the Greenbackers was lower in Benton County, at thirty-seven years, when compared with an average age of Democratic candidates of fifty. As to occupation, the two groups were similar: overwhelmingly farmers. The Greenbackers included eight farmers, one physician, and one candidate whose occupation is unknown. The Democrats included nine farmers (one of whom was also a blacksmith), one machinist, and one individual whose occupation is not recorded. All of the candidates from the two parties were white men.[48]

We can gauge the relative wealth of the Benton County candidates by examining their personal property tax returns for 1879. Among the items assessed were cattle, horses, mules, sheep, goats, hogs, wagons, pianos, organs, watches, jewelry, silverware, guns, knives, merchandise, money, and money at loan. The personal property tax records, then, provide one good index of wealth, probing the size of a farmer's operation, and weighing the value of "luxuries" in the taxpayer's life. By looking also at a random sample of 131 Benton County residents, it is possible to compare the two parties' candidates with the citizenry as a whole.

> Democratic candidates' average assessment: $582
> Greenback candidates' average assessment: $181
> Random sample of citizens, average assessment: $ 96

Thus, although the Greenback candidates owned almost twice as much valuable personal property as the average citizen, the Democrats in turn outvalued the Greenbackers more than three-to-one in assessed personal property.[49]

Another important question has to do with change in economic status over time: were these Benton County candidates maintaining their wealth, increasing it, or losing ground? If we compare the 1879 personal property tax assessments with the assessment made two years earlier, the differences between the two Benton County tickets are again significant.

> Democrats' assessments increase, $518 → $582
> Greenbackers' assessments decrease, $208 → $181
> Random sample, assessments decrease, $132 → $ 96

Thus in Benton County we have two tickets, both made up largely of farmers; the Greenback candidates were far less wealthy than their Democratic counterparts and were losing status while the Democrats gained. The average citizens were also much poorer than the Democratic candi-

dates. Like the Greenbackers they were losing ground, and in November the citizens elected a Greenbacker legislator and a number of Greenback county officers.[50]

Most Mississippians would have agreed with the Greenbacker who observed, "The Republican party of Mississippi has had no vitality since 1875 or 1876." Although there were still many black voters who were Republicans at heart, and some white leaders, the Greenbackers quickly took away Republicans' status as Mississippi's "second party"—holding far more seats in the legislature, for example. Still, in 1878 and 1879 Republicans did continue to run candidates, especially along the Mississippi River and in the southern part of the state, two areas where the Greenbackers were weak. In 1878, for example, Republicans ran two congressional candidates. In the sixth, "worm" district that followed the Mississippi River for the length of the state, white Republican attorney J. B. Deason won just over 12 percent of the vote and carried his home county of Lincoln. In the fifth (southern) district, Republican candidate E. J. Castello carried Adams County (where Natchez is located), while winning 17 percent of the vote across the district.[51]

In 1879, Republicans won some important victories. For example, they won two of the state's twelve district attorney's races, and in Vicksburg's Warren County a Republican was elected sheriff in a tough campaign. Throughout the late 1870s and most of the 1880s the capital city of Jackson was run by a city government dominated by white Republicans. Republicans also held a number of positions in river counties ranging from Adams to Bolivar to Issaquena; the latter county was over 90 percent black. In most cases, however, the Republican officeholders in the Delta counties were elected only after striking an "office-sharing" deal with the Democrats. Typically such agreements would give the Republicans half of a county's legislative seats, two of the five county supervisor positions, and several lesser county offices. The Democrats would retain the all-important sheriff's and treasurer's offices, and control of the board of supervisors. There were several advantages to office-sharing. Violence, intimidation, and fraud were avoided, while Republicans still were given some voice in government. Still, office-sharing was far from being a system of genuine two-party electoral politics.[52]

The most important leader of the Mississippi Republicans was John R. Lynch, only thirty-one years old in 1878. Born into slavery, at Civil War's end Lynch became a photographer. After entering politics he rose quickly

from justice of the peace to state legislator, then to speaker of the state house of representatives, and finally to congressman. Although defeated for reelection to Congress in the tumultuous 1876 election, in 1880 Lynch again announced his candidacy for the congressional seat from the sixth (river) district. After a stiff fight in the Republican convention, Lynch won nomination on the eighty-fifth ballot. The long, narrow sixth district had a great majority of black voters, so that in a fair election there would be little doubt of the Republican candidate's victory.[53]

Lynch had been watching Mississippi elections for years, and in 1880 he proved himself a particularly savvy candidate. He knew, for example, that in some counties Democratic election officials were likely to count Republican ballots as Democratic. On the other hand, he knew that these election officers were unlikely to issue returns for more votes than the actual number cast. Claiborne County had a large majority of black Republican voters, but was thoroughly controlled by Democratic election officers. In Claiborne County, therefore, Lynch took the surprising step of quietly advising his supporters not to vote at all! This way, there would be no Republican ballots to count fraudulently as Democratic. "The result was that the Democratic majority [in Claiborne] was five hundred less than it otherwise would have been," Lynch later recalled.[54]

In Adams County fair elections were usually the rule, but in 1880 Lynch knew that newspapers from other counties were asking what was wrong with Adams—why couldn't the Democratic leaders there insure a Democratic victory? On election day in Natchez, therefore, black voters were forced to stand in a separate voting line from whites, and their line moved with excruciating slowness. Many black voters gave up and went home; many others were still waiting in line when the polls closed. At the rural precinct of Kingston, Lynch watched in dismay as the election officers took the ballot box away from the polls as they went to lunch. The candidate protested, but to no effect. Lynch feared a ballot box stuffing; when the votes at Kingston were finally counted they showed a Democratic majority at a predominantly black, predominantly Republican precinct.[55]

Lynch's greatest hope was Warren County, where the great black majorities in and around Vicksburg might salvage his election. A white Republican deputy sheriff there organized a squad of one hundred white men, most of them Democrats, who were willing to work to assure an honest election. Other Democrats had perfected a plan for lunchtime ballot box stuffing. Just at noon, however, the deputy sheriff's squads descended on each precinct, ready to guard the boxes. Poll managers were

incredulous that white Democrats would prevent a ballot box stuffing, but each poll manager gave in easily because he assumed that his precinct was the only one where the plan for fraud was going astray. In reality, however, the plan to stuff the boxes failed at every polling place. Warren's Republican majority of two thousand votes was enough to insure Lynch's victory.[56]

Finally, in desperation, Lynch's opponent James R. Chalmers seized upon a phrase in the state election laws that said ballots must be "without any device or mark by which one ticket may be known or distinguished from another, except the words at the head of the ticket." This provision of the law was aimed at discouraging voting by illiterates, who recognized ballots by their prominent engravings of roosters (Democratic) or Lincoln's face (Republican). Chalmers claimed that the printer's dashes that separated groups of candidates on Lynch's ballot were "distinguishing devices," and that these ballots should not be counted. On this basis 5,358 of Lynch's ballots were disqualified, chiefly in Warren County, and Chalmers secured the certificate of election. After a long contest in the U.S. House of Representatives Lynch was seated, but with more than half of his term already gone. No sooner was he seated than he had to begin campaigning for reelection.[57]

Like the Republican Lynch, Mississippi's Greenbackers entered the 1880 congressional races with high hopes. Having won over 44 percent of the reported vote in the second district only two years earlier, and over 40 percent in the first district, Greenbackers dreamed of moving on to victory in 1880. In the first district the party tapped T. W. Davidson, a farmer from Clay County. The party was not strong in east Mississippi counties like Clay, and Greenbackers hoped Davidson could help increase its popularity in that region. But this first district race was a fiasco: Davidson won just under 6 percent of the vote, as most black voters chose to vote instead for the Republican candidate, former Reconstruction-era congressman Joseph L. Morphis. Taken together, the two opposition candidates received barely more than one quarter of the total vote.[58]

In the second district, Greenbackers laid aside their prejudice against lawyers and nominated Holly Springs attorney Thomas W. Harris. Harris began an arduous campaign tour in September, agreeing to "divide time" with Democratic speakers. Democratic papers in the district pointed out that Republicans had nominated a candidate too—George M. Buchanan —and that Harris was part of a three-way race. The *Holly Spring South* asked, "Is Colonel Harris willing to be the instrument of electing

Buchanan to Congress" by dividing the white vote? The Greenback *Batesville Blade* retorted that the Democratic candidate was just as guilty of dividing the white vote. But as in the first district, black former Greenbackers now supported the Republican candidate, and with largely white Greenback support Harris won just over 12 percent of the vote, carrying Yalobusha County only. Republican Buchanan won almost 35 percent of the reported vote but carried no counties. The secretary of state declared Democratic candidate Vannoy H. Manning elected, with just under 53 percent of the official vote.[59]

In the third (north-central) congressional district, the Greenback party decided to run a candidate for the first time. The district included a few counties where the party had demonstrated some strength (Sumner, Calhoun, and Grenada), but also included counties where few Greenback votes had ever been polled (Leflore and Neshoba). The party's nominee, J. B. Gunn, was a native Mississippian and former Confederate, but the Democratic papers criticized him because he attacked the Democratic party, yet "handled the Radical party very tenderly." Gunn must be a Republican in disguise, the papers concluded. In the absence of a Republican opponent, Gunn did a little better than Davidson or Harris, winning 19 percent of the ballots cast.[60]

A fourth and final Greenback candidate tried for Congress in 1880; this was William P. Patterson, who ran in the fifth (southern) district. The fifth district included only a couple of counties with active Greenback organizations, and these two counties (Hinds and Lincoln) also had a strong history of Republican strength. Patterson had three opponents— two Republicans and a Democrat—but party leaders begged him to run in order to help give persons "in the humbler walks of daily toil" a candidate. Patterson agreed to work to help "avert an impending thraldom of the laboring classes of America" and accepted the party's nomination, but in November he won only 222 votes (almost exclusively in Hinds and Lincoln counties), less than one percent of the vote cast. The two Republican candidates taken together won about 35 percent of the vote, and so the fifth district returned a Democratic congressman, as did every district in the state except Lynch's. Across the South, Greenback congressional candidates suffered similarly embarrassing defeats, and in fact Gunn's percentage of the vote in Mississippi's third district was the second highest percentage won by a non-fusion Greenback candidate in the region.[61]

State Greenbackers had one final hope for 1880, and that was to win a strong showing for their presidential candidate, James B. Weaver of Iowa.

In this effort, though, the party suffered repeated setbacks. Weaver's letter of acceptance of his nomination suggested that former Union soldiers be given a bonus to make up for the fact that they had been paid in greenbacks instead of gold. The Greenback *Batesville Blade* explained that Weaver made the suggestion only to make a point—that it was unfair to pay U.S. bondholders in gold while the poor soldiers had been paid in less valuable greenbacks. The paper criticized its Democratic counterparts: "You make a great racket about paying the soldier, but bend pliant knee in submissive obedience to the bloated bondholder!" Still, the state's Democratic press was able to exploit image of the Greenbackers being friendly to the Union conquerors.[62]

A second problem arose when Democrats outside Mississippi began to circulate a forged letter, purporting to prove that James B. Weaver was in the pay of Republicans who hoped Weaver would draw off Democratic votes. The Jackson *Weekly Clarion* broke the story in Mississippi, and other papers were quick to copy. Few white Mississippians would be willing to vote for Weaver if he really were taking money from the hated northern Republicans. Weaver won less than six thousand votes in Mississippi in 1880, only about 5 percent of the votes cast. He did carry one county—Yalobusha—and placed second in six others. Perhaps party members could take heart from the fact that Weaver won a higher percentage of the vote in Mississippi than in any other southern state except Texas, and the seventh highest percentage of *any* state. Still, if 5 percent of the vote in some way looked good, the party clearly was in trouble. One scholar has stated that the poor Greenback showing in 1880 only demonstrated that Mississippians saw the party as "primarily an instrument for expressing dissatisfaction within the state rather than in the nation." Yet many of the most important planks of the Mississippi party's platform were goals that could be realized only at the national level.[63]

Still, it was not time for despair. The party did control seventeen seats in the legislature, and some county offices in eight counties. Greenbackers had replaced Republicans as the chief opposition in these eight counties as well as many others. The party could continue to grow if it held onto the counties it now controlled, and added others in the 1881 legislative and county elections. Two things were essential, however. The Greenbackers must prevent further erosion of their black support; this erosion had cost them dearly in the various congressional races of 1880. Also, the party must develop a way to fight the fraud and violence that had hurt them badly in several counties in 1879. Even in 1880, Greenbackers were still

dealing with the fraud and violence they suffered in 1879. A review of two of the contested races from 1879 will show what the Greenbackers feared as they looked toward 1881.

One of the most hotly contested elections in 1879 was the race in Yalobusha County. At the edge of the Delta, Yalobusha was just over half black; overwhelmingly rural, the county boasted only two very small towns, Coffeeville and Water Valley. Early on, the 1879 contest seemed to be going in favor of the Greenbackers; Democrats redoubled their efforts, throwing an elaborate barbecue and inviting all the Greenbackers to come enjoy themselves and listen to persuasive Democratic speakers. After the votes were counted it was clear the Greenbackers had elected their legislative candidate, M. D. L. Stephens. Both parties, however, claimed to have won the county offices. Soon two sheriffs patrolled the county. Two treasurers guarded an empty treasury, and three Greenback supervisors governed the county while two Democratic supervisors stayed away. From other counties, newspapers reported the difficulties in Yalobusha. For example, the two claimants for chancery clerk alternated in possession of the office; "First one is in, then out." In a bizarre set of legal proceedings, a Democratic chancellor issued an injunction that forbid two Greenback claimants from contesting their offices in the courts. The *Grenada Sentinel* reported that "It is feared that a serious difficulty will yet occur."[64]

The most bitter controversy centered on the sheriff's office. Details of the dispute have not survived, but suffice it to say that both candidates considered themselves elected. Greenbacker R. V. Pearson received the certificate of election and entered upon his duties. But in various judicial proceedings the courts declared Democrat L. R. Wilson the victor; for a time both men were collecting fees and filing routine reports to Jackson. Soon after the Democrat Wilson finally gained full possession of the office, Greenbackers discovered that Wilson, who had been an incumbent candidate, owed the state money he had collected as sheriff and never sent to Jackson. A number of witnesses testified that they had paid Wilson certain liquor fees, but the state auditor had never received these funds. The jury, made up of eight Democrats and four Greenbackers, found against Wilson, and he was declared ineligible to be sheriff. A special election was ordered for August 1880.[65]

Yalobusha Greenbackers were determined that, unlike the state's Republicans, they would not permit themselves to be abused by fraud, violence, and intimidation. The editor of the state party's organ, the *Batesville Blade*, denounced the Democrat Wilson as a thief of the county's money

soon after the conclusion of the court case against him. Wilson angrily denied the charges in letters to Democratic papers. But the editor of the *Blade* made a tough rejoinder: "If Captain Wilson did not like the articles . . . he knew his remedy." More appropriate than letters to newspapers would be "a note from him . . . demanding the satisfaction due a gentleman." This would have been "more proper and businesslike, and would have received prompt attention," the Greenback editor concluded.[66]

As the special election campaign for sheriff continued, with Greenbacker R. V. Pearson again contending for the post, feelings between Yalobusha's two political parties continued to run high. Just before the election both groups convened at Coffeeville for Saturday rallies. Both hoped to use the courthouse, but the Greenbackers got there first. Later, as the Democrats paraded, Pearson accosted W. Thomas Spearman, a black participant in the parade. Pearson was angry with Spearman because although the governor had appointed Spearman a non-Democratic election commissioner, he was parading with the Democrats and wearing a Democratic badge. State law required that county election commissioners were to be three men, not all of the same party; the governor typically appointed a half-hearted black Republican to the non-Democratic slot. Pearson denounced Spearman, struck him, and a general firing of guns followed.[67]

Pearson was shot twice, once in each leg; he walked to the corner, then turned and fired at the Democrats, hitting two of them. Finally, after being hit in the lung, Pearson was carried away by his fellow-partisans. Shortly after "The Coffeeville Riot," Pearson won the special election, receiving a majority of seventy-three votes. Although elected, the Greenbacker was so severely injured that he could not enter upon his duties for a full three months. It was a costly victory for the party, but by refusing to be intimidated, and perhaps by doing some intimidating of their own, the Greenbackers were able to maintain Yalobusha County as their stronghold for the next several elections.[68]

A similar course of events transpired in Holmes County, another agricultural county at the edge of the Delta. No official returns exist from Holmes County for this election; the ballot box at Acona precinct was stolen and never recovered. Nevertheless, all newspaper accounts agreed that the Greenbackers had won an impressive victory in Holmes. Some Democratic papers reported that the Greenbackers swept all the offices, while at the county seat the *Lexington Advertiser* stated that Greenbackers lost only three offices, including state senator. The Greenback senatorial

candidate died of natural causes soon after the election, and the party reluctantly acquiesced in the seating of a Democratic senator. The two parties sharply contested the three state house of representatives seats from Holmes; although several Democratic legislators argued that all three Greenbackers should be seated, the house finally seated two Greenbackers and one Democrat.[69]

As in Yalobusha County, however, it was the sheriff's office that most interested the two feuding parties. In Holmes there was little doubt that the Greenbacker J. J. Baker had been fairly elected. But in a reversal of the Yalobusha County events, Holmes Democrats now brought suit to show that Baker was ineligible to be sheriff, because he owed the state $2,100 he had collected as deputy sheriff many years before but had never paid into the state treasury. State courts agreed and ruled that Baker's opponent, Democratic incumbent J. S. Hoskins, should continue in office until a special election could be ordered. Sheriff Hoskins used his newspaper, the *Lexington Advertiser*, to argue that a special election would be a waste of money, and that he should be allowed to continue in office until the regular elections of 1881. Two months later, however, Hoskins was forced to use the columns of his paper to inform Holmes County citizens that he himself owed the state $6000, which he was unable to pay. He claimed he was guilty only of extravagance in running the office, but he resigned, and the governor appointed Democrat Joseph E. Ashcraft to be sheriff.[70]

Meanwhile the board of supervisors announced a date for a new sheriff's election, and three men announced their candidacy: sheriff Joseph E. Ashcraft, the Greenback candidate J. J. Baker, and a Republican attorney named Dyson. The special election was held on the day of the congressional election, in November 1880. As citizens were voting in Lexington, Sheriff Ashcraft's father made a sneering comment to Greenback Chancery Clerk T. J. Lockhart to the effect that Lockhart had not really been elected the previous November. Lockhart then struck the elder Ashcraft; Sheriff Joseph Ashcraft next shot Lockhart in the abdomen. Lockhart retaliated by shooting the sheriff in the chest, and a general exchange of gunfire followed. Among the injured was editor of the Greenback *Holmes County Times*, C. M. Hull. Sheriff Ashcraft died immediately; Lockhart lingered a few days but he died as well. Editor Hull was arrested for his part in the affray, as was a Democratic election officer named H. T. Allen, who was indicted for "attempted assassination of a Greenbacker at the polls."[71]

Soon the state's newspapers carried a singular official notice from

Holmes County. The notice stated that Holmes would hold a second special election, this one for sheriff and chancery clerk, "to fill the vacancies caused by the death of these officers on election day." To many, it must have seemed as if the Greenbackers were carrying an awfully big chip on their shoulders; Greenback violence with little provocation had precipitated both the fracas at Coffeeville and the one at Lexington. But by appearing strong and even threatening, Greenbackers sent a message to other Mississippians that they would not be overawed into oblivion as had the Republican party in 1875. Testifying during a congressional committee's investigation of the 1880 election, A. T. Wimberly described how Democrats inevitably went to the joint political meetings heavily armed. This forced the Greenbackers to go armed as well, Wimberly explained, as "we were not inclined to be bulldozed and run off the track by the Democratic mob." Asked if the election officers provided a fair election in Yalobusha County, Wimberly replied in the affirmative: "We made them give it to us."[72]

Threats and intimidation were very severe problems for any non-Democratic party in Mississippi. A. T. Wimberly, chair of the Greenback State Executive Committee, once received a warning from Coffeeville that he must retire from the 1880 campaign "or I would be a dead man before midnight." Although Wimberly gritted his teeth and replied that he would die "when God called me away and not until then," he did rush to pay up his dues at his fraternal lodge so that his wife would receive the burial benefits. Reports of these death threats were heard as far away as Indianapolis, where a Greenback rally passed resolutions applauding Mississippi Greenbackers' bravery. But in allowing reports of the threats to reach the north, Wimberly (a native Mississippian) left himself open to the charge that he was "waving the bloody shirt" and attempting to malign Mississippi in the eyes of the world.[73]

Black Greenbackers, too, had to worry about intimidation, which could range from blatant to subtle. This report of the actions of some young white men in Noxubee County, for example, was intended to sound innocent enough, but undoubtedly describes a more serious intimidation. The *Macon Beacon* reported that while black voters in 1880 were waiting in line at the court house door, "A few jolly young men amused themselves, in pulling off [the blacks men's] hats, jerking their coat-tails, tickling them, &c., and some of the darkies got a little mad at it, and being tired of waiting their turn to vote, left without voting." These Noxubee County black voters were being assaulted in a partly successful attempt to keep

them from voting. Had they stayed, they risked an escalation into real violence, which could have proved very dangerous to their safety. Although a black majority county, Noxubee cast little more than three hundred votes for Greenback candidate J. B. Gunn, the Democrats' only opponent.[74]

Of course, one way for Independents, Republicans, and Greenbackers to counter fraud and violence was to bring criminal prosecution against the perpetrators. Successful prosecution was not likely at the state level, since most of the state's district attorneys and all its judges were Democrats. There were, however, federal election laws, passed during Reconstruction, that could be used to punish many kinds of fraud, intimidation, and violence. In fact, U.S. attorneys in Mississippi did bring many prosecutions under these federal statutes, more than in any other southern district in the post-Reconstruction period. Moreover, they won a high conviction rate. Yet two factors meant that these successes in the federal courts made little difference. First, Mississippi's federal judge, Robert A. Hill, handed down very small fines and no prison sentences in the election prosecutions of the 1880s. And second, limited funds and a small staff of federal attorneys meant that only a fraction of the election frauds would actually be prosecuted.[75]

In Monroe County in the 1880 congressional races, three Republican voters complained of the actions of two Democratic citizens of West Point. The two men were indicted for conspiring to prevent the three Republicans from publicly supporting the Republican candidacy of Joseph L. Morphis; a second count alleged that "By illegal force & threats of force" these Democrats kept the three Republicans, and others, from voting. The case went to trial on January 5, 1881; the men pleaded nolo contendere (that is, they made no defense). Judge Hill then levied a five dollar fine on each. When the U.S. attorney general heard reports of this and similar cases in January 1881, he noted sourly that Hill's lenient punishments amounted to a "deliberate trifling with the execution of the laws of the United States."[76]

Fraud was widespread in the second congressional district in 1880, and Greenbackers and Republicans joined forces to provide witnesses for election prosecutions. In Greenback-controlled Panola County, the three election commissioners (appointed by the Democratic governor), refused to register certain voters who were known to be Greenbackers or Republicans. These three men also pleaded nolo contendere and also received very light fines: ten dollars each.[77]

A third case, this one from Clay County in the first congressional district, involved three election commissioners at Big Spring precinct in 1880; they were charged with refusing to publicly open the ballot box and count the ballots after the polls closed, as required by law. By implication, the men were suspected of stuffing the ballot box or fraudulently counting the votes, but without witnesses these latter charges could not be made explicit. The federal attorney pulled out all the stops in trying this case; he summoned twenty-two prosecution witnesses including Greenback congressional candidate T. W. Davidson. The cost of the two-day trial was $1,281, an almost unprecedented expense. All three election officials were found guilty; the fine, however, again was ten dollars each.[78]

Another prosecution from Clay County directly charged three young men with ballot box stuffing; they pleaded not guilty, and a four day trial followed, ending in conviction. This time, because of the grave nature of the crime, Judge Hill levied a more severe fine of $250 each. The young men, however, returned home and were welcomed by a cheering crowd. A local woman delivered a poem she had composed in their honor; the poem began,

> Our welcome, gallant trio,
> Clay County's free-born sons!
> Convicted of true manhood
> Thrice welcome honored ones.[79]

The crowd passed resolutions promising to raise money to pay the young men's fines by sponsoring a concert and a shooting match, and in fact the young men's fines were quickly paid. It was clear that with only a fraction of the election crimes resulting in prosecution, and only very light fines assessed on those who were convicted, the federal courts offered little in the way of a solution to the problems of Mississippi's opposition parties.

Fraud and intimidation was one thing Greenbackers would have to meet in the future. Another problem for the party was Democratic co-optation. Although the Greenback platforms were very popular among hard-pressed Mississippi farmers, Democratic politicians soon endorsed these very same policies. In Panola County, Democrats hoped to overcome the 60 percent majority won by the Greenbackers by adopting a county Democratic platform that read like a Greenback party document. Panola Democrats called for free and unlimited coinage of silver, for example, and like Greenbackers they urged that U.S. bonds be immediately paid off with a new issue of greenbacks. Benton County Democrats offered a similar

platform to offset the Greenback party's inroads in northern Mississippi. Further, the Democratic *Ashland Register* gave a long review of currency matters before the Congress and convincingly showed that the Democrats had a good record on matters important to the Greenbackers. For instance, reported the *Register*, Democrats had introduced a bill to allow states to tax U.S. bonds—an idea the Greenback party had been calling for. In the house of representatives, sixty-three Democrats had supported the bill, while none voted against it. Among house Republicans, eight supported the bill, and seventy-seven voted against it. The *Register* concluded by urging men of Greenback sentiments to vote Democratic.[80]

Yalobusha Democrats liked to point out that the Greenback party was "insignificant" at the national level. The Greenback party had no U.S. senators and only a dozen or so congressmen, while the Democratic party, supporting the same principles, controlled both houses of Congress. "Which do you think most likely to succeed and afford you that relief you want right now?" asked the *Water Valley Central*. At the state level, the well-known Democratic leaders were often very popular with farmers. Even Democratic lawyer-politicians could win the warm support of white small farmers. United States Senator James Z. George, for example, was a lawyer; he had, however, been born into poverty, was raised on a farm, and as a politician supported such popular causes as the state Agricultural and Mechanical College. Mississippi farmers considered George the father of the U.S. Department of Agriculture. The Democratic senator also supported state and national railroad regulation and the regulation of monopolies. Ethelbert Barksdale, chair of the Democratic State Executive Committee during the first two Greenback election campaigns, was also a Granger and would win the warm support of farmers during his later congressional candidacies.[81]

The Greenbackers also had to be concerned with the fact that the overwhelming majority of the state's newspapers were controlled by Democratic editors and publishers. This led to a number of problems. The Democratic press repeatedly gave readers the impression that the Greenback party enjoyed very little popular support. In reporting an 1879 party rally in Rankin County, for example, the Jackson *Weekly Clarion* told its readers that although a large crowd attended, most were "curious citizens," and only fifty-two actual Greenbackers were present. The Greenbackers, according to the Democratic paper, paraded without music while carrying an American flag on a cane fishing pole. Finally, the paper quoted

a little boy as saying of the Greenback parade, "It's the derndest, dirtiest nosed, hungriest crowd I ever saw." Perhaps. But on election day more than one thousand Rankin Countians voted with the Greenbackers—about 43 percent of the participating voters.[82]

In an even more biting, sarcastic report of a Greenback gathering, the Jackson *Weekly Clarion* reported on a Greenback mass meeting at the rural Hinds County community of Forest Hill. Most of those present, the Democratic paper claimed, were not Greenbackers but Democrats; in fact, only "three and a half" Greenbackers attended. The "half" supposedly was a drunken black Greenbacker, who went to sleep upon his arrival. Because the Democratic *Clarion's* report is the only account we have of this Forest Hill meeting, we cannot tell how accurate it is. There were certainly more than three or four active Greenbackers in the neighborhood, however, and in fact on election day the Forest Hill precinct returned a majority for most Greenback candidates. The phenomenon of Democratic underreporting of Greenback support was a serious problem. It was hard for the new party to win supporters and mobilize voters when newspapers were reporting, inaccurately, that the movement was dying at birth.[83]

The Democratic press also took advantage of its domination to explain to Mississippians just who the Greenbackers were. In one of the earliest reports of the new movement, the Democratic *DeSoto Press and Times* in August 1878 alleged that the old Republican partisans "confront us under the filmy guise of a new name—the Nationals." A year later the paper was making the same claim, warning DeSoto Countians that "The Greenbackers, alias Republicans, are fully organized." Across the state, Democratic papers applied to the Greenbackers the odious label previously reserved for Republicans: "Radical." In a memorable passage the *Clarion* editorialized, "This [Greenback] movement comes to us under a new name, but when you apply the probe to the putrid carcass you will find the old Radical corpse covered with a thin layer of Greenbacks." If the Democratic press could succeed in making *Radical* a synonym for *Greenbacker*, the party would be in trouble because of the ugly connotation to many white voters: *radical* made whites think of carpetbaggers and black domination. The papers listed similarities between the old Radical Republicans and the new movement: Not only fife and drum music, but secret "midnight meetings" were returning to Mississippi. Greenbackers countered by saying they held political meetings at night so that working men could

attend, and they pointed out that at these nighttime conclaves Democrats were present and were offered equal time. Yet the Democratic accusations were given more space in the press than Greenback defenses.[84]

In speaking to black voters, the state's Democratic press confused the issue by now claiming that instead of being former Radical Republicans, Mississippi's Greenbackers were actually men who had violently fought black rights in the fearful election of 1875. In black majority Monroe County, the *Aberdeen Examiner* claimed that the only difference between the old Radical Republican meetings and the current Greenback meetings was that now carpetbaggers had been replaced by former bulldozers who wanted offices. In Holmes County, another county where a majority of the population was black, the *Lexington Advertiser* noted that some people said the Greenback party had no record. The *Advertiser* was quick to retort that in fact the Greenbackers did have a record—a record of violence and intimidation they had practiced as Democrats in 1875. The Greenback *Weekly Independent* pointed out that it wasn't fair of the Democratic press to accuse the Greenbackers of being both former Republicans and former bulldozers; "Every manly and outspoken movement" is lied about, and the lies in this case would come back to hurt the Democrats, the *Independent* argued, hopefully.[85]

In telling the state's newspaper readers just who the Greenbackers were, the Democratic press had other labels and other accusations. One common label, in addition to "Radical," was "Sore-head." This epithet was widely used across the state, and implied that the Greenbackers were former Democrats who left the party because they had been denied a nomination. In 1879 the Jackson *Weekly Clarion* denounced the "little go-cart of a party" that was "conceived in sin, brought forth in iniquity, and for no other purpose than to satisfy the lust for office." The *Clarion* listed a number of Hinds County Greenback candidates, and attempted to prove they were sore-heads. One had lost a Democratic primary two years earlier (before the Greenback party was organized). Another was a Democratic senator who joined the Greenbackers because he believed he would not be reelected, according to the *Clarion*. In perhaps the weakest accusation of all, the paper claimed that one Greenback candidate was running because his son had been denied the Democratic nomination for a county office. These sorts of accusations were easy to make because almost anyone with a political past has been denied a nomination at one point or another. Interestingly, there seem to be no cases of Greenback candidates who had been denied the Democratic nomination the same year they ran

as Greenbackers. There were a few cases of "Independent," bolter candidates who fit this description, but no Greenbackers.[86]

Yet another Greenback label created by the state's Democratic press was "mongrel party," alluding to the fact that both whites and blacks supported the Greenbackers. The *Weekly Clarion* in 1879 claimed the Hinds County Greenback ticket had little support, owing to "its weak men and mongrel mixture."[87] When a largely black Republican ticket entered the county race, the *Clarion* welcomed the addition, saying it was better to fight "thorough-breds" than "half-breeds and scrubs." In an even more direct use of racial descriptions, the newspaper pointed out that the two black Hinds County Greenback candidates were "both nearly white in color" and did not represent the interests of the county's black voters.[88]

The label-pinning of the Democratic press was arguably the most serious threat to the Greenback party. If the state's white citizens did in fact begin to call the Greenbackers radicals, sore-heads, and mongrels, the party would find it impossible to win new white supporters. One solution to the threat of the Democratic press was obvious: found new Greenback newspapers. Several important county papers had defected from the Democrats to the new party in 1878; these included, for example, the *Batesville Blade* in Panola County and the Ashland *Benton County Argus*, as well as the *Houston Patriot* in Chickasaw County. Several new papers were added in 1878, 1879, and 1880, including the Corinth *North Mississippian*, and Lexington's *Holmes County Times*. By 1880 eight Greenback papers were being published in the state, with more being planned.[89]

These Greenback papers had a variety of formats. Some, such as the *Batesville Blade*, were general-purpose newspapers, reporting not only on party activity but on crops, crime, gossip, and church activities. The *Blade* was widely read in north Mississippi, and was an important voice in answering Democratic newspapers. The *Blade* pointed out the inconsistency of Democrats in calling Greenbackers both "Radicals" and "former bulldozers." When Democratic papers in 1880 urged Greenbackers not to throw away their vote on presidential candidate James B. Weaver but instead to vote for Democrat Winfield Scott Hancock, the *Blade* asked pointedly just after election day, "On whom were the most votes thrown away, Weaver or Hancock?" Although editor Henry W. Thaten reported that a few potential advertisers promised their patronage if he would drop his support of Greenbackers, he refused, and pointed out that in fact he really had no shortage of advertisers. The *Blade* benefited economically from the fact that it won the county printing contract from the

Pennsylvania will elect auditor general and State treasurer

Virginia will elect part of its senate and its full assembly.

Mississippi will elect its legislature. Those county officers whose term is two years, and about half those that hold four years, and district attorneys, as well as all beat officers

---

Milwaukee, October 29.—A Waupun special to the Sentinel says : S. J. Hudson, of Belvidere, Ill, who came here recently with two children in search of his runaway wife, found her masquerading in male attire under the name of Frank Dubois. She was living with Gertrude Fuller, having been married to her early last spring by Rev. H. L Morrison at the home of the bride's mother. the deception had not been suspected, but many thought Frank Dubois had many characteristics of a woman. Under the name she had solicited odd jobs of painting, and was earning enough to support both.

POSTMASTER--GENERAL GRESHAM has made another pass at the lottery business which cannot but result in putting a stop to it, basing his action upon section 3894 of the Revised Statutes, as follows :

"No letter or circular concerning (illegal) lotteries, so-called gift concerts, or other similar enterprises offering prizes, or concerning schemes devised and intended to deceive and defraud the public for the purpose of obtaining money under false pretenses, shall be carried in the mail. Any person who shall knowingly deposit or send anything to be conveyed by mail in violation of this section shall be punishable by a fine of not more

pretenses and abominable injustice.-- Natchez Crusader.

GRAND

GREENBACK RALLY.

There will be a Grand Greenback Rally at

SARDIS, NOVEMBER, 2ND 1883.

BATESVILLE, NOV. 3RD, 1883.

ALL THE PROMINENT

Greenback Speakers

OF THE COUNTY WILL BE

PRESENT!

There will also be speakers from a distance to address the people.

The *Batesville Blade* served the Greenback party from 1878 to 1885, making it the party's most durable publication. Its columns regularly reported on party events and rallies. (From the *Batesville Blade*, November 2, 1883)

Greenback-controlled board of supervisors. This was also true of several other Greenback papers, including the Water Valley *Yalobusha Standard* and the *Benton County Argus*. Greenbackers also published the Jackson *Weekly Independent*, which was intended to be a statewide publication emphasizing party news and not a local Jackson paper.[90]

As 1880 drew to a close, leaders of the Greenback party had much to be proud of. In two short years they had won elections in many counties and had made strong beginnings in many others. They could boast seventeen members of the legislature, and were beginning to enjoy the excitement of planning for the 1881 elections. In 1881 the state's voters would chose a governor and other state officers, a legislature, and county and beat officers. By refusing to give in to intimidation in counties like Yalobusha and Holmes, the party had served notice on Democrats that the tactics used in 1875 could not be used to defeat Greenbackers. Although black defections to the Republican party had hurt in the 1880 congressional and presidential races, already Greenbackers were developing strategies to capitalize on the black vote in 1881. And while the domination of the Democratic press made it difficult for the party to elude labels like "radical" and "sorehead," the Greenbackers had founded eight newspapers and were preparing to launch a like number of new titles. The future seemed bright for Mississippi's Greenbackers.

THREE

Fusion, Confusion, Republicans, and Independents

THE CHARGES SURFACED EARLY IN THE 1881 GUBERNATORIAL campaign. "Independent People's candidate" Benjamin King sometimes went shirtless and was in the habit of wearing coarse brogan shoes. In a flourish of fair play, the Democratic *Jackson Comet* noted that the allegations were surely untrue: "It is absurd for the papers to start any such report." Yet King himself soon admitted the truth of the charges, saying that "he dressed to suit himself." Moreover, the *Comet* reported that although King was wearing shirts while campaigning, he often went without a shirt collar: "Now he would be a pretty specimen to put in the executive mansion." The Greenback newspaper, the Water Valley *National Record*, argued that it should not be held against King that he wore brogan shoes instead of stylish boots. King's own campaign organ, the Jackson *Crisis*, mocked the state's journalists for their horror over King's workingman's dress, and pleaded, "No, no, friend, in pity raise not that issue. Do not crush us to earth with your gloves, and your beaver hats, your rose water and cologne, your delicate silk handkerchief, your powder and cosmetics."[1]

Benjamin King was a popular state senator from Copiah County, a former Whig who had been a Democrat since the Civil War. The idea of asking King to run for governor as the representative of Greenbackers, Republicans, and Independents, was conceived by Republican leader John

Roy Lynch. If all three dissident groups combined their strengths, chances were good they could beat the Democrats in 1881. King, however, was himself a loyal Democrat. When Lynch told him of the plan King was shocked, but did not immediately say no, and finally he agreed to run so long as he did not have to join the Republican or Greenback party. Both the Greenbackers and the Republicans nominated King for governor, and each of the two parties took three of the lesser state offices on the "Independent People's ticket."[2]

For both Republicans and Greenbackers, the biggest issue of the campaign was Campbell's Code, which the legislature had passed in 1880. This was a codification of all Mississippi's laws, including some laws newly added in 1880. Of all the provisions of the code, none was more controversial than the crop lien section, which provided that a farmer's crop could be seized to satisfy his rent obligations.[3]

Small farmers, both black and white, hated the crop lien provisions of Campbell's Code. The state Grange declared that it would oppose all legislative candidates who did not promise to fight this system. Small farmers believed the crop lien law was a type of class legislation, favoring the landlord and merchant class over the renter class. Arguments marshaled by the state's Democratic press to defend the lien law were often far from convincing. The Democratic organ the *Jackson Comet* first argued that landlords would not support laws that hurt their renters; on the contrary, "The interest of the landlord is to have a prosperous, satisfied, and happy tenantry." Second, no one was forced to submit to the crop lien law, since no one was "required" to rent land. In short, explained the *Comet*, the crop lien section was enacted to help renters. Landlords would not rent their lands unless they could be sure to get their rent payments. Without the crop lien law, the Jackson paper concluded, many poorer farmers would not be able to find land to rent. While it was true that to cover a farmer's rent obligations "all that he has" was subject to seizure, "*This is for his benefit.*" Small farmers disagreed, and this one issue was a potent force in uniting black Republicans and white Greenbackers behind Benjamin King.[4]

While the crop lien system did provide King with one galvanizing issue, there were problems with his candidacy more serious than the clothing he wore (or did not wear). Loyal members of both the Republican and Greenback parties were irritated by King's repeated insistence in stump speeches that he himself was neither a Greenbacker, nor a Republican, nor a member of any formal Independent movement. Democrats raised issues of

loyalty, as they pointed out that even as he campaigned, King was a duly elected Democratic state senator. Democrats also alleged that less than a year earlier King had masterminded a gerrymandering plan that would have denied opposition candidates any possibility of winning congressional races. Appealing to the racism of white voters, King's opponent Robert Lowry claimed that the Democratic party was "the only party in Mississippi that relies upon the intelligence of the state for its main support." The source of King's support was the state's black population, Lowry concluded, and he warned that "the stream cannot rise higher than its source."[5]

Many voters did have trouble conceptualizing King's candidacy; if he was neither Greenbacker nor Republican nor Independent, just what was he? Democrats made much of the fact that a few prominent opposition party leaders had refused to support the Independent People's ticket. Well-known Delta Republican Robert J. Alcorn spoke out against King, while the editor of the Greenback *Batesville Blade* announced that his paper would not actively support King, since he was not a Greenbacker. Further, as many of the Democratic speakers pointed out, King must be an opportunist, since he was asking the support of two formal parties that had very little in common.[6]

To this charge the Independent People's leaders had a ready answer. Mississippi Democrats, too, often turned to "fusion" with strange bedfellows. In 1872 the state Democratic party had united behind the Liberal Republican presidential candidacy of Horace Greeley, and the following year they supported moderate Republican James Lusk Alcorn for governor. Furthermore, in many counties with black majorities, the Democrats regularly offered county tickets in fusion with the Republicans. But it was true, especially at the national level, that the Greenbackers and Republicans differed on a number of issues. National Republican leaders shuddered at Greenbackers' desires to inflate the money supply, to cut the power of the national banks, and to allow states to tax U.S. bonds. Yet in Mississippi, the black Republican farmers and the white Greenback small farmers were united by two great issues. As we have seen, one was the crop lien law. The other was fraud and violence in Mississippi elections.[7]

King emphasized this latter issue in his many joint appearances with his opponent Lowry. At one such speaking, King rattled off a long list of state election frauds of the last few years: two ballot boxes had disappeared in DeSoto County in 1879, while two others had vanished in Tate that same year. One had disappeared in Panola County, and was later found in a

sinkhole. But the Democrats complained bitterly about King's charges. "He started up in Tate and recited what somebody said was done with the ballot-boxes there; then what another somebody . . . said was done in DeSoto." It was all hearsay, the Democrats argued.[8]

Robert Lowry himself attacked King on this issue, pointing out that if King's charges were true—if election fraud was widespread—then federal judge Robert A. Hill must be incompetent or corrupt for not punishing such crimes. On the contrary, Lowry added, Hill was a widely respected jurist. To Lowry's attack, King was ready with a response. He produced records from Hill's Oxford court proving that in fact election frauds *had* been investigated by federal officers, many indictments found, and some convictions won. Many of the defendants had pleaded guilty.[9]

Yet it was difficult for King to score against Lowry on the elections issue. King worked himself up to a fever pitch, discussing the notorious election frauds in Yazoo County. He pointed out than in a black majority, Republican majority county, GOP presidential candidate James A. Garfield had received ridiculously few votes. How did this happen, asked King. Lowry answered, "Garfield was not popular in Yazoo!" In other speeches, according to a Greenback paper, Lowry admitted that "there may have been some [election] irregularities, and bad boys may have acted improperly," but the overall results of the elections were not affected. Besides, Lowry had another potent charge. If King was so concerned about peaceful and honest elections, had he never wondered how he himself had been elected a Democratic state senator from a county with a Republican majority? He must not have found out how it was done until now, when his term was almost over, Lowry chuckled. Or, as the *Comet* put it, "If ever there was a ballot-box stuffing in this state, don't every man know that Mr. King was elected to the Senate by this means?"[10]

On the other hand, Democrats did have a spotted record in this 1881 campaign. Reports came in regularly of intimidation of Independent People's ticket supporters. In Winston County the Democrats were running Henry J. Gulley for the legislature. Gulley's name was a household word across the nation, as he had been a leader in the mob murder of the former Republican sheriff of Kemper County in 1877. Prior to election day, the worst incident of the 1881 campaign occurred in Sharkey County. There, one or more hidden gunmen fired into a crowd of blacks as they passed down the road to a political meeting. Three were killed, and two others wounded. The Greenback papers were furious, and pointed out that Lowry had said earlier, "If there is bloodshed on the 8th of next

November, let no colored man say he was not warned in time . . . . For if a conflict should occur, you know who will be the victims."[11]

In fact, throughout the campaign Democratic editors used up prodigious amounts of printer's ink in addressing Mississippi's black citizens. The *DeSoto Times* told blacks that if they "drew the color line" and voted en masse for King, they would be demonstrating "hostility toward the white," which could be dangerous since blacks could not succeed economically without help from white citizens. The *Jackson Comet* told the state's blacks that if they antagonized whites by going into the new political movement, feelings of kindness toward blacks, now common in white breasts, "would fade and die out." More ominously, "there will again be bitter conflict as there was in 1875." Respected Democrat L. Q. C. Lamar warned, "the intelligence of this state [will] never again see Mississippi turned over to the rulers chosen by that solid mass of ignorance."[12]

Since the 1881 race was wholly a state and county election, federal attorneys and marshals made it clear they would not be involved in election law enforcement. Still, the Independent People's candidates had two hopes for an honest election. The first was that by getting some of their supporters appointed county election commissioners, they could prevent ballot-box stuffing and fraudulent counting. Under state law, the governor appointed three election commissioners for each county, with no more than two of the three being members of the same party. The Independent People's campaign committee sent Governor John M. Stone lists of men they wanted appointed from each county. Stone appointed some of the men on the list, in counties where the Democratic party was almost certain to be victorious. In the hotly contested counties, however, the governor declined to appoint the men recommended by the King camp and instead appointed men whom he claimed were Republicans.

King's backers accused the governor of appointing illiterate, pliable, possibly dishonest black men to represent the opposition movement, thus facilitating ballot box stuffing and fraudulent counting. The situation in Oktibbeha County was typical. The governor appointed a black man named Randle Nettles to be one of the county election commissioners. The Greenback and Republican executive committees produced evidence that Nettles had in fact supported the Democratic ticket during the last three election campaigns, but the governor refused to reconsider his appointment. The opposition leaders filed dozens of complaints with the governor's office, alleging that many of the appointees were densely igno-

rant, some were morally corrupt, and that none of them in the closely contested counties were partisans of the King movement. No changes, however, were made. As historian Vernon L. Wharton noted, the appointment of these election officers by the Democratic governor "made all things possible" in counting the votes and preparing returns.[13]

One other way to try to salvage an election free of intimidation and fraud was to talk tough and make it clear that King and his followers would not meekly submit to bulldozing and ballot fraud. As we have seen, the Greenback leaders had some experience in employing aggressive talk and action, and their aggressiveness had helped insure their electoral victories in many counties. King was quick to imitate the Greenbackers' use of tough words. If the new Campbell's Code did not provide legal protection for would-be voters, King announced, his followers would rely more "upon a number of little 'six-barrelled codes.'" In other words, opposition voters would carry revolvers if necessary to assure their right to campaign and to vote. Lowry's *Jackson Comet* was quick to seize upon King's words and give the Democrats a new issue. "The Democrats cry peace," the paper trumpeted, but King's supporters "cry no peace, no reconciliation. . . . The people deserve the olive branch of peace."[14]

The Grange newspaper *Patron of Husbandry* supported a number of King's followers in legislative races and was adamant that "if any middleman or politician gets in the way and tries to obstruct the Grange wagon, *it will be bad for him.*" In the words of the state's chief Grange leader, the Grange was going to involve itself in politics, and "no earthly power" could prevent them. In Jackson, the editor of King's organ *The Crisis* reported that he had received a threat, but added coolly, "Gentlemen may spare themselves a good deal of trouble if they reflect that we are here until the crisis is over."[15]

Most hotheaded of the campaigners was Greenbacker A. T. Wimberly, who was the nominee for state auditor on the King ticket. Democratic newspapers constantly drew attention to Wimberly's provocative actions and words and argued that Democratic campaigners were more likely to bring peace and calm to the state as a whole. At a speaking at the Tate County courthouse just before the election, Democratic and People's Independent candidates made a joint appearance. When the Democratic sheriff nominee interrupted a King speaker, Wimberly stood up, put his hand on his revolver and said, "G-d d—n you, what have you got to do with it?" Even though Tate County had a Greenback-controlled govern-

ment, Wimberly soon found himself under arrest for disturbing the peace. Although the only account we have of this altercation is from a Democratic newspaper, it is in line with other provocative actions by Wimberly.[16]

The tough talk and actions of King partisans was an issue that could cut both ways. True, King's men had to demonstrate to the state's Democrats that they could not be intimidated into near-extinction. On the other hand, Democratic newspapers were continuing to use the hated label "Radical" to describe King's followers, and when King made threats of using six-barrelled codes, and with Wimberly and other campaigners spoiling for a fight, many voters must have wondered if in fact the Democratic newspapers were not correct.

Several other issues played an important role in the 1881 campaign. The Independent People's leaders made an early appeal to factory workers, and attacked the system of child labor, through the pages of their paper the Jackson *Crisis*. In textile factories near Wesson, the paper reported, more than a thousand workers worked nearly twelve hours a day. Many of these workers were children, who "in the winter months of the year only see the sun rise and set while looking through the mullions of the windows and listening to the eternal drone and whir of the spindles." Yet under Democratic policies, child labor flourished, and the factories were exempt from taxation. The *Crisis* editors concluded, "We say save the land from such Democracy."[17]

Another issue popular with farmers was the elective judiciary. After the Civil War, judges in Mississippi were appointed by the governor instead of being elected by the people, and many farmers saw no reason why the state should not return to a system of elected judges. They assumed the judges appointed by the governor were likely to be friendly to moneylenders and to corporations such as the railroads. But many Democratic papers warned that the tumult and back-room dealing of popular elections would not result in a better judiciary. The governor "sees the importance of having competent, pure and able men to sit on the bench," and the governor has "more capacity for judging than the people." These Democratic assertions did nothing to squelch small farmers' desire for a return to the elective judiciary, however.[18]

One final issue was a topic raised in many previous campaigns. This was the Democrats' assertion that under Republican rule taxes had been extraordinarily high, and that only a return to Democratic rule had protected the people from such oppression. Therefore, Democrats urged, only the Democratic party could continue to shield the people from high

taxes. Each side produced tables and charts showing its interpretation of the state's tax history. By choosing carefully what it included in such tables, each side was able to support its case statistically. The truth seems to be that Democrats in fact did lower taxes dramatically after the Republican Reconstruction. They accomplished this reduction, however, by shifting some functions of government back upon the counties. So, while the state tax rate dropped from 9¼ to 6½ mills, many citizens saw their county tax bills increase sixfold or even more. Democrats countered that perhaps county taxes were high because the counties were paying interest on debts contracted during Reconstruction. This explanation, however, does not account for the *increase* in county taxation over the several years prior to 1881, nor for the high taxes in counties that had never been governed by Republicans.[19]

After the balloting on November 8, the Mississippi secretary of state released the official election returns, which showed King winning 40 percent of the vote. For opponents of the Democratic party, this was certainly better than the previous gubernatorial election, where no opposition nominations were made and Democrat John M. Stone won with 98.8 percent of the vote. King's percentage of the vote was comparable to that of the Greenback congressional candidates of 1878—although the 1878 figures had been for two congressional districts, while King won 40 percent *statewide*. The official returns showed King carrying some fifteen counties, including old Republican centers of strength such as Adams, Coahoma, and Sharkey counties, and Greenback strongholds Benton, Sumner, and Tate counties. In Greenback-dominated Panola County, King won by an unprecedented 1,200 votes.[20]

But King had won considerably more than 40 percent, according to the state's Greenback and Republican leaders. Several days after the election the *Daily Memphis Avalanche* reported "suspicious delay" in the reporting of county returns in Mississippi. The newspaper reported that this delay was "believed to be caused by the Democratic commissioners holding them back until it is ascertained how many votes are wanted to elect Lowry." John R. Lynch believed the problem was that while the count was watched closely in Greenback counties where the King leaders were respected white men, in Republican counties the King men did not have the power to prevent fraud. "After the polls are closed the election really begins," a Louisiana politician once observed, and this was now Lynch's allegation about Mississippi. In Lynch's estimation the Democrats won, "not by the vote but by the *official returns* of the black belt."[21]

Some support for Lynch's argument is found in statistical studies made by political scientist J. Morgan Kousser. Using a technique called ecological regression analysis, Kousser prepared reliable estimates of the voting behavior of black and white Mississippians in the late nineteenth century. The most remarkable thing about Kousser's figures for the 1881 election is the large number of blacks that voted Democratic. According to Kousser's estimates, based on official returns, one third of blacks who voted, voted for Lowry. This figure is questionable in a state with a history of nearly unanimous black voting for Republican candidates. Democrats in the state constantly accused blacks of "color line voting."[22]

Of course there are a number of possible explanations of why one third of black votes might have gone to Lowry. Blacks may have decided that only Democrats could bring peace and calm back to the state. Blacks may have been intimidated, even forced, into casting Democratic ballots as they came to the polling places. Yet the most likely explanation is that John R. Lynch was right in his general assessment of Mississippi elections. In black counties, Lynch said, election managers did not fabricate ballots that were not cast, but they did fraudulently count Republican ballots as Democratic. According to Lynch, this fraud in the densely settled Delta region of the state was sufficient to deny King his rightful election. The *Daily Memphis Avalanche* observed that "the sagacity of Gen. Stone in fixing up the election boards with anti-Ben King men is now apparent."[23]

King, the Greenbackers, and the Republicans conferred in Jackson, trying to decide what to do to protect their interests. They told the press they had evidence of fraud and "the grossest irregularities ever before known." When two King men traveled to Washington, rumors were abundant that they would attempt to get the United States government to investigate the election or to intervene in some other way. There were rumors that the King men intended to set up a "dual government," since they believed themselves rightfully elected. Actually, the Democratic *De-Soto Times* was correct when it explained that only "a very few visionaries" in the King camp were actually considering any of these actions. In south Mississippi the *Brookhaven Ledger* noted the rumors, then blamed King for all the violence and unpleasantness of the campaign. "Let him not tempt the Caucasian race further," warned the *Ledger*. "He is beaten for Governor. He had better rest."[24]

Of course the Republicans were beginning to get used to defeat, since they had enjoyed relatively few victories since 1873. The Greenbackers were the most disappointed by the gubernatorial race of 1881. Three years

earlier they had won above 40 percent of the reported votes in two congressional races, then in 1879 had won seventeen legislative seats and control of a number of county governments. The Greenbackers had held high hopes for the 1881 statewide race. But now the *Daily Memphis Avalanche* wrote in a somber vein of the Mississippi Greenback party: "The day seems in the far distant future when the party will be able to win another county." The Grange *Patron of Husbandry* noted with dismay the victories of many conservative Democratic legislative candidates over Greenback and Independent farmer candidates. "They will tolerate no opposition from the 'lower classes,' as they call those who gain their living in the sweat of their brows," the Grange editor concluded. But the *Patron of Husbandry* was more optimistic than the *Avalanche*, arguing that since the "masses" were starting to work together, the day was not distant when the professional politicians would be toppled, and "the toiling millions will cast their votes untrammeled by the dictation of scheming politicians."[25]

The 1881 election was not only a race for statewide offices; it also featured contests for control of county offices and seats in the legislature. Although Benjamin King's ticket for state offices was labeled "Independent People's," there were few "Independent People's" county tickets. Instead, Republicans ran in counties where they had been recently strong, while Greenbackers attempted to follow up successes in north-central counties. In several west-central counties such as Copiah, Madison, and Yazoo, earlier Independent movements again sprang to life and ran candidates. Lauderdale County was home to an "Anti-Monopoly Party." To complicate matters further, a number of counties featured a fusion of two parties, either Democratic-Republican or Republican-Greenbacker. Hinds County had both.

Among the strongest of the Republican counties was Warren, where Vicksburg was located. Here as in many other river counties Democrats attempted to cope with the black majority of voters by offering a fusion ticket that included both white Democrats and a number of black Republicans. Warren Republican leadership, however, felt confident enough to offer a "straight-out" Republican ticket to challenge the Democrat-Republican fusion ticket. There was a calm, peaceful campaign in Warren, and on election day the King ticket carried the county by 1,100 votes. The Democratic-Republican fusion carried the legislative races, while the straight-out Republicans (led by sheriff candidate R. F. Beck) won most county offices. Warren County proved to be an island of tolerance in the

troubled seas of Mississippi politics. The *Vicksburg Herald* was an unswerving Democratic newspaper, but it denounced Democratic tactics of violence and intimidation in nearby Yazoo County, and declared, "We want free speech, free schools, a free ballot, and freedom of all sorts." The *Herald* concluded: "There can never be any real permanent prosperity in this state until [these rights] are enjoyed by all."[26]

Panola County was home to a very strong Greenback party and a flourishing Greenback newspaper, the *Batesville Blade*. The party's ticket seemed almost invincible, and when the Democrats held their county convention one delegate suggested that Republicans be given some places on the ticket. The debate was acrimonious, and the convention refused to admit the press. Finally the Democrats gave three places on their county slate to black Republicans; only one black man was included on the Greenback ticket. The local Democratic organ, the *Weekly Panola Star*, explained that since Democratic-Republican fusion had worked so well in Delta counties ranging from Bolivar to Washington, the Panola Democrats had vowed to try fusion as a "display of conciliation." The *Star* accused the Greenback party leaders of expecting blacks to provide a majority of Greenback votes, but "that party has never given them anything like a fair share of the offices." If Panola blacks would compare the two tickets, they could easily see that they would get "more" from the fusion ticket.[27]

The *Batesville Blade* editors seemed to enjoy the fact that their opponents were in a fusion movement. The *Blade* quoted the *Weekly Panola Star* as denouncing the fusion ticket of Ben King; the *Star* had declared that it would be a "damnable disgrace" to elect the "conglomerate crew." The *Blade* rejoined: "And suppose the 'conglomerate crew' running for office in Panola County is elected. . . . Such a calamity would set this county back at least ten years." Over and over state Democrats denounced the evils of a fusion of two parties that had little in common, and the *Blade* editors gleefully reprinted their comments and applied them to the Panola fusion of Democrats and Republicans. In joint meetings the Greenbackers won farmers' votes by discussing national banks, inflation, and the taxation of U.S. bonds; Democrats pointed out that county officers could do nothing to affect the nation's money supply, but their points failed to make much of an impression.[28]

Democrats were also hurt by the feeling among many blacks that the Republicans on the county fusion ticket were not the *best* men, and by rumors that many white Democrats planned to scratch the names of Republicans off their ballots before casting them on election day. Just before

election day a prominent black Greenbacker was ambushed and shot in the back; the *Star* alleged that he had been guilty of browbeating blacks who wanted to vote Democratic. But this assault helped insure that Panola blacks would vote Greenback. On election day the Greenbackers swept the county offices and Benjamin King carried the county by some 1,400 votes. The Greenbackers' only disappointments came in the legislative races, where the Democratic-Republican fusionists won two of the three seats in the lower house, and the county's senate seat as well.[29]

Two counties in eastern Mississippi featured hotly contested races, even though these counties were home to moribund Republican parties and few Greenbackers. The most dramatic race was in Lauderdale County, location of Meridian, one of the state's largest towns. Unfortunately, the records that document this election are few, and no copies of the county's newspapers have survived. For the early campaign, we have only the statement of the *Patron of Husbandry* that a slate of "farmers and mechanics" was challenging the more elite-oriented Democratic ticket in Lauderdale. The Grange paper applauded the "Anti-Monopoly" ticket, saying that working men would never be respected until professional politicians were turned out of office and farmers and workingmen put in their place. After election day the *Patron of Husbandry* editor wrote, "We deeply regret the defeat of the anti-Monopoly ticket in Lauderdale County." This newspaper must have been the only one in Mississippi that failed to comment upon the most dramatic event in the county in 1881, which occurred on election day.[30]

The trouble apparently began when crowds of blacks supporting both Benjamin King's state ticket and the Anti-Monopoly county ticket gathered in the town of Marion. As one newspaper later put it, an elderly white man was angered by their "insolence" and struck one of the black men over the head with a stick. Gunfire and a general riot followed. For one of the few times in the history of race riots in the Deep South, blacks clearly had the upper hand at Marion, at least at the beginning. Most accounts say that the blacks heavily outnumbered the whites on the streets of Marion, and quickly three white men were shot and killed, three wounded, and one black man was wounded when he attempted to help the whites. The rioters retreated to the house of one of their white allies, a Republican named Ed Vance.[31]

When a sheriff's posse arrived from Meridian the thirty or so blacks at first refused to leave Vance's house, then most of them fled the house with guns ablaze, forcing the posse to retreat. One of Vance's sons was shot and

killed in this latter altercation, as were four blacks and one white member of the posse. Soon white reinforcements came from Meridian, "fresh and eager to carry the war into Africa," as the state's newspapers put it. Gradually blacks were arrested and taken to jail. A Democratic paper reported that black fugitives were being shot, and said grimly, "The negroes and Anti-monopolists started this thing and they must look to the divine master to stop it." The *Vicksburg Herald*, like many of the state's papers, asserted that the Marion killings were "the first fruits of Col. King's six-barrelled code." King and his followers countered that they had never intended to encourage violence, but only to ask their followers to refuse to be intimidated. In Mississippi elections, this could be a fine distinction. The tough words of King and of the state's Greenbackers may have prevented much Democratic intimidation, but when both parties in an election are talking tough there is a strong possibility of violence. The shooting of blacks in Sharkey and Panola counties and the shooting of whites and blacks in Lauderdale County were only the most visible fruits of a tense political campaign.[32]

Tension was also thick in Noxubee County in east-central Mississippi. Despite the county's large black majority, Noxubee Republicans kept a low profile, and it was former Democrats and a few Greenbackers who formed the county's Independent ticket in 1881. The Democratic *Macon Beacon* claimed that although the Independents pretended to be interested in issues such as the crop lien law, actually they were only hungry for office. When the *Beacon* spoke of the Independent movement, its words were strident: "Stamp it out, Democrats, at the polls ere it becomes a formidable force in the state! . . . Democracy and white men forever, should be our battle cry." The Democrats were worried that black Republicans would vote the Independent ticket, and they warned that any black Independent voter "should be spotted and remembered for all time as an avowed enemy of the white people" and should be treated as such. Turning to white Independents, the *Beacon* did not moderate its tone. Democrats who had gone over to the opposition should realize "that they are digging their political, social, and financial graves." In November, the official count showed the Noxubee Independent ticket winning only about 37 percent of the total vote.[33]

Statewide, the 1881 election was a tremendous disappointment for opponents of Mississippi Democrats. Gubernatorial candidate King was soundly defeated either by the will of the voters or—more likely—by election commissioners' fraud. Greenbackers suffered a horrendous set-

back as they watched their seventeen seats in the legislature dwindle to two. Greenbackers also lost control of several county governments, retaining power in Panola and Yalobusha counties only. In Hinds County the Greenbackers probably lost because of fraudulent counting. In Tate County the Greenbackers lost control of the county because they could not win a three-way race that pitted their party against both a Democratic and a Republican slate. Tate County Democrats capitalized on a divided opposition and won with less than a majority. Candidates calling themselves Independents and supporting King won control of Copiah and Madison counties and of the sheriff's office in Kemper County. The new legislature, like the previous one, would have three of these Independents.[34]

The only good news for any of the opposition groups came in the Republican races for the legislature. Mississippi Republicans jumped from having one senator and six representatives to having three senators and fourteen representatives. The reason for the Republicans' good showing was easy to discern. In some formerly Greenback areas, black Republicans' fusion with Democrats in county races paid off, while Greenbackers went down to defeat. In the river counties, the Greenback party had never been strong; here Democrats continued to experiment with office-sharing with the Republicans, and accordingly the Republicans took about half the legislative seats in such counties as Adams, Coahoma, and Washington. These kinds of local fusion and office-sharing were clearly important in giving Republicans a voice in state and local government and kept alive a voice of opposition within the legislature. Yet it was also clear that there was no county in Mississippi where Republicans were winning simple Democrat-versus-Republican races.[35]

There were several reasons the opposition movements won so few successes in 1881. Of course, Democrats' use of color line politics hurt. By making it seem the duty of every white man to vote Democratic, the party could entice whites away from the opposition. Whites who refused to return to the Democratic fold were threatened with social ostracism. Of course, Democrats charged that it was really the opposition that employed color line politics, and that black leaders insisted that members of their race vote to a man for the Benjamin King ticket. But if few influential whites supported the opposition at a given precinct, the Democrats could manipulate the count or stuff the ballot box.

The opposition continued to suffer from domination of the state press by the Democrats. Democratic papers could underreport attendance at

King rallies and could misquote Greenback and Independent speakers or twist their words. This was not, of course, grievous behavior on the part of Democratic editors; Greenback and Republican editors sometimes did the same thing. The problem was that there were so few opposition editors. The King campaign did have the support of two Jackson newspapers that functioned as official campaign organs: *The Crisis*, founded by Greenbackers as the campaign began, and the *Mississippi Republican*, started two years earlier. Greenbackers began several new papers in 1881, including the Holly Springs *National Advocate*, the *Senatobia Herald*, and the Terry *Greenback Flag*. The Grange paper *Patron of Husbandry* supported many Greenback and Independent county tickets and reported favorably on the strength of the King candidacy. The new Greenback titles were partly offset, however, by the folding of a couple of the party's older papers, including the *Corinth Harbinger* and the *Houston Patriot*. Republicans published only one or two titles outside Jackson. There *were* more opposition newspapers in 1881 than there had been in 1879; the anti-Democrat movements had a total of about fifteen titles now. But they were up against the hundreds of titles published by the Democrats. The Democrats clearly did a better job of getting their message out.[36]

As in the earlier Greenback races of 1878 and 1879, the Democratic press in 1881 continued to hurt the opposition by pinning labels. If the newspapers could succeed in getting average citizens to call the King slate the "radical ticket," half the battle was won. Because of connotations dating back to Reconstruction, white voters believed "radicals" stood for high taxes and mass black office-holding. Other labels referred to the King ticket's inclusion of Greenbackers, Republicans, and Independents. Democratic newspapers soon called it not the fusion party but the "confusion party," "the mongrel party," the "conglomerate concern," the "hybrids," and the "hash party." A favorite Democratic label referred to a new food product: the King movement was the "oleomargarine party," a poor imitation for a good product, containing a mass of assorted, poor quality ingredients. Alleging that many King supporters had committed treason against their former party, the Democrats, the party press also used the labels "deserters," and "sore-heads." Finally, arguing that the King movement had no real political agenda, the *Jackson Comet* repeatedly called the movement "the coalition to get the offices." Again, there is nothing wrong with this kind of name-calling; it is all part of the rough-and-tumble of politics. Yet the King partisans, with a much smaller collection of news-

papers, had trouble retaliating. Many voters would have supported King, except that they had decided years before never to vote a "radical" ticket.[37]

For opponents of Mississippi's Democrats, the most tragic aspect of the 1881 race was that it offered no hope for the future. Maybe the voters really wanted King, and only fraud defeated him. Yet even if this were true, how could fraud be avoided in the future? Greenbackers, almost voiceless now in the legislature and controlling only a two-county region of north Mississippi, felt no new encouragement to lay bold plans for the future. In Copiah and Madison counties, Independents had won some successes, but in very ugly campaigns. Republicans now held more offices than any other group save the Democrats, but nearly all of their offices had been won only by cooperating closely with their enemy, the Democratic party.

Despite the disappointments for the Greenback party, it can hardly be said that fusion was a mistake in the 1881 race for statewide offices. The party had no leaders and few supporters in large areas of the state, including the river counties, south Mississippi, and the east-central region. Furthermore, in some Greenback strongholds such as Panola and Holmes counties the party could not win without black votes. If black voters wanted a Republican presence on the state ticket, Greenbackers were not in a position to deny them. A three-way race could be disastrous for the opposition, as seen in Tate County, where Democrats won offices with only a plurality of the votes. So fusion with the Republicans offered Greenbackers an assurance of the continued loyalty of black voters in several Greenback-dominated counties and a promise of votes in the river counties. Republican leaders such as John R. Lynch favored fusion because of a feeling that their ticket needed a larger base of support by well-respected whites. These respected men could help assure a fair count and could belie charges that the election of 1881 was simply a contest between a white party and a black party.

Still, given the discouraging results of the 1881 race, the opposition had little hope going into the congressional races of 1882. One advantage of congressional elections was that United States marshals and attorneys could work to prevent some of the fraud or to punish the fraud if it did occur. But unless the state's Greenbackers, Republicans, or Independents were the recipients of some good fortune, they could expect little from the 1882 contest.

Fortune did smile on the opposition leaders. In the newly drawn third (north Delta) district, Republicans were able to offer a highly respected

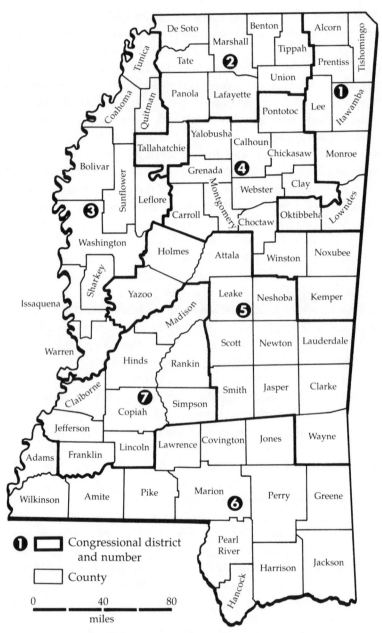

Map 2. Mississippi's Congressional Districts, 1882–1900

moderate candidate named Elza Jeffords. Jeffords was a lawyer and former judge; although he was an Ohioan by birth and a Union veteran, he was widely admired by Delta residents, white as well as black. The good fortune that fell into Jeffords's lap was the Democrats' decision not to field a candidate. Democrats realized that the third district had a black majority of 17,000 votes, and party leaders feared that if they did not conciliate the area's blacks, soon there would be all-black tickets for county and city offices. Jeffords's candidacy, then, was a part of the larger idea of office-sharing in the Delta. Not all Democrats were willing to give the congressional seat away to the opposition, and in fact a man named V. E. Waddell offered himself as an Independent Democrat. But the local Democratic organs said Waddell's course was "unadvised and injudicious," and that if an active campaign were initiated the Republicans would only be encouraged to strengthen their organization. The Republican lawyer won just under 70 percent of the vote and soon traveled to Washington and took his seat as one of Mississippi's seven congressmen.[38]

Another piece of good fortune for the opposition came with the defection of one of the state's most popular Democrats. James R. Chalmers was a former congressman and was the 1880 congressional candidate whom John R. Lynch had defeated in a controversial election. Chalmers was angry that Democrats had given him only lukewarm support in his contested election case; he also believed he was the victim of gerrymandering, as the state legislature had redrawn district lines and put Chalmers in the overwhelmingly black third district, with few counties that had been part of his former district. After this redistricting in the spring of 1882, Chalmers decided to move back to his old home of Panola County in the second district and challenge incumbent Democratic congressman Vannoy H. Manning. Of course, Panola County had a Greenback-controlled government, and Chalmers was quick to win the nomination of the Greenback party, and later the Republican party of the second district. So, like Benjamin King the previous year, Chalmers won the support of Greenbackers, Republicans, and Independents. Unlike King, though, Chalmers was very well known and very popular throughout Mississippi. A native Virginian, Chalmers had lived in Mississippi since 1839; during the war he had served as a Confederate brigadier general and had ridden with Nathan Bedford Forrest's renowned cavalry.[39]

Many black Republicans were lukewarm or even hostile toward Chalmers; after all, he was the man who had attempted to take Lynch's seat with a specious technical argument. Well-known white Republicans, including

George McKee, Henry Clay Niles, and Greene C. Chandler, welcomed the new addition to the battle against Democrats. From Washington, black Mississippian Blanche K. Bruce (now register of the U.S. Treasury), urged state Republicans to "Give Chalmers a chance at the Bourbons." Republican President Chester A. Arthur, putting little faith in the future of the southern Republican party, was glad to help foster Independent movements in the region. He put some federal patronage at Chalmers's disposal, and Republican sources in Washington sent cash contributions to the Chalmers campaign, probably about $2,500. Yet what made Chalmers a strong candidate was not the small amount of aid he received from Washington but his status as a popular former congressman and his record as a Confederate general and associate of Nathan Bedford Forrest.[40]

Chalmers's platform contained several planks of interest to Mississippi's small farmers, including the Greenback Party staples of "free silver, free ballots, and a fair count." Chalmers also opposed the power of national banks and favored an elective judiciary. The candidate made a number of joint appearances with his opponent Manning; at one point feelings between the two men ran so high that they exchanged notes, and a duel was barely averted. Chalmers had long been noted for his combative personality; this coupled with his small stature had won him the nickname "the little gamecock." Remembering what they believed was the fraudulent defeat of congressional candidate J. H. Amacker in 1878 in this same region, Greenbackers announced that Chalmers would be "Amacker's avenger."[41]

Chalmers's platform was generally a popular one with the farmers of his north Mississippi district; his partisans also appealed to voters by attacking the record of the incumbent Manning. The *Batesville Blade* pointed out that although Christian Mississippians had supported Manning in the past, he had betrayed them by voting against a bill to punish Mormon polygamists in the territories. According to the *Blade*, farmers had supported Manning, but he betrayed them by not supporting the Agriculture Bureau Bill. Some men of Greenback sentiments had voted for Manning, but he failed to oppose a bill rechartering the national banks.[42]

Meanwhile a black candidate named Ham Carter also entered the race as an Independent Republican. Carter brought out Chalmers's war record, which included leadership at Fort Pillow, where black soldiers were killed as they tried to surrender. Carter also blamed Chalmers for the deaths and injuries of blacks in past election campaigns. Greenbackers led the fight against Carter. When Carter attempted to campaign in the town of Sen-

atobia, he was arrested by Greenback town officers and charged with using profane language. The *Batesville Blade* then gave publicity to the charge that Carter was foul-mouthed.[43]

More ominous to Carter's chances was the Greenbackers' charge that he was "a hireling and tool of the Bourbons." The *Blade* produced evidence that Manning's managers had offered $750 to two black Greenbackers if they would publicly support Carter. Finally, late in the campaign, Greenback papers published a letter they had obtained, written to Senator Lamar by his private secretary. The letter reported that Manning was going to see to it that Carter "has a little money," and added that "What funds reach [Carter] from Democratic sources should go anonymously." One final attack on Carter was a physical one. W. H. Bruton, editor of the Greenback *Water Valley Index*, shot at Carter on the streets of Holly Springs. Newspaper accounts do not record what provocation, if any, led Bruton to make the attack. The Greenbackers continued to nurture the image of men who were far from pacifists.[44]

Of course, just as Chalmers had some good reasons why the voters should abandon Manning, Manning's campaign leaders had a list of reasons why citizens should not vote for Chalmers. They pointed out that Chalmers's indifference to the high tariff was an affront to small farmers. The Democratic *Ripley Advertiser* argued that Chalmers's success would mean "the active revival of the Radical party in the State and in all the counties," and the horrible campaign of 1875 would have to be fought again. The *Ashland Register* took issue with Chalmers's claim to be a Greenbacker and Independent. Since in his speeches Chalmers attacked Democrats and conciliated Republicans, "a blind man can see that he is a Republican," the *Register* asserted. Admitting that Chalmers had many friends and was an excellent orator, one Democratic speaker urged voters to "reject the deceitful kiss of former personal friendship," and "disregard the nectared sweets of the insidious silver tongued orator."[45]

As election day approached, Chalmers and his supporters began to worry about the possibility of ballot box stuffing or a fraudulent count. The U.S. attorney and marshal for north Mississippi, both Republicans, promised their support. But the state attorney general issued an opinion informing state election officers that U.S. marshals and their deputies had very little power at the polling places. Federal attorney Greene C. Chandler carried the question before U.S. District Judge Robert A. Hill. Hill ruled, first of all, that even though federal law allowed special deputy marshals for election service only in towns of more than 20,000 inhabi-

tants, the marshal could nevertheless appoint *regular* deputies as needed to enforce United States laws. These deputies had the right to be present at the polling places, and to "keep the peace." They might also arrest any election officers who violated U.S. election laws by, for example, refusing to accept the vote of a lawful voter. Hill also appointed federal election supervisors, who were more in the nature of observers. "Bulldozing the nigger will not work at this election," proclaimed the *Batesville Blade*; "neither can the counting out business be successfully worked."[46]

On election day federal election supervisors were active at many precincts in the second district, especially in Lafayette, Marshall, and DeSoto counties. These men wrote down the name of everyone who came to the polling place and everyone whose vote was not accepted. They also kept a written tally of the votes as the count was being made. They kept an eye on the ballot box and insisted that election officers not touch the voter's ballot. The *Blade* was grateful for the help of the federal supervisors but observed, "It is a disgrace to Mississippi that United States marshals have to be appointed to see that HER OWN citizens have a free ballot and a fair count—it is like calling in a policeman to settle a difficulty between a man and his wife." The state government continued to insist that it would not brook interference by federal marshals or supervisors, and on the eve of election Chalmers sent a telegram to the attorney general. "What shall we do if we must summon a posse to arrest state officers who attempt to arrest the Deputy Marshals?" Chalmers added, "We will fight for our rights if necessary." On election day, however, U.S. Marshal Joseph L. Morphis telegraphed the attorney general to report that the election had been quiet and fair.[47]

Both the Democratic and the Greenback newspapers were in agreement: Chalmers had won a clear victory. Ham Carter won a paltry 129 votes, while Chalmers won 9,729, or better than 52 percent of the total. Both sides believed the federal marshals and supervisors had played an important role. The *Ripley Advertiser* echoed the "great indignation" felt by the district's Democrats at the "outrages" at many polling places, where, they claimed, federal officials had usurped many of the functions of the state election officers. The Greenback *Blade's* editor, on the other hand, was ecstatic: "Chalmers Elected!" screamed the headlines. "Col. Van H. Manning Defeated! Carter Snowed Under!" The editor believed Manning must be thinking "of 'what might have been' had there been no United States supervisors of election appointed."[48]

Democrats undoubtedly felt threatened by Chalmers's victory, coming

as it did with federal aid to the Greenback-Republican candidate. Soon the scheming began, and when the official returns emerged from the secretary of state's office, Manning was listed as the victor. It seemed that in Tate County Chalmers had won no votes; a clerical error in Tate's official return had given J. R. Chalmers's votes to "J. R. Chambless." With no votes in Tate, Chalmers was defeated. To their credit, many of the state's Democratic newspapers spoke out against this fraud, which was even more absurd than the fraud Chalmers himself had perpetrated upon Lynch in 1880. The *Macon Beacon*, usually a fiery Democratic organ, urged that Manning not be given the seat by "jugglery." The *Beacon* also pointed out that even with a Democratic Congress, Chalmers would undoubtedly be awarded the contested seat.[49]

It is impossible to know whether Mississippi's secretary of state really expected that a Democratic Congress would permit Manning to take his seat. By giving Manning the certificate of election, though, two things were accomplished. First, most of Chalmers's term was frittered away in a lengthy election contest in hearings before a congressional committee. Second, as the hearings progressed the Democrats were able to air their grievances about some of Chalmers's campaign tactics.

Marshal Morphis testified that he had appointed thirty-eight deputy marshals for service on election day, but he denied that they played a heavy-handed role. Democrats did prove that Republican-appointed federal office holders in Mississippi played a large role in the campaign, working for Chalmers's election while drawing a government salary. Most notorious of the appointments was Chalmers's own as an assistant U.S. attorney to prosecute election cases. Just after the election, Chalmers and the U.S. attorney went to Holly Springs where the election officials were about to throw out six hundred votes because a precinct officer had not signed the return. The two attorneys warned the election officers that they could be liable to federal prosecution if they did not count the votes. They suggested that the precinct manager could still be asked to sign the return. Congressional Democrats alleged that the attorneys intended to overawe the opposition, but Chalmers and his superior simply believed they were doing their duty to ensure a fair election. Undoubtedly, the administration would have acted more wisely had it appointed an assistant attorney who was not a candidate for office in the election being investigated.[50]

Chalmers's side, too, was able to air some grievances about the way the election was conducted. Two black Chalmers supporters testified that Democratic campaign managers offered them money to switch their pub-

lic endorsement from Chalmers to Carter. Chalmers produced witnesses who testified that the governor had ignored their suggestions for election managers and had appointed ignorant black men whom he claimed were Republicans but really were not. Mississippi Republicans also testified that in Lafayette County, Manning supporters had been careful to keep on the voter rolls the names of eighty Ole Miss students who were actually not legal voters; many had left Oxford several years earlier. Keeping these names on the books facilitated the voting of fraudulent ballots. Chalmers was awarded his seat on June 25, 1884—just in time to begin making plans for his bid for reelection in the fall.[51]

The other congressional races of 1882 may be briefly considered. In the new fourth (north-central) district, the Greenback congressional nominee in was Jackson Taylor Griffin, a sixty-six-year-old farmer whom local papers called "Griffin the Greenback Granger." Few people had any real criticism of Griffin; the *Macon Beacon* simply urged his defeat because no respected citizen could hesitate when the choice was between a Democrat and "any form of opposition." Griffin won 26.5 percent of the vote, a higher percentage than was won by any of the Greenback candidates two years earlier.[52] In the first district, Republican congressional candidate Theodore Lyon won 18 percent; in the seventh, noted black Republican leader James Hill captured 33 percent of the votes, winning his support in the southern river counties. In the fifth district, Democrats had no declared opposition, although white Republican Henry Clay Niles received fifty-seven votes.[53]

Incumbent Congressman John R. Lynch faced a tough battle because the old "worm district" of the Delta had been abolished and the new sixth district included many eastern counties such as Jones and Covington that had few black residents. Since railroads had not yet touched many of the sixth district counties, Lynch embarked on a long journey by wagon across his new district. In some areas he had trouble finding lodging because of his race; one night in desperation he secured a room by passing for white. The light-skinned Lynch then amazed his hosts with stories about Ulysses S. Grant and James G. Blaine, and finally he was forced to admit that he was in fact Congressman Lynch. His hosts continued to treat him cordially. At Leakesville in Greene County Lynch had no trouble getting a room in a hotel run by whites, and the local judge adjourned court so citizens could go to Lynch's campaign meeting. At Williamsburg in Covington County he attended an all-white camp meeting. Lynch was glad to receive courteous treatment in the district, and glad that the

John R. Lynch ably represented his delta district in the U.S. House of Representatives. Elected to Congress as a Republican three times, in Reconstruction and afterwards, he did not survive the redistricting following the 1880 census. (Photo courtesy of the Mississippi Department of Archives and History)

election seemed to be completely honest. But in his new white-majority district Lynch could not repeat his earlier victories, although he did win a respectable 47 percent of the votes cast.[54]

Taken as a whole, the 1882 congressional races did infuse new enthusiasm into opponents of Mississippi Democrats. Far from declining in strength in the years after Reconstruction's end, the opposition was reviving. These figures show the increase in non-Democratic votes in congressional races:

1878: 28.9 percent of the vote for non-Democrats
1880: 33.1 percent of the vote for non-Democrats
1882: 39.5 percent of the vote for non-Democrats

The 1882 results were encouraging enough for Greenbackers, Republicans, and Independents to launch a new bid to gain a larger voice in the legislature. In November 1883 all seats in the state house of representa-

tives, half the seats in the senate, and all county offices would be filled in the general election. As in 1881, each county followed a different pattern. Most had only one opposition ticket, either Republican, Greenback, Independent, People's, Independent Democrat, or Anti-Monopoly. The 1881 pattern of Democrats in heavily black counties offering fusion tickets, with some black Republicans included, was continued in 1883.

A state convention of the "People's" movement wrote a platform that was endorsed by most of the county tickets opposing the Democrats. This 1883 "People's" convention was attended by followers of all the movements opposing the Democratic party. The platform stressed most of the same issues raised in earlier opposition campaigns, including honest elections, an elected judiciary, and railroad regulation. The platform also suggested that elections be held every two years instead of annually (in other words, that state and county elections be held in the same years as congressional races). This would not only save the taxpayers some money but would also mean that the federal government could play a larger role in insuring fair state and county elections.[55]

A look at Hinds County will show many of the issues of the 1883 campaign that were discussed across the state of Mississippi. One of the chief voices of the Hinds "People's Party" was T. D. Pace, a leader of the state's Knights of Labor. The ticket included a number of blacks who had previously supported Republicans and then Greenbackers; it also included several white Greenback candidates who had run for office in the last two county elections and believed that they had been "counted out." Pace, secretary of the nominating convention, noted proudly that while Hinds Democrats had an all-white convention, and the Republicans an all-black convention, the People's convention was half-white, half-black. Meanwhile Hinds County Democrats and Republicans sponsored a fusion ticket, as they had in 1881.[56]

As in many counties, in Hinds the People's partisans were again angry at the failure of the governor to appoint competent members of their movement to the county election commission. Walt Hendricks, People's candidate for the legislature in Hinds, brought suit seeking a writ of mandamus compelling the governor to appoint intelligent men who supported a non-Democratic party or movement. Hendricks argued that in the 1883 election there were only two parties on the Hinds ballot: the Democratic-Republican fusionists, and the People's Party. The governor, therefore, had erred in appointing two Democrats and one Republican to the Hinds election commission, and then claiming that he had appointed men "not

all of one party." Hendricks was joined in the case by Greenback candidates from Monroe and Independents from Madison. But the judge's decision was that the governor and his advisory board had "discretionary powers" in choosing the commissioners, and the judge could not exercise discretion for the governor.[57]

As the campaign in Hinds County continued, the People's Party made repeated efforts to win the support of Hinds County farmers; its mouthpiece the *Jackson Tribune* reminded farmers that the People's convention was on record as opposing the unpopular county law requiring the fencing of hogs. Hinds County agrarians hoped to continue the antebellum practice, common among subsistence farmers, of allowing their hogs to run free until slaughter. The People's party also continued its efforts to win black support away from the fusion ticket. The *Tribune* reminded blacks that the Democratic convention nearly broke up over the inclusion of one black candidate on the board of supervisors slate. While in principle the Democratic delegates had agreed that blacks should have one supervisor's seat, each of the five beats argued stridently that it should not be "the one." Finally the Democrats drew straws, and Utica beat was given the distinction of having a black supervisor candidate; Utica Democrats continued to grumble. This was not a party that respected blacks, the *Tribune* concluded. But the People's party could not overcome the fact that such popular black Republicans as John R. Lynch had endorsed the Hinds County fusion with Democrats. Lynch believed fusion with the powerful Democrats offered the only realistic way of electing some Republican officials. After the ballots were counted, only two People's partisans won election in Hinds County, both elected to the board of supervisors. People's candidate for the state senate L. W. Carraway lost with 42 percent of the reported vote, and other candidates lost by similar margins.[58]

In other counties, too, the opposition candidates won a small proportion of the offices. One Greenback supervisor was elected in Tate County, for example, while the Greenbackers elected Webster County's treasurer and chancery clerk. Republicans continued to win many county offices in the Delta through office-sharing agreements; former Governor James Lusk Alcorn was elected to the Coahoma board of supervisors. Independent candidates won many county offices in Madison and Grenada counties.[59]

In two counties the Greenback party swept the offices, and showed there was still some life in that movement, at least in a very limited area of the state. In Yalobusha County, Democrats were demoralized after los-

ing the last several county elections to the Greenbackers, and they were also badly split over a proposal to divide the county into two court districts. The Democrats made no official nominations, although a number ran as individuals, and the Greenbackers easily retained power in Yalobusha County.[60]

In Panola County, Democrats again offered a Democratic-Republican fusion ticket, but the party's leaders blundered by first offering the sheriff's nomination to a black Republican, then insisting that he make way for a white man. Panola Democrats claimed that only the Democrats could save the state from the past extravagances of Republican governments, but the Greenbackers countered that Democrats, too, had been guilty of an extravagance that "demands their removal by a political revolution in this State." Greenbackers won a major victory in Panola County in 1883. After the election, in a flourish of tongue-in-cheek fair play, the *Batesville Blade* editor promised that he would not crow over the results; the campaign was simply an unequal contest "between a well organized political party under a . . . platform of sound principles, against an office-hunting rabble, who had thrown political principles to the wind."[61]

One Mississippi county captured the attention of the entire nation in the 1883 county elections. This was Copiah, where an Independent movement was again expected to capture a number of offices. All the Copiah County Independent candidates were native to the county, and all were white. Most were former Democrats and Confederate veterans. On the other hand, black votes would be important to any Independent victories. Democrats countered the Independent threat by organizing a paramilitary company of 150 mounted men that rode at night through predominantly black beat three. One black Independent was shot and killed in his cabin, and his wife mortally wounded; others were whipped or threatened. Many blacks slept in the woods for as long as three weeks to avoid these nighttime assaults. The case of black Independent Wallace Gilmore was typical. The white men broke down his cabin door while he and his wife were asleep; "they dragged him out of the house, compelled him to get on his knees, presented pistols to his face, demanded to know how he was going to vote, and told him if he was going to vote the Independent ticket he had better 'dig his hole and make his box before he went.'"[62]

White Independents were not immune either. Copiah Democrats alleged that the Independent candidates were making "incendiary speeches." Rumor had it that some Independents' speeches had urged blacks to arm themselves during the campaign, although no one was later able to

testify that they had heard such a speech. Witnesses did recall hearing speeches that denounced the local Democrats as a town clique that was ruling the county in a dictatorial way, and that urged blacks to organize and to vote. The *Crystal Springs Meteor* proclaimed that "Incendiary speeches have but one counter-irritant—lead." Just after this appeared in print, Independent leader Amos W. Burnett was shot by a young Democrat in the town of Hazlehurst. Burnett was a local attorney and former leader of the Greenback party; shot in the groin, he did gradually recover. Meanwhile the *Copiah Signal* turned its attention to the county's blacks, and wrote that "If they will not vote with the Democrats it would be best for them and the county that they refuse to participate in the election. The weather might be warm that day and they might possibly get sunstruck."[63]

The Independent sheriff nominee was J. Prentice "Print" Matthews. Matthews was a native Mississippian who had nurtured Unionist sentiments during the Civil War. Physically he was short, light, and "quite lame." His speeches against the Democratic party were bitter and Democrats soon gave them the incendiary label. On the day before the election a Democratic mass meeting passed a resolution: "Whereas it is thought that the public will be served by Print Matthews absenting himself from the polls on election day: Therefore, *Be it resolved*, that Print Matthews be ordered to keep within his own inclosure tomorrow." Matthews, though, was heard to remark that he was going to vote or go to hell in the attempt. When he came to the polling place, just across the street from his home in Hazlehurst, Democratic leader Erastus Wheeler told him, "Print, I would not vote to-day if I were you." Matthews continued preparing his ballot, and finally Wheeler took up a shotgun and shot Matthews in the throat and upper chest. Matthews fell to the floor and died within feet of the ballot box. In its next issue, the *Crystal Springs Meteor* observed tersely, "We have done our duty. No more nigger domination." Three weeks later Hazlehurst's municipal officers appointed Erastus Wheeler town marshal.[64]

At the urging of Senator John Sherman of Ohio, a U.S. Senate committee investigated the Copiah County election. The committee gave little credence to Democrats' testimony that Matthews had been killed for making incendiary speeches, since it seemed no one had actually heard Matthews make any speech that went beyond denunciation of the Democratic party. Democrats testified that Matthews had a temper; but other witnesses characterized him as a man who lived at peace with others, was

generous almost to a fault, and was personally popular, having been elected alderman as late as 1881. Democrats explained that many white citizens felt anger toward Matthews because he encouraged blacks to vote, but the committee noted that nightriders had *encouraged* their victims to vote Democratic. The purpose of the violence was simply to secure the county offices for the Democrats, the Senate committee concluded. In passing, the Senators noted that Madison County had a similar history in 1883; the only difference was that there Independents withdrew their ticket before the election and thus avoided bloodshed. The committee concluded by urging the Senate to consider legislation reducing Mississippi's number of congressmen, under the Fourteenth Amendment provision that calls for such reductions when segments of the male population are denied the right to vote.[65]

Leaving aside the great disappointments for Independents in Copiah and Madison counties, the 1883 election showed the state's opposition movements holding steady. In county races the Greenbackers retained their hold on two counties, while winning a sprinkling of offices in other counties. Republicans continued to control many offices in the Delta and in other black majority counties such as Hinds. Independents won control of Rankin County and a scattering of other offices across the state. In the legislature, the opposition bloc remained about the same size. The number of Republican senators held steady at two, while in the house the party's representation fell from fourteen to thirteen. Greenbackers in 1883 won four seats in the state house of representatives, three from Panola County and the one seat from Webster County. In 1881 they had won only two seats. As in 1879 and 1881, the new legislature would have three Independents, this time from Rankin, Grenada, and Calhoun counties. The Greenbackers, Republicans, and Independents each were still strong in limited areas; perhaps they could resume their growth if they could follow up the encouraging 1882 congressional elections with another good showing in 1884.[66]

This was not to be. In none of the seven congressional districts did the opposition mount a credible challenge to the state's Democrats. James R. Chalmers came the closest in his bid for reelection as a Greenback-Republican fusion candidate. The *Batesville Blade* rallied the state's Greenbackers to Chalmers' banner, defending his support of the high tariff, saying it would protect U.S. industries. The *Blade* noted that a high tariff was favored by national Greenback leaders such as James B. Weaver and by state leaders including Absalom M. West and Reuben Davis. Chalmers

also promised to vote for the Blair Education Bill, which would provide money for the education of poorer children and coincidentally might help reduce county school expenses. But Chalmers was out of step with the voters of his district. The tariff was indeed the key issue of the 1884 campaign, but small farmers did not favor protectionism. The tariff did not protect American agricultural products and it did keep prices for tools and other manufactured goods high. Chalmers won about 41 percent of the vote in his reelection bid and carried only Panola County.[67]

In the first (northeast) district, white Republican Greene C. Chandler based his campaign on calls for a strong federal government that would act to protect home industries, aid public schools, and regulate monopolies. Chandler's joint meetings with his opponent "Private" John Allen were canceled after "some of the hot-headed Democrats became overheated." Still, it is doubtful Chandler could have won a majority of the votes in this district of small farmers even in a free and open election, since like Chalmers he clung to the high tariff issue. Chandler won 18 percent of the votes cast and did not even come close to carrying a county. In several other districts Republicans nominated candidates unlikely to win any white support or even white tolerance. A. G. Pearce and Josh Smith were black politicians who had not won the respect of whites; Pearce won 30 percent in the third district, while Smith won 23 percent in the fifth.[68]

In the fourth district native white Republican William D. Frazee was the candidate; most white Mississippians still remembered him as a radical Republican of Reconstruction days. Frazee, an attorney, won 30 percent of his district's votes. John R. Lynch made yet a second bid to return to the halls of Congress, but although many whites gave him their grudging respect, they did not give their votes, and Lynch won 39 percent in a white majority district. Finally, in the seventh district, former white Greenback leader John B. Yellowly, now a Republican, won 33 percent of the ballots. For the first time since 1878, Mississippi sent only Democrats to Congress.[69]

Nor did the 1884 presidential race offer any encouragement to Mississippi's Republicans, Greenbackers, or Independents. President Cleveland easily won the state's electoral votes over James G. Blaine, who was despised as an enemy of the south by most white Mississippians. Blaine won 43,535 votes, to Cleveland's 77,683. Blaine did carry eight heavily black counties; opposition congressional candidates carried only five. The state's Greenbackers had the honor in 1884 of having one of their favorite sons on the Greenback national ticket: Absalom M. West was the party's vice-

presidential nominee. West was undoubtedly included on the national ticket to balance the presence of Benjamin F. Butler of Massachusetts at the ticket's head. Butler was hated in the South for his role as a Reconstruction-era Republican, and in fact he was *so* hated that Mississippi's Greenbackers made the wise decision to decline to bring out a state Butler ticket. Ironically, then, Mississippians had no way to vote for native son Absalom M. West. Nationwide, the Butler-West ticket won less than 2 percent of the vote, certifying that the national Greenback organization was now devoid of any strength whatever.[70]

Greenbacker farmers began to look for a new vehicle to support their political interests now that their party enjoyed little vote-getting power in the state. One idea was to work within the Democratic party. Agrarians began to flock to the banner of popular Grange leader Putnam Darden, and in 1885 they placed his name in nomination for governor at the state Democratic convention. The convention, however, chose instead the conservative Robert Lowry, and Darden won the support of only 45 delegates to 192 for Lowry. Many small farmers urged Darden to become an Independent candidate, but he refused; nevertheless on election day 1,071 Mississippians wrote in his name, and this non-candidate actually carried Webster County.[71]

The year 1885 may be marked as the year when everything fell apart for the state's opposition movements. While the 1884 congressional races were clearly discouraging, the election of 1885 was a near-fatal blow to the state's Greenbackers, Republicans, and Independents. In a number of counties, including Hinds, dissidents offered no tickets in opposition to the Democrats. Old strongholds of the Greenbackers finally fell: Yalobusha County went Democratic, and the banner county of Panola fell to the Democrats by a margin of more than 1,500 votes. Tate County failed to elect a single Greenbacker. In Warren County the Republican candidate for sheriff, who had served a number of terms, withdrew to prevent an "unpleasant" campaign, and his colleagues on the ticket did likewise. In Monroe County, opponents of the Democrats failed to field a ticket for the first time since 1875. At the state level, no opposition group brought out a ticket to oppose the Democrats.[72]

There are a number of reasons for the failures of 1885. The inability of opposition movements even to return to their strength of 1879 was one problem; voters were beginning to doubt that Greenbackers, Republicans, or Independents would ever again be able to win elections. Democrats

made their most active campaign in many years, sending their best speakers into some of their weakest counties: Tate, Panola, Calhoun, Webster, and Yalobusha. In Calhoun County, Democratic leader Edward Cary Walthall urged voters to spurn the county Independent ticket: "there are but two political parties," Walthall counseled, Democrats and Republicans, and in casting their ballot for a Greenbacker or Independent voters were "casting them to the wind." In Congress, the White House, and the various state legislatures, all battles were between Democrats and Republicans. To vote for an Independent was "equivalent to firing a blank cartridge."[73]

Democratic editors argued that those Independent tickets that did exist were simply examples of old-time radicalism, and that to elect Independents was to return the state to an earlier era of misrule and high taxes. In Tate County, Lieutenant Governor G. D. Shands warned that if Independent or Greenback movements were allowed to prosper, the state would return to the days of blacks marching arrogantly to the polls two abreast and regularly defeating the best white candidates. In Noxubee County white dissidents offered an Independent ticket; the Democratic county chairman sent a letter to the Independent sheriff nominee, warning him that his candidacy was "calculated to injure, to some extent, the prospect for a quiet and peaceable election." The letter was printed in the local paper, as was the Independent candidate's reply. The candidate defended himself by saying he hadn't asked to be the Independent nominee, but argued that he could not prevent his friends from voting for him if they wanted to. Next the local paper ran boldface notices urging Democrats to "Come out strong and vote early and often. There are traitors in the camp." While this message may have been made in a half-humorous vein, it could hardly be considered a joke given the history of recent Mississippi elections. If nothing else, the statement encouraged further disrespect for the electoral system. It may be needless to add that Noxubee County's Independent ticket was soundly defeated.[74]

It would be an appropriate endorsement of the good things accomplished by the Democratic party, argued the Jackson *Clarion*, "if the seventy-four counties in Mississippi should all elect Democratic officers." The *Clarion* very nearly got its wish. Only one county failed to elect the Democratic ticket: Attala County Republicans won the county and legislative elections of 1885. Here white Republican lawyer Henry Clay Niles won election to the legislature with 73 percent of the vote. Attala Republicans had won some offices in the past, but their overwhelming victory in

1885 was made possible by their alliance with the "dry" forces on the prohibition issue. Democrats had taken the less popular stand against countywide prohibition, and thus lost control of this white-majority county. Yet the winning of one county could hardly make up for the massive losses in this election. From holding twenty-two seats in the legislature the opposition groups fell to controlling only eleven: eight black Republicans from the Delta elected in office-sharing schemes, a white Republican from Attala County, and Independents from Wayne and Rankin counties.[75]

After the year when everything fell apart, the opposition offered little resistance in the 1886 congressional races. The only candidates opposing the Democrats in Mississippi that year were three Republicans. Judge Horatio F. Simrall, a white Republican active in the party since Reconstruction days, lost in the third district; Democrats argued that Simrall was motivated only by "personal greed of office, pure and simple." As Chalmers ran again in the second district, Democrats noted that he had finally thrown off his Independent and Greenback disguises and was running as the Republican he had always been. Like a true Republican, Chalmers continued to try to win support for a high tariff but to no avail, and the candidate made his worst race to date, winning only 38 percent of the vote. John R. Lynch again had to content himself with carrying only his home county of Adams; he won 32 percent across the sixth district.[76]

Meanwhile, one by one, the opposition newspapers folded. The *Jackson Crisis* and the *Rankin Free State* did not last into 1884; in 1885 new management purchased the flagship Greenback paper the *Batesville Blade* and merged it with the Democratic *Panolian*. By the late 1880s there were almost no Mississippi newspapers that did not champion the Democrats. The *Jackson Advertiser* was a Republican journal but many party members considered it lukewarm in its support of the GOP. A few black newspapers supported Republican politics at the national level; these included the Columbus *New Light* and the Greenwood *Golden Rule*. The folding of Greenback, Independent, and Republican papers in the state was clearly an effect, not a cause, of the decline of the state's opposition movements. But the two trends were mutually reinforcing, and without an opposition press it would prove almost impossible to win new support for non-Democratic candidates.[77]

With the Greenback party all but dead and Independent movements winning very few victories, the Republican party was the one party that might hope to launch a counteroffensive and again begin to win elections.

Unlike the other two groups, Mississippi Republicans did have a national party that might be willing to help them, and unlike the other two groups the Republicans did control two city governments, some county offices in the Delta and in Attala County, and nine seats in the legislature. But the state Republican party had real problems in the late 1880s, including a serious internal division along racial lines. Blacks in the party argued that since they provided the great bulk of Republican votes in the state, they should be rewarded with places on the congressional tickets and with federally appointed jobs such as internal revenue collector and postmaster. Whites argued that the only way the party could ever hope to win control of counties, congressional districts, or the state, was to offer respected white candidates that whites would be willing to support—men like Delta attorney Elza Jeffords, Attala County lawyer Henry Clay Niles, or the former Republican governor James Lusk Alcorn. If white voters respected the Republican candidates, they might support them or at least acquiesce in their election. Both groups made valid points, but as leaders of the two factions continued to clash the lack of unity made any real progress for the party impossible.

Examples of the friction between black and white Republicans are abundant. In 1882 white opponents of the Democrats joined together and prepared to offer a congressional candidate in the seventh district. They asked the official endorsement of the district's Republicans; whites in the party were amenable, but the black Republicans decided instead to nominate James Hill. Hill was widely admired by the state's blacks, but most whites in the state saw him as a party hack. Hill won no white support whatever. In 1884, when Elza Jeffords announced for reelection as Republican congressman from Mississippi, black Republicans in his district revolted, passed over the incumbent Jeffords, and selected black candidate A. G. Pearce. Pearce's campaign slogan was "Negroes must vote for a Negro." Black leaders were also suspicious of James R. Chalmers and gave him only grudging support. White Republicans, on the other hand, endorsed Chalmers with great enthusiasm and worked diligently in his several campaigns.[78]

Blacks were undoubtedly justified in seeking positions of leadership within the Republican organization; by the late 1880s only some six in one hundred white Mississippians thought of themselves as Republicans. Though they were unlikely to win actual contests with the Democrats, black Republicans could achieve dignity and leadership by serving as county officers under fusion plans, by attending the Republican national

conventions as delegates, by offering their candidacies for Congress, and by winning the appointment of Republican presidents to lucrative white-collar jobs. If Republicans did not win elections against Democratic candidates, by the late 1880s few intelligent observers of Mississippi politics believed this was still possible.[79]

Yet Republican involvement would offer fewer and fewer blacks the dignity and leadership they were seeking. Black Republican William H. Foote was a native Mississippian, a former student at Oberlin College, and formerly a Republican legislator from Yazoo County. In the mid-1880s he was deputy federal revenue collector in Yazoo County, a county noted for its suppression of Republicans and Independents. In 1884 only six voters had gone to the polls and voted Republican in this overwhelmingly black county. Foote was famous for his dignified manner and his refusal to defer slavishly to whites. One account recalls Yazoo whites who did not know him looking in amazement at Foote walking with his head erect, and saying, "Why! look at that nigro; who is he? He has the audacity of a white man!" Yazoo Countians could accept the white Republican postmaster at Yazoo City, but "How could 'our nigros' be made to 'keep their places'" with a well-to-do, dignified black Republican leader like Foote in the county?[80]

Foote's downfall came when he shielded a black man from a whip-wielding white mob. When Foote coolly met the mob and quarreled with one member, general gunfire broke out. Five whites were shot, three fatally. It is not clear whether Foote shot all five, whether blacks in nearby buildings did some of the shooting, or whether members of the white mob killed some of their own number in the confusion and heavy gunsmoke. Even after the shooting, the indomitable Foote refused to leave the county. After he and eleven others were taken to jail, a mob appeared and did a cruelly bungled job of hanging two blacks prisoners; another prisoner was killed by gunshot. When the mob broke down the door of Foote's cell, Foote struck to the ground the first white man to enter, then fought the others until finally he was shot to death. A coroner's inquest ruled that the four black men came to their death at the hands of a "body of unknown men."[81]

Black Republicans were not the only ones who were terrorized into abandoning their politics. For many years voters in the capital city of Jackson had elected a board of aldermen dominated by white Republicans; Mayor John McGill was also a Republican. McGill, a second generation Irish-American, had come to Mississippi in 1833, and during the Civil

War he had served with Mississippi troops. He was a hero of the yellow fever epidemic of 1878 and was a popular member of four fraternal lodges. But now whites in Jackson were beginning to be embarrassed that they were living in one of the last strongholds of the Mississippi Republican party. They were also irritated by the presence of blacks on the city's police force, and they believed the black policemen performed poorly. A convention of four hundred white citizens resolved to nominate a Democratic ticket and carry the city in the 1888 election. Then a mass meeting of the "young white men of Jackson" adopted a resolution promising to carry the election for the Democrats at any cost and warning that any black who attempted to run for any city office would do so "at his supreme peril." Black voting, too, would be punished. Participants in this meeting printed a circular detailing the resolutions; this Red Circular, as it was called, was headed by engravings of a shotgun and two pistols and was printed in red ink. The Jackson *Daily Mississippian* warned whites to watch out for "idiots" who said that "it is unnecessary to use extreme methods" to carry the election.[82]

Black voters responded in self-defense by holding a convention and passing resolutions promising they would not attempt to vote in the city election. The black alderman candidates also withdrew. Divisions within the Republican party may be seen by the participation of several prominent white Republicans in the movement to oust Jackson's Republican government. Among these was the head of the local party's presidential campaign committee, also the chair of the Republican County Executive Committee. Even the Republican editor of the *Jackson Advertiser* called for McGill's defeat. Some of these Republicans apparently were angry at Mayor McGill's anti-prohibition stands. But for most white voters the chief goal of the campaign was to bring a Democratic administration to "the capital city of a Democratic state." No blacks cast ballots in the 1888 municipal election, and without black votes McGill was turned out. Only 37 percent of this white electorate voted to retain the Republican mayor in office. Only one of the five aldermen elected was a Republican.[83]

Once again, a U.S. Senate committee investigated the election. Democratic witnesses explained that the impetus for their movement had come on Christmas eve of 1887. Young white men were drinking and parading and occasionally arguing on the streets with blacks. Finally a black man grabbed one of the young white men and prepared to stab him. Someone was about to intervene, but a black policeman allegedly said, "No, let him go, let him carve him," and the white man was killed. Two other murders

had occurred in the previous eighteen months, and drunken assaults were common. Asked if the new administration had secured the arrest of the drunkards or the murderers, the Democratic witnesses had to admit that it had not. Democrats also admitted that the Republican administration of John McGill had done a good job of paying off the city's debts, and without burdensome taxation. But the Democrats said they were ashamed of the city's well-publicized murders, and ashamed of having a Republican city government. Democrats in Vicksburg also took control of that city in the late 1880s, leaving Mississippi with no Republican city government.[84]

The horrendous opposition losses in the 1885 county and legislative races were no temporary aberration. In the 1887 legislative races, results were essentially the same, except that Republicans lost their one state senator, leaving the upper house entirely in Democratic hands. The house of representatives now had seven black Republican members from the river counties and two Independents. Attala County returned to the Democratic fold after only two years of Republican rule. Republicans ran congressional candidates in all seven districts in 1888, but not one of them won as much as 30 percent of the vote.[85]

By the late 1880s Republicans and Independents were not only losing elections in Mississippi; in an increasing number of counties they were not running at all. Although only incomplete election returns for the state house of representatives have survived, we do have complete returns for state senate races. These figures show that Mississippi voters were having fewer and fewer choices as they went to the polls in November:

1879: 45 candidates for 20 Senate seats
1881: 31 candidates for 18 Senate seats
1883: 33 candidates for 19 Senate seats
1885: 31 candidates for 20 Senate seats
1887: 24 candidates for 20 Senate seats[86]

Other figures show the decline in vote-getting of the non-Democratic candidates. In congressional races, for example, the opposition candidates won a post-Reconstruction high of 39 percent of the vote across the districts in 1882; these percentages fell to 24 percent by 1886 and 22 percent four years later.[87]

It is hardly surprising that Republicans, Greenbackers, and Independents were so dazed by the great losses in 1885 and 1887 that they had little zeal or energy for the 1889 race. Only one member of the opposition groups was excited about running a state ticket in 1889; this was James R.

Few politicians have had as varied a political career as James R. Chalmers, who sought offices on Democratic, Republican, Greenbacker, Independent, and Free Silver tickets. His widespread personal popularity helped lead to his election in 1882 as Mississippi's second district congressman on a Greenback-Republican fusion slate. (Photo courtesy of the Library of Congress)

Chalmers, now firmly in the Republican camp. Chalmers declared his candidacy for the governorship and played the major role in choosing the rest of the slate. Black Republicans acquiesced when Chalmers put white men into the slots on his ticket; only secretary of state candidate W. E. Mollison was black. As John R. Lynch explained, the party hoped that if the ticket were made up largely of former Democrats, "we would at least be permitted to hold mass-meetings." The Greenback party, or what was left of it, also endorsed the Chalmers slate.[88]

Chalmers began making fiery speeches, vowing that he would carry the Republican message into every part of the state and striving to make it clear that he and his followers would not be overawed. Even the Republican Lynch termed Chalmers's speeches "intemperate." When Chalmers vowed to open his formal campaign in Columbus, where "no Republican speech had been delivered" since 1875, threats were made that Chalmers would not leave Columbus alive. In Jackson, a Democratic correspondent of the *Clarion-Ledger* argued that the nomination of a Republican ticket was "a menace to our most cherished institutions—to our liberty—to our

civilization." A delegation of citizens from West Point, both Democrats and Republicans, formally called on Chalmers and asked him not to meet in their town for fear that a riot or massacre would result. The candidate received warnings from the town of Okolona as well. In the face of the many threats, the once-fiery Chalmers abandoned his campaign. In legislative races in 1889, Republicans won only six seats in the house of representatives through office-sharing deals with Delta Democrats.[89]

After peaking in 1881 and 1882, post-Reconstruction opposition movements in Mississippi grew steadily weaker. The Greenback party was in decline nationally after 1880 as the depressed economy improved. The state Greenback party declined for similar reasons, and in addition the state's Democrats embraced many of the Greenbackers' favorite issues, including inflation of the money supply and state taxation of U.S. bonds. In the earliest years of the state's Greenback movement, the Democrats had called the party "radical," or synonymous with the Republicans. In fusing with Republicans in 1881, the Greenbackers seemed to publicly admit that the charge was true. These various problems kept the Greenbackers from expanding from their north Mississippi base and winning any real support in the rest of the state.[90]

Republicans continued to be weak because of color-line politics. Democratic campaigners made it clear that it was the duty of every white man to support the Democratic party; whites who supported the Republicans were traitors to their race and were working to bring black domination to the state. Accordingly, by 1889 there were only about two hundred white men in Mississippi who were willing to play a leadership role in the Republican party at the county or state levels. It is true that Mississippi was a black majority state, and that a huge majority of blacks favored the Republican candidates. But whites dominated society, the economy, and the government, while blacks very often seemed powerless. Without prominent whites to break the color line and to publicly insist on a free and fair election, the Republicans could not take control of the state or of individual counties.

By the late 1880s, some of the most important voices of opposition in the state belonged to Independents, some of whom still considered themselves Democrats while others were non-partisans. In counties ranging from Calhoun and Noxubee to Lincoln, Rankin, and Wayne, Independent candidates ran for office and in many cases were elected. But these candi-

dates had a number of obstacles to overcome. With no national or state organization to support them, and no permanent county organization, it was difficult to oppose the well-oiled Democratic machine. In most cases they had no newspapers to support them, and the Democratic press charged that the Independents were actually helping the Republicans or were themselves "radicals." Even in an honest election these candidates would have trouble winning, and given the Democrats' control of the election apparatus, honest elections might not take place. Calhoun County Independents, for example, won the county election in 1887, but Democratic officials threw out their ballots because of the printer's dash at the top of their tickets. As in the Lynch congressional race of 1880, the printer's dash was declared a "distinguishing device" contrary to state law. This time the ballots were thrown out in an overwhelmingly white county, but the Independents were less powerful than the Democrats and were able to make only feeble protests.[91]

Greenbackers, Independents, and Republicans often expressed their hopes that the United States government would help them secure free and honest elections in the state. Congressional committees did investigate the defeat of Greenbacker Reuben Davis in 1878, of Copiah County Independents in 1883, and of Jackson Republicans in 1888. None of these investigations resulted in any action being taken, however; no new support was given to the U.S. attorney general for his efforts to secure honest elections, and no real effort was made to reduce the state's congressional representation under provisions of the Fourteenth Amendment. Democrats may have been right when they said that the purpose of these investigations was to give northern Republicans ammunition to use in national election campaigns against the Democrats.

Still, federal election laws were on the books, and during most years the U.S. attorneys and marshals in the state were Republicans. But federal law enforcement officers had little success in punishing election law violators. After the 1882 congressional races, for example, grand jurors handed down indictments against fifty individuals charged with election law violations in north Mississippi. The judge or prosecutor dismissed twenty-one of these cases for technical problems or a lack of witnesses, while petit jurors found nineteen defendants not guilty. Three defendants pled guilty, while juries reached seven guilty verdicts. In cases of obstructing deputy U.S. marshals and election supervisors, Judge Robert A. Hill typically assessed fines of five dollars each. Such small fines offered little deterrence

to future violations. In fact, in many cases the defendants became heroes. Democratic congressional candidate Vannoy H. Manning bragged to the voters that he had defended, free of charge, J. J. Brooks, a Democrat accused of ballot box stuffing. Brooks, though, publicly contradicted Manning, saying that the attorney's fees had been paid by the Democratic party and by individual Democratic citizens.[92]

Opponents of the Democratic party of Mississippi faced an uphill battle in the 1880s. All across the state, Democratic editors and Democratic stump speakers attacked the idea that the opposition movements were seeking to bring progress to the state. "The most absurd political dogma ever advocated," asserted the editor of the *Macon Beacon*, "is that two political parties are necessary in a state situated as ours is." Then attacking Greenback-Republican fusion directly, the editor added, "Fusion means Radicalism; Radicalism means negro; and negro means ruin." The columns of the *Aberdeen Examiner* reported in November 1885 that for the first time since Reconstruction the Monroe County Democrats had no opposition. Far from showing concern about the development of one-party rule, the *Examiner* congratulated Monroe citizens "on their happy escape from the excitement and ill feelings engendered by heated and bitter campaigns and closely contested elections."[93]

Yet even if Greenbackers, Republicans, and Independents were gasping for breath in Mississippi, it is not true that voters had no political choices to make. There was active competition within the Democratic party. In some counties the opposition movements were so lifeless that the Democrats felt safe in making no nominations at all, and allowing Democrats to run freely against each other in the general elections. In Tishomingo County in 1883 six Democrats ran for sheriff in the general election, while eight ran for circuit clerk. In 1889 the Democrats made no nominations in Alcorn, Greene, Hancock, Calhoun, Jones, Lee, Prentiss, Smith, and Tishomingo counties. In those counties where the Democrats did make nominations, the competition was so fierce that it sometimes took conventions more than three hundred ballots to settle on a Democratic candidate. Moreover, Greenbackers and Independents were not the only candidates offering to represent small farmers. Some popular farm leaders did run for office as Democrats in the 1880s, and many were elected. In 1887, for example, a host of small farmers was elected to the legislature, and popular agrarian C. B. Mitchell was elected speaker of the state house of representatives. Still, many small farmers chaffed at the firm grip that conservatives usually held over the Democratic party.[94]

By 1889, farmers were becoming more passionate about politics than they had been in at least ten years. But they had scant interest in pursuing Greenback, Independent, or Republican politics. Farmers in the 1890s would find new vehicles for their political interests.

FOUR

A New Constitution
and New Directions
for Agrarians

ON HORSEBACK, F. M. B. "MARSH" COOK RODE TO HIS NEXT
speaking appointment. Marsh Cook was one of a handful of white native
Mississippians working to keep the state Republican party alive. In 1888
he had run for Congress, winning one fifth of the votes cast; now, in July
1890, Cook was the only Republican outside the Delta trying for a seat in
the upcoming state constitutional convention. A committee of men recently had approached him, warning that he must not make any more
speeches in behalf of his candidacy. Cook replied that "he would at his
next appointment speak, or die in the attempt." The Republican leader
died in the attempt.[1]

As he approached a log schoolhouse in a lonely section of Jasper County
in east-central Mississippi, five men inside thrust shotguns through the
chinks and fired at Cook when he was at his closest. Cook died a lonely
death; only hours later did a woman happen upon his body, riddled with
shot. Cook had proudly called himself "an uncompromising Republican."
In nearby Meridian, a newspaper labeled him "a prominent and offensive
Republican of Jasper County." The Republican leader's "offense" seems to
have been that he warned voters that the constitutional convention was
likely to limit the right to vote, and he urged Republicans (a large majority
of whom were black) to organize and work against disfranchisement. The
population of Jasper County was almost perfectly balanced between blacks

and whites; Democratic leaders there wanted to ensure that few blacks would be voting in the future. The ambush and murder of Marsh Cook sent a message to blacks living in the area: 1890 would mark a new era in voter participation. Precisely who would be voting in the future remained to be seen, but it was clear that most black citizens of Jasper County had already seen the inside of a polling place for the last time.[2]

The killing of Marsh Cook received extensive coverage nationwide, and an embarrassed Governor Stone offered a reward of $500 for the capture of the assassins. Cook's brother tried to interest U.S. authorities in the case, arguing that Cook's civil rights had been violated, but he was told the case was hopeless. A federal prosecutor wrote to the attorney general reporting the murder, adding that he had heard only one white man denounce the killing. As was true with the majority of political killings in the state, no one was ever tried for the murder of the Jasper County Republican.[3]

The agitation for a new constitution for Mississippi had begun in earnest in 1886; among the loudest voices demanding a new document were those of agrarians. They denounced the old constitution, first of all, as a "putrid reminiscence" of Reconstruction days, written by "a conglomeration of white and yellow adventurers, camp followers, [and] carpet baggers." The fact that many conservative Democrats seemed satisfied with the old constitution was proof enough that change was needed, many agrarians thought.[4]

Experiencing distress in their increasingly commercial, cash-crop brand of agriculture, white small farmers had three chief goals as they sought a new organic law for the state. First, they wanted reapportionment of the legislature. Black-majority counties held over half the seats in the legislature yet paid less than half the taxes and had fewer voters than the white counties. Agrarian editor Frank Burkitt liked to draw a comparison between the black-majority county of Yazoo and white Itawamba County:

> Yazoo in 1889:   300 votes cast, for 4 legislators
> Itawamba in 1889: 1,600 votes cast, for 1 legislator

Farm leaders wanted to end this domination by the black counties, since the planters, merchants, and lawyers elected from these counties opposed the fondest goals of yeomen farmers.[5]

As an added bonus, a reapportionment in favor of the white counties would also give those counties a stronger voice in the Democratic party.

This was true because representation in the state party convention was based on the number of legislative seats each county held. Leaders of the small farmers believed that if the white counties had had their equitable share of delegates in the 1885 state Democratic convention, Grange leader Putnam Darden would have won the gubernatorial nomination. Agrarians also sought an elective judiciary. Farmers hoped that under this system the judges would be less likely to rule in favor of creditors, landlords, merchants, and railroads.[6]

Finally, many agrarians were interested in black disfranchisement. They recalled the 1881 loss of People's Independent gubernatorial candidate Benjamin King, and credited his defeat that year to the fraudulent counting in the Delta of many black voters' ballots as Democratic. Independent congressional candidate Chalmers lost many votes for the same reason in 1882. Moreover, farmers were becoming increasingly vocal in support of prohibition. To secure countywide prohibition, a "local option" election was held; many farmers believed that prohibition forces lost these elections either when blacks' votes were purchased or when "dry" votes were fraudulently counted as "wet" in black precincts. If black voting could be eliminated, agrarians believed, elections would be more fair and honest, agrarian candidates would be more likely to defeat conservatives, and prohibition would be easier to achieve in many counties.[7]

The movement for a new constitution made steady progress. A bill calling a convention passed the state senate in 1886 but failed in the house of representatives. In 1888 a similar bill passed both houses of the legislature, but Governor Robert Lowry vetoed it. "It is better to bear the ills we have," Lowry intoned, "than fly to others we know nothing of." The turning point came in 1889. In the national election of the year before, Republicans had swept both houses of Congress and elected the president. Congressman Henry Cabot Lodge of Massachusetts then introduced a bill to provide federal supervision of congressional and presidential elections. Democrats angrily dubbed the proposed law the "Force Bill," implying that the federal government wanted to force Republican victories on the South. When Mississippi Republicans nominated a straight state ticket in 1889, for the first time in sixteen years, many state Democrats believed it was time to end black suffrage. Senator James Z. George gave his vocal support to the movement for a new constitution in October 1889, and the momentum became unstoppable. Both houses of the legislature passed a convention call, and Governor John M. Stone gave the measure his signature.[8]

Delegate elections were set for July 1890. Each county was entitled to the same number of delegates as it had members in the state house of representatives, and there would also be fourteen state at-large members. Republican participation in this election was modest at best. The party's state executive committee announced that it would not field a slate of at-large candidates, but would encourage Republican candidacies for county delegates in any areas where there seemed to be "a chance of success." Outside the Delta, only Marsh Cook believed he saw "a chance of success"; as we have seen, he was mistaken.[9]

In the river counties, Democratic conventions met and nominated slates of delegates. In two cases they agreed to give places on their ticket to Republicans: former governor James Lusk Alcorn in Coahoma County, and Horatio F. Simrall in Warren County. In Adams County, the Republicans made nominations, then withdrew them for reasons that went unmentioned in the press. In Bolivar County, where there was a nine-to-one black majority, Republicans nominated one black and one white Republican for the county's two delegate seats. County Democrats also nominated two men.[10]

Outside the Delta, agrarians worked to achieve the election of some of their number. The Farmers' Alliance, a strong agrarian group, was pledged to refrain from partisan endorsements, but it did encourage farmers to play an active role in the delegate elections. In most cases the agrarians contended for the Democratic nomination for delegate. In the Lincoln County convention farmers worked long and hard to have an agrarian nominated, only to see a lawyer win after 384 ballots. In the south Mississippi county of Marion, when the Democrats nominated a "town politician" for delegate, agrarians brought out Independent candidate Elias Polk. The county newspaper, the *Pearl River News*, complained that Polk's ideas sounded like "anarchism" and "socialism." What the county really needed, the *News* argued, was a careful, reliable delegate who could work constructively on framing a new constitution. Official returns showed Polk winning only one fifth of the votes cast in Marion.[11]

The most vigorous race waged against a Democratic nominee was in the old Greenback stronghold of Webster County, a white-majority county in the northeastern part of the state. Here Democrats nominated G. W. Dudley, a newspaper editor. Webster had never been without opposition movements, and now the Independents, together with a small number of white Republicans, began to criticize Dudley's record. Unlike the agrarians in most other counties, Webster County Independents were fearful of

the constitutional convention, even resentful that a convention was to meet. They had the foresight to fear that limiting the suffrage would actually hurt, rather than help, agrarians. They attacked Dudley's record as a legislator for voting in favor of a constitutional convention. Dudley claimed that the journal of the house of representatives contained an error and that in fact he had not favored a convention unless the voters approved of one in a referendum. Dudley produced affidavits of some witnesses who were present at the roll call vote, but one of his attackers in Webster County had been present at the vote, too, and he said Dudley had voted "aye." On the day of the July general election, the Independent candidate won over 52 per cent of the vote. This candidate, John E. Gore, was a farmer and part-time preacher who still called himself a Greenbacker.[12]

The turnout in Mississippi's 1890 delegate election was the lowest of any election since the Civil War. Only about 15 percent of the state's adult males turned out to vote. In Sharkey County four voters turned out; in Union County thirty-two citizens cast ballots. Agrarians certainly did not win the domination they had hoped for. While approximately fifty-five delegates were members or supporters of the Farmers' Alliance, this was far from a majority of the 134 seats. Looking simply at occupation, only forty-seven of the delegates were farmers, while fifty-six were lawyers.[13]

As to party, two white Republicans were elected in office-sharing arrangements with the Democratic organizations in Delta counties. In Bolivar County the Republican ticket was victorious over the Democratic one; the GOP ticket included the only black delegate who would sit in the convention, Isaiah T. Montgomery. The white member of the Bolivar County Republican ticket, planter George P. Mechoir, was prominent in Republican circles; by the time the convention roster was drawn up, however, he was calling himself a Democrat. The convention also included Greenbacker John E. Gore and two Independent Democrats who defeated the regular party nominees. These Independents were J. J. Rotenberry of Yalobusha County and C. K. Holland of Calhoun County. With three avowed Republicans, one Greenbacker, and three other men who defeated the Democratic nominees, the convention obviously had a very small contingent from the opposition groups. Yet the work of the convention would prove of overwhelming importance to the future of opposition parties in the state.[14]

Although proponents of a constitutional convention had been highly interested in reapportionment and an elective judiciary, it was the pro-

posed suffrage restrictions that most captured the attention of state residents and, in fact, of citizens nationwide. The need, felt many Mississippians, was clear. As one citizen wrote to the Jackson *Clarion-Ledger*, "The old men of the present generation can't afford to die and leave their children with shotguns in their hands and perjury on their souls, in order to defeat the Negroes. The constitution can be made so that this will not be necessary." Republican delegate Alcorn favored creating a black-led house of the legislature so that blacks could have a voice while still being kept in their own separate political sphere. Most delegates, however, preferred to keep blacks out of politics altogether. Ideas of how to accomplish this (without violating the Fifteenth Amendment by mentioning race in the new suffrage rules) were legion. Simrall, the Republican delegate from Warren County, suggested that voters be disqualified if they had lived in their precinct less than one year. This way, Simrall believed, transient black tenant farmers would be disfranchised, while the more stable white population and a smaller number of blacks would vote.[15]

Other plans focused on the fact that few blacks owned land. One Democrat suggested giving property owners one vote for every forty acres owned. Others suggested allowing women to vote if they or their husband owned at least $300 in real estate. A few delegates proposed making many county offices appointive by the governor, so that even black majority counties would never again see persons of color winning office.[16]

The plan that was finally framed by the committee on suffrage had many separate parts. First, all adult males would be assessed a poll tax of at least two dollars per year for the benefit of the public schools. Sheriffs could not compel payment of this tax, but only those who had paid the tax for two consecutive years would be permitted to vote. The idea here was that blacks (and undoubtedly other poor men) would choose not to pay the tax and would thus give up the right to vote. While four dollars (for two years' taxes) may not sound like much, in fact it represented a serious obstacle to voting for a small farmer whose annual cash income would typically be about fifty dollars—if he finished out the year in the black at all.

A second provision stipulated that in order to register to vote, a citizen must be able to read or to express his understanding of a part of the state constitution when it was read to him. Like the poll tax, this provision had the potential of disfranchising white voters as well as black, since many white farmers were illiterate or barely literate. The genius of this section, however, was that all discretion was left up to the registrar, who almost

invariably would be a white Democrat. Easy "understanding tests" could be given to white would-be voters, while extremely difficult questions could be asked of black applicants. Even if the black applicants gave a strong answer, the voting registrar could deny registration with a simple "No, that wasn't good enough."

Another kind of literacy test was added by the constitution's prescription of an "Australian ballot." Under this provision, instead of the political parties printing and distributing their own ballots with their candidates' names, the counties would print up ballots with *all* nominees' names included. The voter would have to be sufficiently skilled at reading to pick out the names he wanted to vote for (not labeled by party, and in no particular order on the ballot). The voter would then mark an X in ink by each name selected and deposit the ballot. Poorly educated voters would have a difficult time with the new Australian ballot, even if they had managed to pass the literacy or understanding test.

Opposition to the suffrage provisions recommended by the convention's suffrage committee was limited. Even the lone black delegate, Isaiah T. Montgomery, announced that he would acquiesce, for the good of the state's race relations. By assuring white control, hatreds and tensions would fade, Montgomery mused, and perhaps the better class of blacks would be permitted to vote. Conservative Republican Alcorn shook his head in disbelief at the idea of an understanding test based on the voter's interpretation of the constitution: "The construction of the constitution is a matter over which the most erudite lawyers and statesmen have always differed." Alcorn predicted that tens of thousands of white as well as black voters would be disfranchised unless the registrars "put easy questions to the white voter." Webster County's Greenbacker delegate opposed the entire disfranchisement scheme, fearing that one faction of whites could use the literacy test against another faction of whites. The faction in power could register its own supporters, black as well as white, while denying hundreds of its opponents the right to register under the subjective understanding clause.[17]

In other matters, the agrarians got little of what they were seeking. The elective judiciary was defeated by a vote of fifty-five to thirty-six. Moreover, although the new constitution awarded a number of new legislative seats to the white counties, the black counties still enjoyed a sixty-nine to sixty-four majority in the state house of representatives. In perhaps the most controversial move of all, the constitutional convention rejected by a vote of eighty to twenty-six a proposal to submit the new document to the

Isaiah T. Montgomery has been a controversial figure in Mississippi history since his decision in 1890 to support the new state constitution. Montgomery was the only black delegate in the constitutional convention. He is also noted as the founder of Mound Bayou, an all-black town in Bolivar County. (Photo courtesy of the Mississippi Department of Archives and History)

voters for their approval. Eight delegates voted against the new constitution on the final vote; four delegates refused to sign the document. Two of those who refused to sign were at the forefront of agrarian leaders: Gore of Webster County and Farmers' Alliance state lecturer Frank Burkitt of Chickasaw County. Both men objected to the suffrage sections, and both decried the failure of the convention to seek the people's ratification.[18]

The state press also denounced the new constitution. The *Clarion-Ledger* spearheaded the opposition and at one point listed thirty-four newspapers, including most large papers in the state, that opposed the constitution as drafted. In Claiborne County, the *Port Gibson Reveille* complained that while many states suffered from election irregularities, "it was reserved for the state of Mississippi to make its very constitution the instrument and shield of fraud." By November, the *Clarion-Ledger* noted that while some newspapers continued to complain bitterly, it was a "useless fight."[19]

The new constitution brought two immediate changes affecting the near future of Mississippi politics. One was that all state and county officers, including legislators, were now to have four-year rather than two-year terms. The constitution extended the terms of current officers through January 1896. This meant, for example, that Governor Stone, elected in 1889, would serve six years instead of two. Any new efforts to defeat the state's Democratic officeholders would come later rather than sooner.[20]

The other change came with a new statewide registration of voters prior to the 1892 presidential election. This would provide a first test of how the new suffrage rules would work. In this first registration, the understanding test proved not to be the grossly unfair procedure that many had feared. Of those illiterates who qualified to vote by passing the understanding test, approximately 49 percent were black. One county, Quitman, was left with a black majority of voters even after the new registration. On the other hand, in Delta counties white election officers could still manipulate the black votes. For instance, it is curious that despite Quitman County's majority of black voters, Republican Benjamin Harrison won only fourteen votes there in 1892, while the great majority of the county's votes were reported as Democratic. The explanation for the low opposition vote in Quitman County is not clear. It may be a case of fraudulent counting; it may be a case of blacks having been won over to the Democratic party by whatever means. It *is* clear that even if blacks registered in substantial numbers in some counties, the Democratic party was not necessarily put in any danger.[21]

The other point to remember about the new 1892 registration is that while many blacks did successfully use the understanding test to register, the overall numbers of voters registered now stood at 8,615 blacks and 68,127 whites. Black voters would not be an important factor in state elections for over seventy years. This made impossible any resurrection of a Mississippi Republican party—unless the party found a way to win mass white support.[22]

In his influential *Southern Politics in State and Nation*, V. O. Key argued that the disfranchising laws and constitutions in the South were of comparatively little importance, since really they reflected a fait accompli. Using Texas as an example, Key showed that three trends usually attributed to the disfranchising laws had actually preceded these new laws. These three trends were: large numbers of blacks staying away from the polls, the defeat of Populism, and a reduction in the size of the overall

electorate of more than 50 percent. Historian J. Morgan Kousser strenu-
ously attacked Key's fait accompli thesis, and a long and careful study of
Mississippi politics before and after disfranchisement verifies that the thesis cannot be successfully applied to the Magnolia State.[23]

Of the three trends cited by Key, *none* describe Mississippi very well for
the period prior to the drafting of the new constitution. While certainly
substantially fewer blacks voted in 1888 than in 1876, it is striking that the
largely black Republican party won one of every four presidential votes in
the state in 1888 and carried seven heavily black counties. Further, Mississippi's disfranchising convention was held two years before the Populist
party even appeared in the state. Finally, although the overall size of the
electorate fell between 1876 (its peak) and 1888, the drop was 29.7 percent, not in excess of 50 percent. In fact, after a sharp drop between 1876
and 1880, the number of votes cast held steady through 1888.[24]

The three trends cited by Key for Texas became realities in Mississippi
only *after* passage of the 1890 constitution. Estimated black voting dropped
nearly 70 percent between the elections of 1888 and 1892. At the same
time, votes for the Republican presidential candidate fell from 26 percent
of the total in 1888 to less than 3 percent in 1892. The Populist party died
in the state several years after the passage of the constitution; the role of
the constitution in limiting Populist success will be examined in chapter 5.
Finally, the overall size of the electorate was cut in half in just four years,
between 1888 and 1892; this cut reflected reductions in the numbers of
white as well as black voters. Clearly it is inaccurate to say that Mississippi's constitution of 1890 simply formalized the conditions that were already present. The new constitution brought impressive changes to Mississippi's electorate and to its political system. Only in a limited sense is
Key's thesis valid for Mississippi: the general weakening of the state's
Republican, Greenback, and Independent movements in the late 1880s
allowed the Democratic party to work its collective will in the constitutional convention. Since the Democratic delegation was largely conservative, the disfranchisement of both blacks and poor whites in Mississippi
was quite thorough.[25]

Early in the 1890s, Mississippi's powerful Farmers' Alliance began to show
a keen interest in politics. At a meeting of the Southern Alliance in Ocala,
Florida, held in 1890, a majority of delegates rejected the proposed formation of a national third party; Alliance members were still willing to work
within the Democratic party. The convention did, however, adopt the

"Ocala Demands." If Democratic candidates would endorse the list of demands, the Farmers' Alliance would support them. If not, farmers would bring out other candidates to oppose them. At a later meeting, delegates promised, they would again consider forming a third party.

The Ocala Demands included many of the old Greenback party goals. Among these were an increase in the money supply, in part through silver coinage, a low tariff, abolition of national banks, and an honest and economical government. Newer agrarian goals included making commodity speculation a crime, government regulation or ownership of railroads, and direct election of U.S. senators. The most novel idea found in the Ocala Demands was the proposal for a "subtreasury system." Under this plan, the federal government would build a series of warehouses; farmers could store their crops in these warehouses and wait for a favorable time to sell. Meanwhile, they could borrow from the government up to 80 percent of the crop's value, at not more than 2 percent interest. If the farmer did not sell his crop within one year, the government could sell it to satisfy the debt. There is no doubt that the plan was wholly radical; the U.S. government had never played such a major role in the economy. There is also no doubt that American farmers, especially in the South, were wildly enthusiastic over the subtreasury proposal. They believed the plan gave them a glorious new opportunity to get out from under the thumb of bankers, merchants, and commodity speculators. Here was a chance, they believed, to regain some of the independence yeomen farmers had enjoyed in the antebellum period. Of all the Ocala Demands, none captured the attention of Mississippi farmers as successfully as the subtreasury proposal.[26]

In the 1890 congressional elections, the state Farmers' Alliance managed to elect two congressmen who were wholehearted supporters of the Alliance and its goals. Both were also loyal Democrats, elected as the regular nominees of their party. In 1891 the Alliance turned its attention to Mississippi's United States senators. The legislature elected in 1891 would serve four years, and would have the opportunity to elect both of the state's U.S. senators. Prior to the 1891 campaign, a Carroll County chapter of the Farmers' Alliance sent letters to U.S. senators James Z. George and Edward Cary Walthall, asking their views on the Ocala Demands and particularly on the subtreasury. Both men answered that the subtreasury was impractical, unconstitutional, and would represent a dangerous growth of government size and power. Both senators recommended that farmers trust the Democratic party's traditional policies of a

low tariff coupled with moderate inflation of the money supply to help the nation's farming folk.[27]

Democratic editor Frank Burkitt, who ran the Alliance newspaper *Chickasaw Messenger*, opened a campaign against the two men with an editorial headlined, "Good-bye, Senators." Walthall soon announced he was not a candidate for reelection, and Alliance congressman Clarke Lewis announced for Walthall's seat. Most attention, however, focused on Burkitt's editorial efforts to oust Senator George. The agrarians chose Ethelbert Barksdale as their candidate to replace George, and urged voters to elect legislators pledged to Barksdale. (Senators were elected by the legislature in this period.) Barksdale, like Burkitt, was a loyal Democrat who had long been an agrarian. He had edited a Jackson newspaper and served in Congress in the 1880s. At first the anti-George campaign seemed weak and disorganized. Most of Mississippi's congressional delegation supported George, as did the governor. The state Alliance's own organ, the Jackson *New Mississippian*, did too. Several local Alliance chapters dramatically turned in their charters rather than see the organization become so embroiled in an election, but Burkitt snorted that these were only "town Alliances," not chapters made up of real farmers.[28]

As the campaign progressed, the Barksdale movement picked up steam. Pro-Barksdale legislative candidates appeared in almost every county. In many cases they won the Democratic nomination, while in others they ran as Independents. In some counties both the Barksdale men and the George supporters claimed to be the true Democratic nominees. In Yalobusha County one group was "the Democrats" while another called itself "Democrats No. 2." In a few cases where the agrarians won the Democratic nomination, they were opposed by pro-George Independents. The most dramatic example of this situation came in Chickasaw County, where Frank Burkitt sought election to the legislature. Burkitt, the state's most vocal Barksdale supporter, won the Democratic nomination but soon found himself facing an Independent Democrat pledged to George. The campaign in Chickasaw was an ugly one. Burkitt's *Messenger* burned to the ground at 3:30 one morning, under mysterious circumstances; Burkitt was certain the burning "was an outgrowth of the bitter and unrelenting war made on me as . . . a supporter of Major Barksdale." Feelings ran high in Chickasaw. Burkitt was shot in the head by his opponent, although the shot was "a glancing one" and the Alliance editor soon recovered.[29]

Similar incidents occurred across the state. In Pontotoc County the voter registration books disappeared, apparently stolen by George supporters who hoped to prevent the election from being held in that agrarian county. Barksdale and George met face to face in a number of debates, but their joint campaign soon had to be abandoned to prevent riots. In a debate between Barksdale and Congressman Hernando D. Money, Barksdale accused Money of having accepted a bribe from the railroads. Money hotly retorted that Barksdale was a liar, and Barksdale threw a lawbook at the congressman, striking him in the head. The meeting quickly erupted into fistfights. Meanwhile pro-George newspapers unleashed bitter attacks on the agrarians. Farmers should not support "a fetid amalgamation of political debauchery," urged the *Tupelo Journal*. Like a mule, the Barksdale faction had "no pride of ancestry or hope of posterity." The *Natchez Democrat* warned voters to stay away from "a sickly political embryo that can never reach the entity of a party."[30]

A political observer in Grenada County surely spoke the truth when he described the 1891 campaign as "one of the most exciting and serious we had ever witnessed in the state." It was also an especially grueling race. Frank Burkitt visited nearly every county in the state, traveling eight thousand miles in the first half of the campaign alone. Barksdale similarly exerted himself, but the results of the election were disappointing for the agrarians. Barksdale's supporters did win victories in some of the more agrarian counties such as Pontotoc and Webster. A pro-George editor in Webster County wrote angrily, "Ethelbert Barksdale, the seeds that you have sown have brought their fruit; but . . . the army of political bastards you have reared will bring shame and disgrace upon your aged head and curse you yet." In Webster County, Greenback candidate John E. Gore again defeated a Democratic opponent; Gore was pledged to Barksdale. Yet statewide only about one third of the new legislators were Barksdale agrarians.[31]

When the legislature met and balloted to choose the U.S. senators, George received 101 votes, while Barksdale won only 53. The coy Senator Edward Cary Walthall, who had earlier declared no interest in being reelected, received 135 votes, while Alliance candidate Clarke Lewis garnered 21. The agrarians could not content themselves by vowing to try harder next time. They had used every bit of energy, and every resource they could muster. The Alliance leaders saw one major reason for their defeat. The Democratic party ran the elections in Mississippi, and the party machinery was in the hands of professional politicians rather than

farmers. In most counties George's supporters had run the polling place, counted the ballots, and sent the returns to Jackson. Governor Stone, a George man himself, had not appointed a single Barksdale partisan to the county boards of election commissioners. The biggest problem, however, was that Democratic nominations for office in most counties were made by county conventions. Insiders, party regulars, and professional politicians dominated these conventions, the farmers perceived, and chances for nominating a genuine agrarian were slim. Mississippi's Alliance leaders began to think that their only hope for winning elections lay outside the Democratic party.[32]

By early 1892, Farmers' Alliance leaders across the country were talking in earnest about forming a new political party. In a number of Mississippi counties, farmers took concrete steps to leave the Democratic party and join the new movement for a People's party. One of the leaders of this movement was James S. Madison, speaker of the state house of representatives. Physically a huge man (weighing in at more than three hundred pounds), Madison was a successful farmer from Noxubee County. He opened a People's party office, and issued a call for a third-party convention to be held in Jackson on June 22, 1892. At a steady clip, many Mississippi farmers abandoned their support of the Democrats. Early in June a meeting of the Choctaw County Farmers' Alliance was opened to the public and transformed itself into a People's party convention, electing delegates to attend the state convention. In the southwestern county of Copiah, where there had been few Independent candidates since the murder of Print Matthews in 1883, the Democratic county convention unexpectedly declared itself a People's party convention, and also selected representatives to the state convention. A number of Democratic newspapers went over to the People's party, or Populist, side. These included the *Pontotoc Democrat* (soon called the *People's Banner*), the *Choctaw Plaindealer*, and the Kosciusko *Alliance Vindicator*.[33]

The People's party state convention met in Jackson with delegates from twenty-four counties. The convention organized a state executive committee, selected a presidential elector slate, and chose delegates to the Omaha National Convention. The platform of the state party was firmly based on the Ocala Demands of 1890. In Omaha, the Mississippi delegates heard sobering words from reform leader Ignatius Donnelly, who warned: "We meet in the midst of a nation brought to the verge of moral, political, and material ruin." To stave off the impending national crisis, the convention adopted a national platform of inflation of the money supply, eco-

nomical government, the subtreasury, and government ownership of the railroads. The Mississippi delegates undoubtedly cringed when the convention left the tariff issue out of its platform, and included it only in a set of auxiliary resolutions. Calls for a lower tariff were popular with Mississippi voters. Still, the rest of the platform contained goals that were likely to please Mississippi farmers. The convention tapped General James B. Weaver of Iowa, the Greenback candidate of 1880, to be its standard bearer. For vice-president, the ticket was balanced geographically by the choice of a Confederate veteran, James G. Field of Virginia.[34]

As Mississippi's 1892 presidential and congressional campaign got underway, it was clear that two men would bear the brunt of campaigning for the Populists. One was Frank Burkitt. A native of Tennessee, Burkitt had served in the Confederate cavalry, rising to the rank of captain. By 1867 he settled in Chickasaw County, Mississippi, where he taught school briefly, practiced a little law, and was elected justice of the peace. In 1872 he and a partner purchased the *Chickasaw Messenger*, giving Burkitt a mouthpiece for his political ideas. By 1883 he had joined his father in the legislature, where he won a reputation as a watchdog of state expenses. He was also active in the Grange, and later was state lecturer of the Farmers' Alliance. Some observers said Burkitt knew more Mississippians than any other man alive thanks to his Grange and Alliance work. He was a man of simple tastes, usually wearing a farmer's wool hat and old, patched clothes. Sometimes he even wore his durable Confederate uniform to meetings of the legislature. He wrote a statute that prescribed a uniform (denim pants and vests) for students at the state agricultural college, "to prevent any distinction in dress" among the students.[35]

Burkitt first attracted statewide notice in 1886, when he published the so-called Wool Hat pamphlet. In this tract, he attributed the state's deficits to wasteful expenditures for the state's public colleges, especially the agricultural college. He also complained that of the three hundred graduates of this college in its first seven years of operation, only three had become farmers. While the college administration later provided its own statistics and defenses, Burkitt's pamphlet attracted more notice. As chairman of the house appropriations committee in 1887, Burkitt sponsored deep cuts in state government expenses. By the late 1880s he was calling for tough regulation of railroads and denounced the pro-railroad regime of Governor Robert Lowry. Lowry retaliated by coming into Chickasaw County to support an Independent running against Burkitt in 1887, but

without success. Most recently Burkitt had denounced the suffrage planks in the constitutional convention and had spearheaded Barksdale's bid for the U.S. Senate. In the latter campaign Burkitt was defeated for reelection by a pro-George Independent Democrat. Burkitt, like Barksdale, initially opposed formation of a new third party in 1892, and in fact he had accepted the Democrats' nomination as a presidential elector candidate. Unlike Barksdale, Burkitt finally did cast his lot with the Populists, and he resigned his place on the Democratic elector slate.[36]

The other great People's party activist of 1892 was Thomas P. Gore of Webster County. Initially people flocked to hear Gore out of curiosity. He was, first of all, only twenty-two years old, yet had developed a reputation as a great speaker. Furthermore, Gore was blind, having lost the sight in each eye in two separate accidents. But if people initially came out of curiosity, they left with respect for a man who clearly deserved his status as an orator of the first rank. Gore was a Webster County native; after teaching school briefly he had studied at the Cumberland University School of Law in Tennessee. In 1892 he was just beginning his practice.[37]

Gore fell into the People's party quite naturally. His home county of Webster had long been one of the greatest hotbeds of agrarianism and independent political action. Between 1874 and 1889, Webster County had been home to Independent, Greenback, People's, Independent People's, Anti-Monopoly, and Union Labor tickets. Repeatedly, the opposition had won some county offices and legislative seats. The Gore family was at the forefront of these anti-Democrat movements; Thomas Gore's uncle John E. Gore twice had won election to the legislature as a Greenbacker. By the early 1890s seven members of the family were leaders of the Populist party, but none could win converts as effectively as young Thomas Gore.[38]

The Democratic newspapers had little that was negative to say about the young Populist speaker. True, the *Grenada Sentinel* editor found it "amusing" to hear so young a man style himself an expert on national issues, but the editor added that Gore was clearly a speaker "of ability and talent." Like Burkitt, and Benjamin King before him, Gore cared little about his dress (he usually went sockless), but farmers and even merchants and lawyers were captivated by his speeches. The Democratic flagship newspaper the *Clarion-Ledger* reported that Gore's ability was "amazing." Despite his handicap, he cited statistics and quoted unerringly the Bible, Shakespeare, and Grover Cleveland. Gore was expert at varying his deliv-

ery, the Jackson paper reported: he was "bitter, amusing, and pathetic in turn." He advocated Populism with "courage, intelligence, and force," the *Clarion-Ledger* concluded.[39]

The time seemed ripe for the appearance of a new party in a cotton state like Mississippi. Cotton prices had slipped from just over nine cents per pound to just over seven cents during the previous two years, and more ominously, farmers were facing a much smaller crop in the fall of 1892. Dry, cool weather had caused a shedding of the plants, and crop yields were down by 30 to 40 percent. Furthermore, the Democratic presidential candidate was no agrarian. While Grover Cleveland did have a reputation as an honest and economical administrator, he was also seen as a politician who oriented himself toward his banker and businessmen supporters. He was, for example, far from an avid silver supporter. Rumors circulated across the South that Cleveland's wife had refused to attend ceremonies dedicating a statue of Robert E. Lee, fearing that she might meet Jefferson Davis's widow there. Another rumor alleged that Cleveland had invited black leader Frederick Douglass to a White House reception. In a published letter, Cleveland denounced the first rumor, while admitting the truth of the second.[40]

Actually, Mississippians faced a presidential ballot with three locally unpopular candidates. Populist candidate Weaver had the reputation of a loser—he had carried only one Mississippi county as the 1880 Greenback nominee. Further, Weaver had moved from the Republican to the Greenback to the Populist party; was he not simply an opportunist? The biggest problem for Weaver's candidacy was his record as a Union general, which was trotted out, exaggerated, and given great publicity. General Weaver had militarily occupied the area around Pulaski, Tennessee. Faced with the problem of feeding homeless refugees, he had seized farmers' crops. The distorted version of the general's wartime record, which ran in most Mississippi newspapers, was that he had seized crops and shipped "meat and cotton back to his home in Iowa" for his own profit. Any food that was not sent to Iowa, the Democratic press alleged, was used not to feed good citizens, but "negroes and sorry white men." Soon the state press was calling the Populist candidate "J. Banditt Weaver" or, more commonly, "South-hating Weaver."[41]

Weaver came to Mississippi and made speeches at Meridian and Tupelo; predictably, the Populists pronounced the speakings highly successful, while Democratic papers reported that Weaver won not a single convert while in the state. Populist vice-presidential candidate James G. Field also

James B. Weaver ran twice for the presidency on the Greenback and Populist party tickets. In Mississippi, his status as a former Union general hurt him. Still, Mississippi ranked second among the southern states in its support for Weaver in 1880, and third in 1892. (From *Cyclopaedia of American Biography*)

visited Mississippi, speaking at Grenada and Jackson; most observers reported that the elderly Field was no spellbinder. The reputation of the Populist national ticket sank so low in the state that a few of the party's rank and file vowed they would not vote for it. Congressional candidate J. H. Jamison tried to salvage some support for Weaver by pointing out that all occupying generals have unpleasant duties, including the seizing of food. Even Robert E. Lee in his invasion of Pennsylvania had acted no differently from Weaver, Jamison told an audience at Winona. But the otherwise friendly audience shouted back that Lee was *not* a general who stole property.[42]

If Mississippians had reasons to react to Cleveland in a lukewarm way and to disdain Weaver there was of course no chance at this late date that the Republican candidate would carry Mississippi. A large majority of blacks were now disfranchised, while only a small percentage of whites would support the party of Lincoln. Just to make sure, Democratic papers

in the state gave wide coverage to a spurious quotation alleged to have been uttered by candidate Benjamin Harrison. Like many Republicans, Harrison favored the Lodge Election Bill, which would have provided federal oversight of congressional and presidential elections. Discouraged at the Republican party's existing prospects in the South, Democratic newspapers claimed Harrison had said, "I wash my hands of the South. It is a land of rebels and traitors . . . and I will never be in favor of making a campaign down there until we can place bayonets at the polls." In this clumsily manufactured quotation, Harrison allegedly concluded, "I am now more than ever in favor of ramming a force bill down their throats."[43]

Making one final decisive attack on Weaver, the state press warned that Weaver's candidacy really was designed to help the Republican party by dividing southern Democrats. This same ploy had been used effectively to attack Weaver's 1880 candidacy. A headline in the *Tupelo Journal* informed the voters that "The Third Party Is A Scheme Of The Republican Plutocrats." Other Democratic papers pointed out, correctly, that in neighboring Alabama, Republicans and Populists were cooperating. Alabama still had many black voters and an active Republican party, which was not the case in Mississippi; still, why give support to a party that was helping the enemy in an adjoining state? In a more serious but unsubstantiated charge, the *Pearl River News* editor reported that the Republican National Committee was providing funds for the Populist campaign in Mississippi. The editor's source? A prominent (unnamed) Republican in Chickasaw County had told the editor's (unnamed) friend that this was true. The state's Populists vehemently denied that they had sought or received any Republican funds. Still, many Mississippi farmers had to ponder the statement of Democratic leaders that if they voted for Weaver, they might be responsible for helping the hated Republican party win the White House.[44]

The two most important issues of the presidential campaign in Mississippi were free silver and the tariff. The Populists picked up the old Greenback party demand that the money supply be inflated, not only by the printing of more currency but by an aggressive program of silver coinage. This inflation would help the indebted farmers, since their income would rise while their previously contracted debts would remain constant. The Populists gleefully pointed out that while Mississippi Democrats might claim to favor the free coinage of silver, their platform was ominously silent on the question. The Democrats responded by saying that the farmers' greatest problem was the tariff. Every time he went to

town to buy a plow, a hoe, or a skillet, the farmer paid a high price. The price was high because if the item had been made abroad, the manufacturer had paid a hefty import duty; if American-made, the item was expensive because of a lack of foreign competition. Democratic speakers wanted to know why the national Populist platform was "as dumb as an oyster" on the tariff issue; Populists responded that it was more important to seek monetary inflation first, and then turn attention to the tariff.[45]

Despite the problems with their presidential candidate, state Populists remained optimistic. One ray of hope came in a special election to fill a vacancy in the office of chancery clerk in Choctaw County. The first election in Mississippi to feature a Populist opposing a Democrat, this August 1892 race resulted in victory for Populist Jesse Hughes, who won over 54 percent of the vote. The election showed that while town voters bitterly opposed the Populists, rural residents could flock to the People's party banner. Populist Jesse Hughes won only 23 percent of the vote in Ackerman (the county seat and only town of any size); in several isolated farm communities, on the other hand, Hughes won more than three quarters of the vote.[46]

In the 1892 congressional races, Democrats nominated lawyers for Congress in all the districts, thus giving Populist leaders cause for hope. If the Democrats won in every district, all seven congressmen and both senators would be lawyers. As in the Greenback heyday of the late 1870s, farmers were tiring of lawyer politicians, and demanding a larger voice for themselves. The People's party nominated congressional candidates in all but the Delta district; their nominees included three farmers and only one lawyer. Their other two candidates were physician S. W. Robinson and Farmers' Alliance editor Frank Burkitt.[47]

Burkitt, running in the fourth district in northeast Mississippi, faced a Democratic opponent who had clear weaknesses. Former congressman Hernando D. Money had retired from the house of representatives and spent six years as a corporate attorney in Washington, returning to Mississippi only in 1891. He was a conservative, and many Democrats believed the party needed to bring out an agrarian to defeat the popular Burkitt. It took 185 ballots at the Democratic district convention for Money's supporters to secure his nomination. During his joint meetings with Burkitt, Money did not pander to the prevalent agricultural sentiment, but remained true to his conservative ideals. He attacked the subtreasury plan as "unconstitutional," an unfair plan that would help farmers at the expense of others. He called government ownership of the railroads an impractical,

"wild scheme." As if these stands did not hurt Money enough in this district of farmers, Populist editors soon resurrected a scandal from one of Money's previous terms in Congress.[48]

While a congressman, reported the People's party editors, Money had accepted funds from railroad magnate Collis P. Huntington. Money, for his part, had introduced a bill to help Huntington's Texas and Pacific Railroad. In the 1892 campaign, Money was forced to spend most of his time defending himself from the charges. He complained first of all that the charges were stale, that they had been investigated earlier without hurting his career. Second, he argued that the funds received from Huntington were a loan for his firm, backed up by collateral. Finally, he pointed out that he had received the loan *after* introducing the railroad bill, so it could not be a bribe. (Of course, it could have been a reward.) Burkitt showed his mastery of politics by taking the high road, leaving it to other Populist editors to keep the charges before the people. In his speeches Burkitt said he did not believe Money guilty of wrongdoing, only of faulty judgment. Money felt so under attack that he actually used Burkitt's words to defend himself, saying in effect: my opponent does not accuse me of dishonesty, only of having poor judgment.[49]

State Democratic leaders, however, were not going to let Money fall. They sent a veritable army of popular speakers into the fourth district, visiting every supervisor's beat. Money was an influential man in Washington, they argued. If Burkitt were sent to the nation's capital, it would take him a long while "to even know where he was at." To the Populists' questioning what the Democrats had done to merit continued support, the Money speakers responded that the Democrats had reduced state expenses and had thrown out the "heavy, sluggish colored men" in the legislature in the mid-1870s. If the party had a less enviable record nationally, they had never since the Civil War simultaneously controlled both houses of Congress and the White House.[50]

An assistant editor of the *Grenada Sentinel* reported that he had met Burkitt several years earlier while the latter was on an Alliance speaking tour. The assistant editor had said he suspected Burkitt wasn't making much money speaking, and that he presumed Burkitt would soon get a good office from the voters. Burkitt allegedly had responded, "Yes, I will, if the damn fool Alliance don't bust too soon. You know you can't keep the damn fools together long." This quotation, and a second one of similar tenor, appeared in nearly every Democratic newspaper in the state. Some papers used the quotations as fillers, printing them dozens of times in each

issue to fill up odd spaces in the columns. Burkitt, meanwhile, denied ever calling the farmers fools.[51]

The most controversial decision the Populists made in Burkitt's campaign was their petitioning a federal judge to appoint election supervisors. Under one of the old Reconstruction-era civil rights laws, citizens had the right to ask for such appointments; the supervisors would have the power to witness the balloting and the official count and could serve as witnesses in any later court proceedings or election contests. Burkitt and his followers knew that in hundreds of recent political races, the non-Democratic candidates had been the victims of stuffed ballot boxes, intimidated voters, and fraudulent counts. Having federal supervisors at each polling place could help prevent such occurrences in 1892. On the other hand, Burkitt gave the Democrats an easy issue. The Democratic press had already alarmed the voters with stories of the Lodge Election Bill, warning that soon federal bayonets would be seen again at Mississippi elections. While Populists denied they favored the Lodge Bill, now Democrats could point out that regardless of their position on that particular bill, Populists did favor federal interference in Mississippi elections. In Burkitt's own county the Democratic *Okolona Sun* stated, "We very much mistake the temper of Chickasaw manhood, or it will resent this insult." As the *Clarion-Ledger* explained, the Democratic party believed that "the voters of each neighborhood have the sense to know how to manage their affairs."[52]

In the other congressional districts, many of the same issues were raised. In some counties outside the fourth district, Populists petitioned for federal supervisors and met the same backlash from the Democratic press. In the fifth district of central Mississippi, the Populist candidate was W. P. Ratliff, a farmer who did a little preaching on the side. Ratliff benefited from his firm stand in favor of prohibition, but Democratic speakers and writers mocked Ratliff's strong church ties. They feared that in Congress Ratliff would read temperance leaflets into the *Congressional Record*, or sponsor appropriations "for the distribution of tracts . . . among the Hottentots." Ratliff also came under fire when he formed chapters of a secret society called Gideon's Band. The bands were made up of a few dozen of the most loyal Populists in each county. They were to mobilize public opinion in their neighborhoods and make sure Populist voters turned out on election day. The Democratic press, however, made the most of the secretive nature of the Gideon's Bands, arguing that perhaps violence and intimidation was a part of their unknown agenda.[53]

By October the campaign had deteriorated into simple name-calling.

Seventh district Populist candidate S. W. Robinson was an "infidel"—he had once suggested leaving the Bible out of the public school curriculum. James B. Weaver was a "characterless political prostitute," and his supporters were "Weaver's weevils." Fifth district candidate Ratliff was "governed by the mad lust of office," the same motive that led Lucifer to rebel against heaven. Refusing to use the dignified Latinate term *Populist*, Democratic papers referred to the "Pops" and to "the one-third party." Populists retaliated by calling the Democrats "the whiskey party." Referring to the fact that both the Democratic and Republican platforms opposed free silver and the subtreasury, Populist speakers referred to the "Demopublicrat" party.[54]

As was true of the election of the previous year, the 1892 race was an ugly one. In the first district, located in the northeast corner of the state, the Populist party was weak and unorganized. Party leaders did not help matters by nominating attorney James Burkitt, brother of Frank, for Congress. Immediately Democrats discovered a letter James Burkitt had written thirteen years earlier, to a black school teacher. In it, the young lawyer promised to help the school teacher get an extra assistant. He also promised to work to get one month's back pay for the assistant for a period before the assistant had yet been appointed or done any work, provided James Burkitt got half of the back pay. The letter's postscript said, "Read and burn." James Burkitt denied any wrongdoing, saying the teacher had been entitled to an assistant for many months; the letter was simply that of an attorney offering to help a teacher get all the funds he was entitled to. Burkitt's "half" was his attorney's fee. The "read and burn" postscript was to protect the county superintendent of education, who had failed to appoint the proper number of assistants.[55]

Of course, the letter doomed an already weak candidate. More seriously, the story of the letter was also used to hurt Frank Burkitt's candidacy in the district just to the south. At one rally Frank Burkitt saw a young man carrying a placard lettered "Read and Burn." Burkitt accosted the man, and the man's father responded by striking Burkitt severely over the head with a cane. Burkitt's brother-in-law then shot at the cane-wielding father, but missed. Burkitt's brother-in-law was arrested. In a similar confrontation over a placard, Burkitt's father attacked Congressman Eaton J. Bowers. In yet a third instance James Burkitt fought with Congressman John Allen. These were not isolated incidents of violence. At McCondy in Clay County, Frank Burkitt accused certain named Democrats of ballot box stuffing. One of the accused men jumped up on the platform, striking

Burkitt so hard that the candidate fell from the platform and was knocked out cold. Populists took up a collection and hired two bodyguards to accompany him. But the *Tupelo Journal* denounced Frank Burkitt's desire to have a bodyguard "in order that he may go around and denounce better men than himself with impunity."[56]

In other instances Democrats used the same tactics they had used to defeat Greenbacker Reuben Davis in 1878. In Copiah County hoodlums made a great noise at a rally at Wesson, preventing Rev. Benjamin T. Hobbs from speaking in favor of Populist congressional candidate S. W. Robinson. The Jackson *Daily Clarion* was unconcerned: the Constitution guaranteed the right of free speech but it "doesn't undertake to make people listen." Even the popular and respected speaker Thomas P. Gore was the victim of this noisy tactic. An elderly Mississippian interviewed in 1942 recalled that his employer had taken him and a wagon-load of employees to a Populist speaking to shout down young Gore. "We did it, too," he added.[57]

Newspaper editors warned Populists that their future was bleak if they did not return to the Democratic party. The *McComb City Enterprise* urged readers to write down the names of Populist voters in a notebook and keep it for future reference. The Populists were dangerous not only in politics, explained the editor, but were "dangerous in commerce, dangerous in church, and dangerous in society." The *Grenada Sentinel* warned that young men should be careful whom they supported, "as a wrong act at this juncture may come back to haunt them through life." When Lee County Populists petitioned for the appointment of federal supervisors of election, the local paper printed the names of those who had signed the petition. Once again citizens were urged to file away the list of names, that they not forget "this motley crew." From Jackson the editor of the *Daily Clarion* praised the "quiet but effective action" of publishing the names of the Populist petitioners.[58]

Of course, the federal supervisors were not the only hope Populists had for a fair election. In each county, three commissioners (not all of one party) were supposed to insure an honest election. These three county commissioners appointed the precinct officers. In a spirit of fair play, Holmes County election commissioners decided to let the Populists choose one officer for each polling place. In nearly every other county, however, Democrats selected all precinct officers. At the county level, the three election commissioners were appointed by the governor, and while he claimed to appoint some Populists to these positions, as well as Republi-

cans, he did not appoint the men specifically suggested by the People's party. The Populists were generally unhappy at the list of commissioners that was chosen. As one observer wrote, the Democrats expected the men appointed were men who "would not make their influence felt."[59]

As it turned out, the most common dirty trick in 1892 was not ballot box stuffing, nor fraudulent counting; the most common trick had to do with the printing of the ballot in each county. This was the first presidential election held with the Australian ballot, and voters were warned ahead of time that they must know the names of the nine electors pledged to their candidate—these would not be labeled by party. Just before the election, Democratic clubs spread the word that to vote for Cleveland, one simply would vote for the first nine electors printed on the ballot. The other twenty-seven elector candidates had their names mixed and scrambled at the bottom of the ticket. A third-party leader in south Mississippi recalled that when he entered the voting booth, his heart sank to see "how difficult the dem. party had made it for any who did not vote the dem. ticket to make out his ballot."[60]

Nationally, James B. Weaver ran the best third-party race seen since the Civil War, actually carrying several western states and winning twenty-two electoral votes. He won more than one million popular votes. In the South, as expected, Weaver won fewer votes than in the West. In Mississippi, Weaver won more than seven times as many votes as Harrison, winning 19 percent of the total. Among the southern states, only Alabama and Texas returned higher percentages for Weaver than did Mississippi. Concerns about his war record clearly hurt Weaver in Mississippi, and as in 1880 he carried only one county—in this case, Chickasaw.[61]

Also as expected, the strongest Populist congressional candidates in 1892 were Frank Burkitt and W. P. Ratliff, running in northeast and east-central Mississippi, respectively. Burkitt carried a bloc of four contiguous counties in the fourth district: Chickasaw, Choctaw, Pontotoc, and Webster. Overall, he won about 39 percent of the reported vote. Ratliff won about 29 percent. In other districts north of the state's center, John H. Simpson won 22 percent in the second district, while James Burkitt of "read and burn" fame won 18 percent. In south Mississippi districts, physician S. W. Robinson won 25 percent, while farmer T. N. "Nat" Jackson won just over 17 percent. Although carrying four counties for their candidates arguably was not a bad showing in the Populists' first congressional race, the party's leaders chaffed at the knowledge that it would be three years before they could follow up by winning county offices and legislative

seats in these and other counties. For unambiguously good news, the party had to look at the national results, which included the election of some fifteen hundred Populist state legislators, three governors, five U.S. senators, and ten members of the house of representatives.[62]

A large group of Mississippi agrarians had made the fateful decision that they could win the reforms they sought only outside the Democratic party. While they did not elect a congressman in 1892, they did win a respectable percentage of the vote and proved themselves locally strong in several counties. The Populist politicians of Mississippi now vowed to redouble their efforts, to launch new People's party newspapers, found new Populist clubs, and make every effort to convert their friends and neighbors. Soon, they believed, their efforts would pay off, and the halls of the state legislature in Jackson would ring with the voices of angry Populist members seeking to enact the party's agrarian goals.

FIVE

Heyday for Populists

IN NOVEMBER 1892, SOME MISSISSIPPI POPULISTS WERE EXPRESsing satisfaction at having made a promising beginning in the congressional races held that month. The state's Democrats, meanwhile, went nearly insane with joy. For only the second time since the Civil War, their candidate had won a clear victory in a presidential race. In the town of Grenada, Democrats held torchlight parades on three consecutive nights, complete with roman candles, tin horns, cow bells, and cannons. On the first night, a coffin carrying the effigy of Frank Burkitt was paraded through town and publicly burned. At West Point, Democrats repeatedly fired a cannon in celebration; in their excitement they put too much powder into the cannon and it exploded, killing three and cutting off both legs of the former mayor. Since the Democrats now held the White House, the town's leaders were quick to petition President Cleveland for a postmastership for their maimed comrade. In a similar incident in Choctaw County, celebrating Democrats were loading an anvil with gunpowder, lighting it, and watching the anvil jump into the air. Again an explosion surprised the crowd, and one Harry D. Tolbert died of his wounds three days later.[1]

Mississippi's Populists got their turn to celebrate one year later. Even distant newspapers, such as the *Rocky Mountain News*, gave wide coverage to Mississippi's "startling political sensation" of January 1894. In that

month the legislature convened in Jackson for a special session. Elected in the 1891 contest that had pitted George supporters against Barksdale agrarians, the legislators were almost unanimously Democrats. Of all the members of the two houses, only three lonely Delta lawmakers declared themselves Republicans, no members called themselves Independents, and only John E. Gore represented the remnants of the Greenback party. For the official roster of the first session, seven members had used the label "Alliance Democrat," but this did not reflect any third-party movement. Then, as the special session convened in the first days of 1894, twenty-two members dramatically "declared themselves out of the Democratic party" and formed their own Populist caucus. Of course, no one was surprised that legislators Frank Burkitt and W. P. Ratliff did not join the legislative Democratic caucus. But few suspected that as many as twenty-two legislators would support the new party. The Mississippi Populists' biggest victory to date came by defection, not election.[2]

Actually, this was not the first such occurrence. Even though county elections would not be held until 1895—more than three years after formation of the new party—the Populists had already captured control of several counties. In Amite County in the southwestern corner of Mississippi, a majority of the board of supervisors went from the Democratic into the People's party. A local newspaper editor called their action a betrayal of the people who elected them and likened the defectors to Benedict Arnold. In Webster County, four of the five members of the board of supervisors joined the People's party. In Pontotoc County, nearly every county officer, from sheriff to coroner, denounced the Democratic party and signed onto the new organization. The only disappointment came when a special election for a legislative seat in Pontotoc County ended in fraud and a loss for the People's party. Although the Populists had been almost certain of victory, Democratic election officers in certain precincts refused to open the polls. Other men took their places, but the Democratic county election commissioners threw out all returns from these heavily Populist precincts. The Democrats won the seat in the legislature, but in so doing they sent many disgusted citizens into the Populist camp.[3]

Who were the Mississippi Populists? The identity of the twenty-two Populist legislators will give one indication. Geographically, these legislators came from nearly every region of the state. Only the Gulf Coast and the sparsely settled piney woods of southeast Mississippi had no Populist lawmakers. At the edge of the Delta, Tate and Tallahatchie counties elec-

ted Populists; in the northeast hills, Prentiss County had a People's party legislator. Other counties included central counties like Scott, south-western counties like Franklin, and east-central counties such as Lauder-dale. In all, seventeen counties were represented by Populists in the state house of representatives. As might be expected, the Populist legislators were much more likely to be farmers than were their Democratic counter-parts. In fact, twenty of the twenty-two Populist lawmakers were farmers, while one was a doctor and one (Burkitt) an agrarian editor. Less than half of the Democratic legislators were farmers, while 35 percent of them were attorneys. Age of the legislators did not differ appreciably by party, nor did their nativity. As in other recent years, all members of the legislature were born in Mississippi or another southern state.[4]

The Populist delegation in the 1894 special session was the largest delegation representing a single opposition party since Reconstruction; not until near the end of the twentieth century could another party boast an opposition bloc of this size. Democrats did take steps, however, to assure that Populists did not hold the "balance of power" on important votes where Democrats were divided. As in the 1880 session with its bloc of Greenback party members, so in the 1894 legislature the Democrats made a number of important decisions in caucus. The retirement of U.S. Senator Edward Cary Walthall because of illness gave the legislature one important task—choosing his successor. It took sixty-seven ballots in Democratic caucus to settle upon Anselm J. McLaurin; on the floor of the legislature the Democrats voted unanimously for McLaurin, while the Populists gave their votes to Frank Burkitt. By choosing McLaurin in caucus, the Democrats were able to prevent the Populists from playing an important role in the selection of Walthall's successor.[5]

An analysis of roll call votes in the state house of representatives in this 1894 special session allows a comparison of the behavior of Populist legis-lators and their Democratic opponents. As might be expected, the Demo-crats had a better success rate: individual Democratic members voted on the winning side an average of 79 percent of the time, while Populist legislators were on the winning side only 59 percent of the time. Populist members were conscientious, having an absentee rate on roll calls nearly 25 percent smaller than that of the Democrats. The index of relative cohesion—showing how often legislators of a certain party vote the same way—provides a way to measure the extent to which ideological party lines were sharply drawn.[6]

On the index of relative cohesion, if all Populist members voted alike on

all roll calls, their score for the session would be one hundred, while if they were perfectly divided on each vote their score would be zero. In this 1894 session, Populist members of the house were somewhat more cohesive than the Democrats. The Populist legislators scored sixty-two on the index of relative cohesion, while Democrats scored fifty-eight. These index scores are substantially higher for both parties than the scores of Greenback and Democratic legislators in the 1880 session (forty-six and thirty-seven, respectively). This indicates, first, that the Populists were more ideologically unified than the earlier Greenbackers, who after all were made up of former Whigs, black former Republicans, and white former agrarian Democrats. The comparison of the two sessions also indicates that by 1894 the Democrats were more likely to act in concert than they had been in the 1880 session. This should not be surprising, since the state was in a severe depression in 1894, and lawmakers were unlikely to raise certain kinds of divisive issues (new land taxes, for example, or new lien rights for landlords).

On individual roll call votes, the Populists did sometimes play a decisive role, despite Democrats' efforts to prevent them from doing so. The Populists' most assiduous efforts aimed to limit state expenditures, thereby averting the need for additional taxation. Former agrarian Democrats like Frank Burkitt were past masters at this kind of action, and the Populists voted to slash expenditures even for very popular state institutions. In the house of representatives, all Populist legislators present voted to reject a proposed home for aged and infirm Confederate veterans. The proposed institution was defeated by a vote of 45 to 64, and the Populists' votes were decisive. People's party members played a similarly crucial role in cutting the appropriation for Confederate pensions. On a technical bill that strengthened the cause of local option prohibition, all but one Populist legislator voted in favor of the law, and again their votes were decisive as the bill passed 57 to 47. Populist members also played decisive roles in cutting the appropriation for the Industrial Institute and College and in placing restrictions on the commissioners who would be buying land for a new penitentiary farm. Populist members were crucial in the defeat of a law that would have given insurance companies more power in determining how to compensate victims.[7]

The People's party legislators introduced several bills or amendments that initially passed but later failed to take effect. Frank Burkitt introduced an amendment to an antinepotism bill that would have increased the number of agencies in which the statute was to be in effect. Burkitt's

amendment passed the house, but then the nepotism bill itself was defeated, despite nearly unanimous Populist support. Attala County's Populist lawmaker W. P. Ratliff introduced an amendment to the tax bill that would have placed a privilege tax on large incomes and inheritances. The measure passed, but after Democratic leaders cracked the whip a number of Democrats changed their minds, and on a reconsideration, Ratliff's proposal was defeated, despite unanimous Populist party support. The story was similar for a state constitutional amendment proposed by a Democratic legislator; this amendment would have restored the elective judiciary to the state. On the first reading the measure passed 66 to 24, with all Populists supporting the measure. But on a second reading the vote was 72 to 37, with enough formerly absent Democrats now voting "nay" to deny the amendment the required two-thirds approval.[8]

Taken as a whole, the Populist members, cooperating with a bloc of agrarian Democrats, were able to play an important role in shaping legislation. Yet while Populists and agrarian Democrats were capable of working together, tensions between the two parties could be severe. After the session closed, the two Attala County legislators (Populist W. P. Ratliff and Democrat S. A. Jackson) returned home to report to the voters. In the Populist newspaper *Alliance Vindicator* Ratliff poked fun at Jackson, saying that Jackson had at one point in the session cast a vote for a Populist for U.S. senator. The Jackson *Clarion-Ledger* later reported that it was clear Ratliff intended "no malice," but Jackson was furious and denied Ratliff's charge. In a private conversation, the editor of the *Clarion-Ledger* urged the Democratic legislator to forget the matter, but Jackson replied that in Attala, "where party lines are so tightly drawn, I do not think I can afford . . . to let him go unnoticed." Jackson therefore published a card in the Kosciusko *Star* that announced: "I, S. A. Jackson . . . EMPHASIZE that W. P. Ratliff, Populite Representative from Attala County, is an infernal, DAMNED LIAR."[9]

The two men met by accident at the court house on a Saturday as they attended a sheriff's auction. An angry Ratliff struck Jackson and got him to the ground; friends separated them, but the two managed to draw guns and begin shooting at each other. Now the sheriff separated them and began to escort Ratliff away. Jackson, however, managed to follow them and again began shooting at his Populist enemy. Ratliff coolly returned the fire, hitting Jackson in the head and instantly killing him. In the barrage of gunfire, two bystanders were also hit; one died immediately and the other was very severely wounded. Ratliff was charged with murder and

manslaughter, but within two weeks of the shooting he was acquitted by a jury that ruled the Populist editor had acted in self-defense. Ratliff's reputation was not ruined by the encounter; in fact, it was enhanced, and he began to prepare for the fall elections for Congress.[10]

The most pressing issue for most Mississippians in this 1894 congressional race was the state of the economy. In the fall of 1894 cotton prices on the New Orleans exchange reached five cents per pound, the lowest level recorded since 1848. This was an absurdly low price, lower than the farmers' break-even point. To make matters worse, a hog cholera epidemic was killing thousands of swine in Mississippi, making many farmers fear a year with little cash and little food. Nationally, the country had entered a terrible depression. Unemployment was high, with bank and corporate failures commonplace.[11]

For many hard-hit Americans, there was one clear villain: Grover Cleveland. Of course, any president who happens to be in office when a depression hits is likely to become a scapegoat. But Mississippi Populists noted that Cleveland had been elected on a platform of free silver and a lower tariff. After getting into office, agrarians charged, he had actually worked against both of these goals. Cleveland had decided that the one clear cause of the depression was the government's failure to adhere to a strict gold standard. He used every bit of influence he had to get Congress to repeal the Sherman Silver Purchase Act of 1890, infuriating advocates of silver coinage. Moreover, while Cleveland was devoted to tariff reform, he was embarrassed by a nearly empty treasury, as imports fell off and tariff collections dropped. Accordingly, the Wilson-Gorman tariff supported by Cleveland was far from reformist. It dropped some tariff rates, but raised many others.

A vast number of southern agrarians saw Grover Cleveland as a politician who did not keep his promises. As a supporter of the gold standard and a high tariff, they mused, he was no better than a Republican. Campaigning for the People's party in north Mississippi, physician A. C. Gore reported that "old gray-headed Democrats, members of the church," now believed that "there is not a man in the United States" who could be trusted. Many angry farmers who had not been registered to vote in 1892 now went down to see the registrar. In some counties the number of registered voters rose markedly from 1892 levels. Sensing victory, Populists in the fourth district sponsored two great caravans across the counties of the district, converging on Sulphur Springs for the congressional nominating convention. It became apparent that in certain neighborhoods,

nearly every resident was now a Populist. In beat five of Attala County, for example, the county Democratic newspaper admitted that the typical Populist "rises in the morning and as far as he can see, Populist smoke rises from nearly every chimney." When he went out on the county road "five out of every six men he meets 'cuss' Cleveland."[12]

The state Democratic party was going through convulsions, unsure what attitude to take toward the unpopular president. Some of the state's Democratic newspapers disowned Cleveland, while many others argued that his shortcomings were exaggerated. In the seventh congressional district, which included the state capital and many southwestern counties, a Democratic convention took 1,151 ballots to dump incumbent congressman Charles E. Hooker, and nominate a Cleveland supporter in his place. In the sixth district, comprising the southernmost counties, from the Mississippi river to the Alabama line, the convention took three days to agree to pass over incumbent congressman Thomas R. Stockdale. Stockdale was a popular Democratic agrarian, but Cleveland's supporters were in control in the sixth and they nominated gold advocate Walter Denny. But in the waning moments of this nominating convention, after many Denny supporters had left, the convention also passed a pro-silver resolution.[13]

Although the People's party had won only 1,054 votes in the sixth district in 1892, the nomination of Cleveland supporter Denny provided Populists with an excellent opportunity to increase their vote, or even carry the election. To oppose Denny, the People's party chose N. C. "Scott" Hathorn. Even the Democratic speakers had to admit that Hathorn was a popular, respected leader; a former legislator and delegate to the constitutional convention, Hathorn invariably had voted with the agrarians. Hathorn assured agrarian Democrats that he had the same goals as the lamented Mr. Stockdale. The *Lawrence County Press* cried foul; Stockdale now supported Denny, the editor pointed out, and all true Stockdale supporters should do the same. Another Democratic editor, however, reluctantly admitted that Stockdale partisans "are very sore over their defeat and openly assert that they will vote the Populite ticket." From Liberty in Amite County, the local editor warned that the Populists were "working like beavers," while Democrats were doing very little.[14]

Democratic campaigners urged voters to stick with the party that had ended Reconstruction and reduced state expenses. They charged that Populist members of Congress had introduced bills that would have cost the nation billions of dollars, including new pensions for Union soldiers. As for the People's party goal of government ownership of the railroads,

Democratic campaigners asked if the country was really ready for another half million members of the corrupt civil service. Government ownership of rail lines was simply an "un-American scheme." Defending Grover Cleveland's record, sixth district Democrats claimed that although some tariff duties had risen, the duties on everyday necessities had gone down. The tariff on flannel shirts, denim cloth, twine, lumber, and cotton bagging had all decreased under the Democratic administration, they said. Finally, Denny's supporters asked where Scott Hathorn had got his campaign funds "in these hard times." Had the money not come from the national Republican party? Hathorn firmly denied receiving any money from Republicans.[15]

Denny, meanwhile, came under attack for more personal shortcomings. The Democratic newspapers reporting his speeches euphemistically described his "conversational tone." Populist papers provided the translation: Denny's speaking style was "a monotone," which would be no asset in the U.S. Congress. Another Democratic newspaper reported the current rumors that Denny "goes on a spree now and then," but added that even if true, voters would prefer Denny to Hathorn. Prohibition advocate Benjamin T. Hobbs described Denny as "a common drunkard." For his part, Hathorn said he did not want to be elected because of someone else's demerits, but his supporters kept up the accusations. Denny did miss a number of speaking engagements. At Columbia he failed to speak at the great Democratic barbecue; Populists chortled that Denny had had such a bad "cold" that he had to be put to bed with his boots on. Without mentioning drinking, Hathorn attacked his opponent's record in the constitutional convention, where Denny had missed twenty-seven of seventy-eight votes. Denny weakly explained that he had not felt well some days, and that on other days he had had to go home for chancery court sessions, since he was chancery clerk. Many south Mississippi farmers were heard to say they would vote for Hathorn because he was a Christian gentleman, while Denny was "a drinking man."[16]

In the districts to the north, many of the same issues were raised. In the fifth district rematch between Congressman John Sharp Williams and Populist W. P. Ratliff, allegations of drunkenness also played a role. Ratliff vowed to fight for prohibition, while rumors were widespread that Williams appeared drunk at a couple of his speaking engagements. Democratic journalists rushed to Williams's defense: "Mr. Williams has touched no wine or intoxicants for many months, as his appearance will plainly show." Ratliff also championed free silver and declared that he had left the Demo-

cratic party in 1892 because he could not stomach the gold standard policies of Grover Cleveland. But many Democratic newspapers in the district, including the influential *Kosciusko Star*, maintained that "the country now has the best president it has had for fifty years."[17]

In the fourth district, caravans of farmers arrived at their district convention and heard a two-hour, scathing denunciation of the Democratic party by Frank Burkitt. Burkitt declined to be considered for the congressional nomination, and the party instead tapped J. H. Jamison, president of the state Farmers' Alliance. The convention passed a resolution condemning Grover Cleveland's intervention in the Pullman strike, calling it an "invasion" of the state of Illinois by U.S. troops against the wishes of the state's governor. After the convention closed, Jamison embarked on an ambitious speaking tour, accompanied by the Jones Family Coronet Band, "the most remarkable aggregation of musical talent in the state."[18]

Supporting Jamison, the Pontotoc *People's Banner* unleashed a vigorous attack on the nation's two old parties. "The Demo-Republicans," charged editor N. W. Bradford, have "put the producing masses of our people on the road to financial ruin." The president had promised that the return to the gold standard would end the depression, but it had not. The president had promised better times after passage of the new tariff bill, but still the economy languished. The *Banner*'s most potent argument, if a demagogic one, was that "The man who votes the Democratic or Republican ticket this fall votes for four cent cotton . . . next fall."[19]

Despite Democratic divisions, despite the discontent borne of the depression, despite Cleveland's unpopularity, the Populists lost all seven of the congressional races. Still, the party did register gains in strength. In the fifth district Ratliff carried one county, Attala; he had not carried any in 1892. In the sixth district, too, Populists improved their record as Scott Hathorn carried Amite and Marion counties and came very close to winning several others. In the seventh district in southwest Mississippi, Populist state legislator A. M. Newman, a physician, came within three votes of carrying Franklin County in his bid for Congress. Fourth district Populists carried four counties, as they had in 1892. The People's party increased its percentage over 1892 in every district except the second. Taking all the congressional districts together, the Populists had won 25 percent of the vote in 1892; this figure rose to 31 percent in 1894. In Scott Hathorn's district, agrarian discontent led to a doubling of the party's vote over that of 1892. In Jamison's fourth district, the Populist percentage now stood at a respectable 42 percent. Populists were proud of their gains,

especially since voter turnout had dropped between 1892 and 1894. This is not uncommon in a midterm congressional election, but the Populists strongly believed that they tended to benefit from high voter turnout. The 1895 races for state and county offices would undoubtedly feature a much higher turnout than either 1892 or 1894.[20]

Nationwide, Democrats met with a defeat in congressional races of stunning proportions. Their loss of 113 seats in the House of Representatives was the greatest loss in congressional history. Meanwhile, in the United States Senate the Populists held the balance of power, since neither of the two major parties could claim a majority. Alabama elected a People's party congressman, while in North Carolina the Populists took control of the state senate and cooperated with the Republicans in organizing the state house of representatives. "Honest Democrat," proclaimed the *People's Banner*, "the cyclone has struck you! . . . Come and sit by the warm and cozy fire-side of the Populist; we have a place prepared for you." Dimensions of the Democratic party's defeat were so great that the *Banner* declared that as a national party, "It no longer exists," and in fact, "The thing can't die any deader."[21]

The Populist party was not the only opposition party in the state of Mississippi. The Prohibition party made its appearance in the state, as in most others, in the late nineteenth century. Prohibition was an important and emotional issue in Mississippi. As we have seen, it was an issue that could lead to a Republican victory in a white county; this happened in Attala County in 1885, when Republicans led by Henry Clay Niles won on a prohibition platform. Populist W. P. Ratliff, too, won many votes by favoring prohibition and, like many others, he attacked the Democratic party by calling it "the whiskey party." Beginning in 1881, state prohibition conventions had been held annually in Jackson, but they invariably had proclaimed their nonpartisan nature. The 1884 convention had assured Mississippians that "the cause of prohibition should not be entangled with party politics." In 1888, however, the convention split, and the "third party prohibitionists" fielded an elector slate pledged to Prohibition party presidential candidate Clinton B. Fisk. With many of the state's temperance leaders refusing to support the presidential slate, Fisk won only 240 votes in Mississippi.[22]

By 1890 the party was again involved in politics, this time supporting the calling of a constitutional convention. The prohibitionists were particularly interested in black disfranchisement. Prohibition party leader

Rev. J. B. Gambrell believed the liquor interests used the votes of "low vicious negroes" in local referenda on the prohibition question. One vocal prohibition leader advocating the call of a constitutional convention was Rev. Benjamin T. Hobbs of Lincoln County. Since 1882 he had used his newspaper, the *Brookhaven Leader*, to advance the cause of temperance and prohibition. In 1892 Hobbs took heart when the People's party state convention declared itself in full sympathy with the prohibition cause. The Reverend Gambrell noted in a letter to a fellow crusader that "It looks now that we will completely fuse with the farmers, & if we do we can carry this state from Gov. down, next election." But he added, "Of course, Prohis will vote the Prohi national ticket." Indeed, Gambrell and his colleagues soon brought out a full slate of elector candidates pledged to Prohibition party candidate John Bidwell. "Prospects for prohibition in Mississippi were never so bright, with a party behind it," said a pleased J. B. Gambrell.[23]

The highlight of this 1892 Prohibition party campaign in the state came in September, when vice-presidential candidate J. B. Cravill visited Jackson as well as the manufacturing town of Wesson in Copiah County. The party also used its limited funds to hire Robert J. Alcorn to canvass the state. Alcorn, a former Republican and cousin of the ex-governor, was a good speaker. But the Democratic editors made sure their readers heard about his earlier reputation as a drinker. Announcing Alcorn's speaking tour, the *Grenada Sentinel* observed snidely, "Judge Alcorn has sounded all the shoals and depths of whiskey and ought to be a good witness against John Barleycorn." Meanwhile the Reverend Gambrell toured south Mississippi too and told his listeners that he didn't see how any Christian could vote the Democratic ticket. Only the Prohibition candidate would be certain to support wholeheartedly the cause of temperance.[24]

Of course, John Bidwell did not do well in his bid for the presidency. Nationally, he won about a quarter of a million votes. In Mississippi, he won about 2 percent of the ballots cast—nearly one thousand votes. Bidwell actually ran ahead of Republican candidate Benjamin Harrison in thirty of the state's counties. State party chairman Henry Ware was angry at the scrambling of the names of non-Democratic electors on the printed ballot but he observed that, "given the handicaps," Bidwell's performance in the state was "by no means discouraging." But hard times for the party quickly followed. Its state organ, Hobbs's *Brookhaven Leader*, was in financial trouble, and had to suspend publication until a wealthy party member provided a fresh infusion of funds. Meanwhile, a plan to hire a party

organizer who would "get away from the railroads and go down among the rank and file of the common people" had to be abandoned.[25]

By the summer of 1894 the *Brookhaven Leader* was back on its feet, and the party treasury had a little money in it. Meeting in Jackson, the Prohibition party convention nominated congressional candidates in five districts. In the first district, Populists had already nominated an ardent prohibitionist, John A. Brown. Accordingly, the Prohibition party simply endorsed Brown, as well as Populist W. P. Ratliff, running in the fifth district. The campaign seemed to go well, although in late October the Prohibition party nominee in the sixth district, George Hartfield, announced his withdrawal from the race. The editor of the *Lawrence County Press* chuckled that "this action . . . was altogether unnecessary, as nobody knew he was running."[26]

In the third (Delta) district, the Prohibition candidate Thomas Mount benefited from the fact that the Republicans nominated no candidate, while the Populists failed to get their nominee on the ballot, except in Bolivar County. Prior to the election Mount published an attack on his incumbent opponent, Thomas C. Catchings. Mount said Catchings was shamelessly exaggerating his role in securing appropriations for levees; actually, railroad lobbyists had secured them. He further charged that in the house Rules Committee, Catchings had blocked an important piece of antiliquor legislation from coming to a vote. Mount also accused Catchings of being "obstinate in his adherence to the single gold standard."[27]

In his published reply, Catchings admitted that throughout the campaign "I have studiously avoided any reference whatever to [Mount] or his candidacy," but now he was forced to respond. Catchings denied being opposed to any role for silver in the money supply but charged that radical silver men like Mount would wreck the economy. He accused Mount of inaccuracy regarding the antiliquor bill. Finally, if Mount believed that the government cheerfully spent money on levees, without the prodding of congressmen, "he is entirely too innocent and fresh to be allowed to go to Washington, but should be kept at home where his friends can look after him."[28]

Even optimists could find little cause for cheer in the results of the Prohibition party races for Congress in 1894. Two of the four straight-Prohibitionist candidates won less than fifty votes each. In the seventh district, Jackson grocer Thomas P. Barr won 173 votes, mostly in Hinds and Lincoln counties. In the Delta district, Thomas Mount did win a higher percentage of the vote than any other Prohibition party congres-

sional candidate in the nation (and there were scores of them). Nation-wide, twelve other Prohibition party candidates won better than 5 percent of the vote in their races but none reached Mount's level of 11 percent. On the other hand, in terms of actual numbers of votes, Thomas Mount received only 207. In the Delta, especially after the constitutional convention of 1890, voter turnout was very low, and even a small number of votes could mean a large percentage of the total.[29]

In January 1895 the Prohibition party convention announced its intention to field a ticket for state offices as well as county tickets wherever possible. The state ticket never materialized, but in Lincoln County the Prohibitionists did field a county slate. Several times the Lincoln County Prohibition party leaders, Hobbs foremost among them, urged the nomination of a fusion ticket with the Populists, but the Populists were not interested, pointing out that in 1892 and 1894 they had won more votes in Lincoln than their Prohibition opponents. For his part, Hobbs argued that most Lincoln Countians favored prohibition, and only the Prohibition party platform offered both control of the liquor traffic and a host of other reforms. As the Prohibition party candidate for state senator, Hobbs stressed the need for a state constitutional amendment outlawing the liquor traffic, and also the need for currency inflation. The party's county platform stressed these same two issues.[30]

The Prohibition party ticket in Lincoln County included Hobbs for the senate, a candidate for the state house of representatives, and candidates for three county offices. The party endorsed the Populist candidates for three county offices and Democrats for three other offices. It was a campaign like no other. Hobbs accused Democratic gubernatorial nominee Anselm J. McLaurin of going on drinking sprees in Jackson; he accused a Democratic legislative candidate of taking bribes over textbook selection. The Democrats responded by calling the Prohibitionists "visionary cranks," and said that prohibition was a moral and not political question. It was as ridiculous to found an antiliquor party, argued Democrat R. H. Thompson, as it would be to found an antilarceny party. But Hobbs responded that if the state government was licensing larceny and taxing it, then an antilarceny party *would* be in order.[31]

Toward the end, the newspaper rhetoric heated up. Hobbs told his readers that if Satan were a U.S. citizen, "he would be either a Democrat or a Republican, but never a Prohibitionist." To the Democratic editors who said that participants in the Democratic primary were honor-bound to vote Democratic in the general election, Hobbs responded that to stifle

The Reverend Benjamin T. Hobbs was a widely respected minister, temperance advocate, and newspaper publisher. His efforts to build up the Prohibition party in the state met little success, and as a candidate for county office Hobbs went down to ignominious defeat. (Photo courtesy of the Mississippi Department of Archives and History)

one's conscience and vote for a corrupt whiskey party was no honor at all. "When God gets into a man, that man will get out of the whiskey party," declared the Prohibitionist editor. In the last issue of the *Leader* before election day, Hobbs urged that before voters entered the polling place, they "offer a prayer to Almighty God that He will give us men to rule over us who are not in league with the soul-damning liquor traffic." Hobbs was sure that if the reader offered the prayer in good faith, "you will vote the Prohibition ticket as sure as God rules."[32]

Either Hobbs was mistaken, or few voters offered the prayer in good faith. The election results showed Hobbs himself winning 11 percent in his race for state senator, while the top Prohibitionist vote-getter for a county office won 18 percent. The Populists did a little better, winning about a quarter of the votes for county offices and electing a supervisor and a justice of the peace. The Prohibitionists began to tire of defeat. They did run one final presidential elector slate in 1896 and hosted presidential candidate Joshua Levering during the campaign, but the party won fewer votes than four years earlier. After 1896, the Prohibition party of

Mississippi stopped running candidates, never having elected anyone or carried a county. The party failed for a number of reasons. First, it was seen, erroneously, as a one-issue party, and one-issue parties rarely prosper. It was true that in certain states and cities the Prohibition party was able to wield some power by holding the balance between Democratic and Republican parties that were nearly equal in strength. In Mississippi, though, there were not two roughly equal parties. There was a Populist party in the state, but Populists and Prohibitionist were both rivals and partners. They cooperated when that seemed a useful avenue for both parties, but usually each jealously guarded its own prerogatives and its own identity.[33]

The chief reason the Mississippi Prohibition party failed is that the prohibition issue was co-opted by the Democrats. By the late 1890s, a majority of the state's Democrats favored prohibition of some kind; one of these was the rising young star James K. Vardaman. At the county level, prohibition was moving forward under Democratic leadership even as the Prohibitionists were running their candidates. Mississippi had forty dry counties in 1890; by 1894 this number had risen to sixty-one. In the early twentieth century legislators passed increasingly tough laws bringing statewide prohibition, and in January 1918 the Mississippi legislature was the first in the nation to ratify the Eighteenth Amendment enacting national prohibition. Were the Prohibition party leaders disappointed that Democrats took over their most important issue? Not at all. When Governor Vardaman announced in 1907 that he hoped to see every saloon in the state "closed by a general statute enacted by the Legislature," Hobbs and the other former party leaders were glad to give him their vocal, long-term support. The state's prohibitionists were able to win their chief goal through the agency of the Democratic party.[34]

The Populist and Prohibition parties did not have a monopoly on opposing Mississippi's Democrats. The state's Republican party was still alive, if not well. In 1890 the party ran congressional candidates in five of the seven districts; the two strongest candidates won about 3,500 votes each, or just under 30 percent of the reported votes cast. In the third (Delta) district, black politician James Hill worked to prevent fraud. In this last election before adoption of the secret ballot, Hill printed up books of Republican ballots with serial numbers marked on them. Party workers distributed the ballots on election day, noting the name of every voter who took a ballot and the serial number on the ballot. Voters then re-

turned to report that they had indeed deposited the ballot. Hill won just under 25 percent of the reported vote, but he contested the election before the U.S. House of Representatives. There was no doubt, the congressional committee soon ruled, that the district would go Republican in a fair election if each side was equally organized, but they believed Hill had not successfully turned out a majority of the votes on election day. While committee members believed the Democratic majorities had been padded, they told Hill he had not convinced them that he was elected. Two years later, George Washington Gayles ran for Congress in the district; Gayles was a black Republican who had served a number of terms in the state senate. In the wake of the new voter registration, however, the Republican candidate won only 159 votes.[35]

By the early nineties the Republican party was winning so few votes that Democratic papers began to charge that party members were only interested in winning appointive offices from Republican presidents—goodpaying jobs like postmaster and internal revenue collector. In fact, charged the Democratic press, the state's Republican party did not even want new members: this would only increase the competition for the lucrative government jobs. Still, Republican leaders *did* make some efforts to increase the party's vote-getting power. In 1895, Jackson Republicans organized a State Republican League, "to educate the colored voter and prevail on him to register." In an effort to regain some elective offices in the city of Jackson, respected Republican businessman George C. McKee pledged to use his considerable influence to bring a new railroad to Jackson, provided that an election be held for city offices in which "all the citizens of the city be allowed to vote." The Democrats called the proposal "monstrous," and refused to consider it.[36]

The best news for the state's Republicans came unexpectedly in the fall of 1895 when the town of Summit held a special election for mayor. Summit was a town of sixteen hundred people not far from the state's southern border with Louisiana. Republicans there brought out Frederick W. Collins to oppose the Democratic candidate for mayor. The *Summit Sentinel* admitted that the Republican Collins was a fine man, but was quick to add, "We do not want to hand Summit over to that party." Many local merchants, while not Republicans, favored Collins over the Democrat and argued that since the office really was more administrative than political, Collins should be elected. The *Sentinel* urged that there was nothing wrong with the lawyer who was running as a Democrat, and the editor added, "We would dislike to see Summit standing out to the public

gaze as the only town in the state of Mississippi with a Republican mayor." Collins was victorious, however, winning over 52 percent of the vote as he benefited from his strong support of prohibition. Yet Summit was far from a hotbed of anti-Democratic activity. One month later the Populist gubernatorial nominee won only sixteen votes in the town, while at about the same time a second special election, this one for a city council seat, featured two Democratic candidates and no Republicans.[37]

In the party's old stronghold of the Delta, Republican office-holding was eroding fast by the 1890s. While as late as 1891 Bolivar County, with its vast black majority, had a sizeable number of black Republican county and beat officers, by 1893 county politics were beginning to change. In that year in a special election for the state senate, Bolivar Democrats chose their candidate in an all-white primary. Knowing that Democrats controlled the counting of the ballots, Republicans did not even field a candidate in the general election. Under the new constitution fewer and fewer blacks voted, and white Democrats began to take all the offices. The earlier office-sharing arrangements became increasingly rare. In the 1895 election, for the first time since the advent of black voting, no blacks, and in fact no Republicans, were elected to the state legislature.[38]

As the People's party faced the gubernatorial, legislative, and county elections of 1895, there was some reason for optimism. Their 1894 performance had been substantially better than that of 1892. Further, the Democrats nationally had suffered a horrendous defeat in 1894, and Mississippi Democrats could no longer claim to be part of a growing national party that shaped legislation in Washington. Furthermore, although the economy seemed to be improving, a drought and an infestation of "cotton worms" meant that the 1895 crop was likely to be much smaller than usual—perhaps 40 percent smaller. Agrarian distress would undoubtedly help increase the Populist vote. The party could point to successful records of governing several counties, such as Webster, where the county books were in the black.[39]

On the other hand, the low cotton yields, which led to increased discontent and helped Populist candidates, were offset by a sharp rise in cotton prices. In one year's time, the price of a pound of cotton had risen 60 percent. Even with the smaller crop, farmers' income was likely to rise in 1895, for the first time in several years. To make matters even better for the farmers, and worse for the Populist party, Democratic boards of supervisors had just lowered taxes in nearly every county. Populists would

not have the opportunity to blame the Democrats for lower farm incomes and higher tax bills. Describing the outlook for the Populists in 1895, the Democratic editor of the *Liberty Southern Herald* predicted, "They can't survive with cotton at 9 cents."[40]

When the People's party delegates met in convention in Jackson in July, they strove to frame a platform that would attract the state's farmers. Delegates called for a reduction of at least 20 percent in the salaries of all state officers, and they criticized the Democratic administration's "weakness, extravagance, and prodigality." The platform called for fair and honest elections, development of industry, and prohibition of land ownership by aliens. The financial planks pledged the Populists to free and unlimited coinage of silver, abolition of the national banks, and a money supply of fifty dollars per capita, to be maintained by issuing silver money and greenbacks.[41]

The convention nominated Frank Burkitt for governor, and for once in his life Burkitt read his speech, so as not to miss any important issues. He praised the platform just adopted and stressed the need for an elective judiciary. Burkitt accused Democratic legislators of paying lip-service to economizing, but then giving in to "the army of appropriations hunters that infest this state, . . . [and] howl clamorously for more pap and more taxes." He asked Mississippians to work with him to secure adequate public school education for all children. If the state could not afford to improve its public schools, then funds would have to be taken from the colleges and the college students asked to pay higher tuition. The public schools were the colleges of the common man, Burkitt added. Burkitt set the tone of his campaign as he made his most dramatic point. Farmers supported the state government with their dollars, which they derived almost exclusively from cotton. If one looked at state expenditures in terms of cotton bales rather than dollars, Mississippi's Democratic legislators were now spending three to four times as much as did the Republican state government during the dark days of Reconstruction.[42]

While Burkitt's point was valid, Democrats were furious at the accusation. No sooner had the campaign begun than they oversimplified Burkitt's statement, charging that the Populist leader spoke "fondly" of Reconstruction and preferred the rule of carpetbag Republicans to that of native Democrats. The Populist nominee compounded his problems when he pointed out, correctly, that the recent defalcation of Democratic state treasurer William L. Hemingway was much larger (at $315,000) than any embezzlement of the Reconstruction era. Again Democrats charged that

Burkitt was defending Republican rule and longing for the days when carpetbaggers and black officeholders ruled the state. Burkitt eventually tried to back away from his allegations, but angry Democrats refused to let him.[43]

At their state convention, Democrats adopted a platform that was virtually indistinguishable from a Populist document. They also aimed to cut into Populist support by nominating a pro-silver candidate, Anselm J. McLaurin, for governor. Congressman Hernando D. Money would also play a large role in the coming canvass, since he hoped that the new legislature would elect him to the United States Senate. Money warned that the Populists must be defeated, since they taught "socialism and the destruction of individuality." Democrats accused the Mississippi Populists of being in league with the GOP, pointing out that white Republican leaders James R. Chalmers and William D. Frazee were quietly supporting Burkitt.[44]

As in 1892, so in this gubernatorial race Thomas P. Gore became one of the most influential People's party campaigners. Gore asked his Democratic listeners how they could support the party of stolen elections and a greatly diminished white, as well as black, electorate. Democratic campaign managers countered by sending an army of popular speakers into Gore's corner of north Mississippi. James K. Vardaman and Earl Brewer, both future governors, led the corps of speakers backing McLaurin. Brewer later recalled, "T. P. Gore was hard to wallop and it took a considerable army from the Democratic party to do it." As in 1892, if strong Democratic speakers were not available, local rowdies simply shouted down the Populist speakers.[45]

Burkitt and McLaurin made a number of joint appearances, including one in Jackson in early October. The People's party candidate led off, telling the audience he had left the Democratic party because it was controlled by "the money powers of the east." Since the East had no interest in free silver, it was up to the party of the South and West, the People's party, to win unlimited silver coinage. While Burkitt admitted that all seven Mississippi Democrats elected to Congress in 1892 had been pro-silver, he charged that by 1893 only three of them were still voting for silver, while the other four were "administration Democrats." He likened this to the problem found in a child's schoolbook: If a frog in a well jumps up two feet every day, and falls back three feet every night, how long would it take for the frog to get out of the well?[46]

By this time Burkitt was really angry, denouncing what he called the lies

of the Democratic party. Democrats claimed that they were for states' rights; well, what about Cleveland's invasion of Illinois in the Pullman strike, over the governor's objections? Democrats claimed that their tariff bill put many items on the free list. Burkitt admitted that this was true, then read a list of such items: rags, skeletons, hoofs, horns, and diamonds. Bibles, on the other hand, were taxed 25 percent. Finally, Burkitt jabbed at Mississippi's Democratic officeholders, saying that while indebted farmers suffered in the hard times, the officeholders were content, since their regular salaries would buy more under the prevailing depressed prices.[47]

When McLaurin got up to respond, he was quick to bring up Burkitt's supposed defense of the Ames administration, and he charged that Burkitt was incompetent in interpreting the statistics of state expenditures. McLaurin said he was as interested in silver coinage as was Burkitt, and progress was more likely to come through actions of the Democratic party than through the election of Populists. McLaurin closed by reading some old editorials from Burkitt's *Chickasaw Messenger*, in which the then-Democratic editor had praised Grover Cleveland.[48]

In races for the legislature and county offices, a variety of issues surfaced in each county. In the old Greenback party stronghold of Panola County, Populists had won few votes in the last two elections; now the Populist candidates for county offices vowed that as a gesture toward economical government they would, if elected, return one fifth of their salaries to the county treasury. The *Weekly Panolian* was probably close to the mark when it observed that the offer showed the People's party couldn't win in the county without "superhuman exertions." In Lauderdale County, Populists appealed not only to farmers, but to railroad workers in the city of Meridian. Populist candidate for the state senate John A. Bailey praised railway union leader Eugene Debs in his speeches, and damned Grover Cleveland for sending U.S. troops to the scene of the Pullman strike. Bailey promised a better day when Populists won elections and the U.S. government ran the railroads. Bailey's Democratic rivals, though, warned that Populism led to "socialism and anarchy" and accused Bailey of stirring up hatreds between management and labor. We should all be "one united, happy people," Bailey's opponent urged. In its last issue before the election, the *Meridian Daily Herald* urged citizens to "Vote to kill populism, socialism, communism, and anarchy."[49]

In many counties, the People's party campaigners followed the lead of physician Rufus K. Prewitt of Choctaw County. In joint appearances with Lafayette Robinson, his opponent for the legislature, Prewitt asked Robin-

son two questions. If elected, would Robinson vote to support a gold standard candidate for the U.S. Senate if the Democratic legislators chose such a candidate in caucus? Also, would Robinson vote for the Democratic presidential candidate in 1896 if the Democrats failed to adopt a pro-silver platform? Robinson surprised Prewitt by answering the first question negatively, but he was evasive on the second. Prewitt then accused his opponent of being a gold standard man who tried to fool the voters by "going around with a fresh, glittering coat of silver paint on him." In other counties the Democrats vowed unequivocally to support *any* duly nominated Democratic candidate, leading the Populists to accuse them of putting politics before principles.[50]

Webster County, governed by a Populist board of supervisors since the Democratic supervisors had defected to the new party in 1892, was the site of a hotly contested race in 1895. Young Populist speaker Thomas P. Gore was now joined by an even younger newspaper editor, Edgar H. Harris, in espousing the Populist cause. Twenty-year-old Harris founded the Eupora *Sun* to serve as an organ for Webster Populists. Harris did a good job of combing the state's Democratic papers for provocative quotations. He quoted the editor of the *State Line Graphic* as saying that while the *Graphic* was a pro-silver paper, it would support any Democratic nominee, "yea, even Mr. Cleveland who is prince of the gold bugs." Harris wondered aloud how any editor could be so willing to abandon his beliefs on such an important issue as the silver question. An important boost for the Webster County Populists came in July, when each party held a county primary. Although observers accused the Democrats of allowing blacks and other nonregistered voters to participate in their primary, the turnout in the Populist primary was substantially larger than in the Democratic. The low point in the Populist campaign came when the *Sun* ran out of money and Harris took a job as editor of a Democratic paper in Biloxi. After a hiatus of several weeks the county's Populists again began publishing their paper, but only after losing a great deal of momentum.[51]

In the southern half of the state, the most interesting race was in Marion County, where Populists tapped 1894 congressional candidate Scott Hathorn to run for the legislature. He had carried the county with 57 percent of the votes while running for Congress. Marion County Democrats were still angry that their party had unceremoniously dumped agrarian congressman Thomas R. Stockdale the previous year, and many of them vowed they would again support Hathorn instead of his Democratic opponent. At the county Democratic convention, a delegate stood and offered a

resolution denouncing as a lie the report that county Democrats were going to vote for Hathorn. Only two out of one hundred delegates present supported the resolution. Marion County Democrats exacerbated their already severe problems by failing to make any nominations. The county ballot, therefore, was a confusing mix of numerous Democrats, Independents, one Republican, and the Populist slate. Despite the rumors of Hathorn's involvement with a young woman, and despite the Columbia *Pearl River News*'s shrill statement to Democrats that they did not have the right "to stab [their] party in the back by voting for a populite," Hathorn's campaign went well. The campaign developed into a race between the townspeople of Columbia and the Populists of rural Marion County. There is some evidence that Hathorn's rural supporters practiced intimidation on their Democratic rivals.[52]

When the statewide returns came in, supporters of Mississippi's People's party were disappointed at the performance of gubernatorial candidate Frank Burkitt, who, according to the secretary of state's figures, won 28 percent of the vote and carried only one county (Choctaw). While Prewitt and Hathorn defeated their Democratic opponents in races for the legislature, none of the incumbent Populist lawmakers won reelection. The Populists did elect over one hundred individuals in 1895, in Amite, Attala, Carroll, Chickasaw, Choctaw, Franklin, Grenada, Jones, Kemper, Lauderdale, Lawrence, Lee, Lincoln, Marion, Montgomery, Neshoba, Panola, Pike, Pontotoc, Simpson, Tate, Tippah, Webster, and Winston counties. Unfortunately for the Populists, most of these victories were for beat offices and were not won at the countywide level. The party did win about half the county offices in Choctaw County, two in Franklin County, one each in Webster and Marion counties, and an unspecified number in Carroll County. Populists won control of the board of supervisors in Webster, Carroll, and (together with the Independents) Marion counties.[53]

The truth of the matter is that the elections of 1892, 1894, and 1895 all were disappointments for most Mississippi Populists. We can discern some of the reasons for the failures. As with the Republicans, Greenbackers, and Independents of the 1870s and 1880s, the People's party candidates had to contend with Democratic control of the election machinery. There clearly was fraud involved in all three of these elections, though it is difficult to say how much. In 1895, Chickasaw County Democrats foresaw a near-certain Populist victory in Burkitt's home county. But Populists who investigated the registration books just before the election found that the

N. C. "Scott" Hathorn, Mississippi's most successful Populist candidate. Hathorn was a farmer who was twice elected to the state house of representatives as a Populist. This is the only known picture of the Marion County legislator, taken from a composite portrait of the legislature. (Photo courtesy of the Mississippi Department of Archives and History)

names of seventy-two taxpayers had improperly been erased, allegedly for nonpayment of taxes. On the other hand, 101 Democrats had been retained on the books even though they had not paid taxes or had moved away. Another ninety-eight names were marked off the books by unknown persons for unknown reasons. To seal their victory, Democratic poll managers allegedly put marks on Populists' ballots, then later rejected the ballots for having marks. Frank Burkitt was sure the frauds were enough to have prevented a Populist victory in Chickasaw, and they probably were.[54]

Old tricks from the days of Reconstruction were resurrected. At a Populist neighborhood in Kemper County, an allegedly drunk man created a disturbance at the polls, shouting and grabbing up a handful of blank ballots. Although balloting resumed after order was restored, the county election commissioners threw out all the ballots from that precinct at the end of the day because of the disturbance. At a Populist precinct in Attala County a Democratic election manager took the ballot box away with him at dinner time, despite the strong protest of a number of voters. Although one defeated Attala County Populist contested the election on the basis of alleged ballot box stuffing, he could not prove the box had been stuffed. In Winston County, official returns showed Populist sheriff nominee T. W. Jackson losing by three votes. Populists felt certain that Democrats had falsified the returns. In Pontotoc County, which had gone Populist in the past, the certificates of election went to the Democratic candidates for

county offices. "How [Pontotoc] voted the outside world will probably never know," sighed the editor of the *People's Banner*. Yet contests before Democratic judges would be useless, he concluded.[55]

While Democrats only rarely charged that the Populists were interested in encouraging black voting, they still found effective ways to use the race issue. In dozens of counties Democrats urged that voters owed a debt to the Democratic party and must therefore continue to support it, since "it was the party that removed the black heel from white necks" in 1875. When Frank Burkitt condemned the new constitution for disfranchising "50,000 of the best citizens in the state," he was referring to poor whites. The Democratic press, however, repeatedly printed the quotation out of context, adding with a straight face that Burkitt was, of course, referring to the state's black voters.[56]

Like the Greenbackers, Republicans, and Independents, leaders of the Populist party in Mississippi had difficulty contending with the Democrats' overwhelming control of the state press. One Leake County Populist complained in a letter to a national newspaper that there were no People's party newspapers in Leake, "and the Democratic dishrags lie on us and slap us in the face." One of the common techniques of Democratic editors was to underreport Populist strength. The People's party campaign rallies across Choctaw County suffered from very low attendance, according to the Democratic *Plaindealer*; at one meeting only one Populist attended. While there is no way to verify the *Plaindealer's* assertion, it is clear that one month later Frank Burkitt carried the county. When James B. Weaver visited Tupelo in 1892, a correspondent of the Democratic *Tupelo Journal* wrote that Weaver was met by "three white men, four negroes, and a yellow dog," and heard "vociferous silence" as he stepped off the train. Yet Populist newspapers described Weaver meeting a crowd of two thousand eager listeners in Tupelo.[57]

Populists knew how important it was to have newspapers supporting their cause. After the 1894 congressional election, editor N. W. Bradford of the *People's Banner* noted that "Our greatest strength has been developed in the counties where we have reform papers." When Populists lost most countywide offices in Webster County in 1895, winning only the surveyor's post, they admitted that no fraud had caused their downfall. The problem was that many People's party supporters had not seen a Populist paper in twelve months and had succumbed to the arguments of the Democratic press.[58]

Some of the earliest papers to espouse Populism were established Dem-

ocratic papers that converted to the new party, including the *Chickasaw Messenger* (soon called the *People's Messenger*), and the *Alliance Vindicator*, published in Attala County. Some of these newspapers had a very large circulation, considering that they were published in farm towns. The Kosciusko *Alliance Vindicator* had a circulation of thirteen hundred, the largest circulation of any Attala County newspaper. Burkitt's *People's Messenger* had a circulation of twelve hundred, and Hobbs's *Brookhaven Leader*, which supported both Populists and Prohibitionists, had fifteen hundred subscribers. Other People's party newspapers had circulations more fitting with their status as rural, county newspapers. The *Phagocyte*, published in Choctaw County, printed 550 copies each week.[59]

Many of the state's Populist leaders felt strongly that there should be an official organ carrying the party's statewide news. Joe Marshall, of Webster County, complained that "We . . . know more about the condition and progress of our own party in Georgia, and the West, than we do in our own state." Marshall was instrumental in the founding of the *Mississippi Populist* in 1894. Speaking of the new publication, editor J. F. McDowell told the state's farmers that although the paper cost money, "You must have it, even if you have to take one less chew of tobacco each week." In its early weeks the paper sent out 2,400 samples of each issue, and party leaders urged the rank and file to build up the subscription list. Meanwhile the *Alliance Vindicator* diversified by bringing out a second title, the *Red Hot Populite*. Physically, the *Red Hot Populite* was a miniature newspaper. Its sole purpose was to win new converts; at fifteen cents per year it was within the reach of every Mississippi farmer. In some south Mississippi counties, Populists made up for the lack of a party newspaper by buying space for a weekly column in Democratic sheets. The editors of both the *McComb City Enterprise* and the *Liberty Southern Herald* accepted this arrangement, though both had to fend off charges that they were weak in their support of the Democrats.[60]

Across the state, Populists started some thirty-eight newspapers between 1892 and 1896. While Democrats clearly did a better job of getting their message out, the Populists did do a much better job than the earlier Greenbackers, who managed to found only about eighteen newspapers. With their thirty-eight newspapers, the Populists entered the fray and did battle with the Democratic press. One of the most common kinds of press fighting was label-pinning. This had worked very well for Democrats in past years, when they had made the label "Radical" synonymous with "Republican," and to a lesser extent, with "Greenbacker." But the Demo-

cratic press did not use the radical label with the Populists, since it would have seemed too farfetched for most voters; the Populists were not carpet-baggers, scalawags, or Negroes. Instead, Democrats generally referred to the Populists by names that gave them little dignity. They were the "Pops," the "Poppies," and "the one-third party." Populists did some label pinning too. The Populist newspapers asserted that the national Democratic and Republican parties were really identical in interests. They were, then, the "Demo-Republican party" and the "Demopublicrats."[61]

The press battles between Populists and Democrats make the political rhetoric of modern newspapers seem awfully tame by comparison. Repeatedly, editors of both parties used emotionally charged words like *slavery, shame, manhood, honor,* and *coward.* The *People's Banner* warned its readers that unless Populism prevailed, the people soon would be living under "tyrannical oppression, slavery, and poverty." In another issue the *Banner* editor urged farmers to "Think of your wives and children who helped you, on scant food, make the cotton that the gold bugs are fattening on, when you go to vote." The editor closed by telling farmers to vote Populist and "vindicate your manhood."[62]

Democratic newspaper editors often focused on the Lodge Election Bill (or Force Bill, as they called it). Only the Democratic party could protect voters from this federal interference in Mississippi's elections; if voters supported Populists or Republicans, they would bring the people of the state to "absolute vassalage" and the "supremacy of the negro." When Populists sought federal election supervisors, their aim was to "strangle the liberties of Mississippians." If a defeat of the Democrats led to passage of the Lodge Bill, Burkitt would be responsible for this attack on "the virtue of Southern manhood and the purity of Southern womanhood." The *Choctaw Plaindealer*, now back in the Democratic fold, warned its readers that if they voted Populist, the shame of it would follow them all their lives and would "roost upon [their] tombstone" when they were dead. The *Grenada Sentinel* warned that a vote for Weaver for president was really a vote for the Republican Harrison. A vote for Harrison was a vote for a return to bayonet rule in Mississippi. Voters of Grenada County must vote Democratic—unless "your liver is white, your blood pale, your manhood shrunk."[63]

In its first three years of existence, the Mississippi People's party proved itself to be, by most measures, weaker than the earlier Greenbackers, Republicans, and Independents. While the Populists did "win" twenty-

two legislative seats by the defection of Democrats to the new party, they won only two seats by actual election in 1895. The Greenbackers, by contrast, had won seventeen legislative seats in the 1879 election. Frank Burkitt's 28 percent of the vote won in his gubernatorial race pales beside the 40 percent won by Independent People's candidate Benjamin King fourteen years earlier. Populists won no congressional races in 1892 or 1894, while a Republican and a Greenback-Republican fusionist had each been elected to Congress in 1882. We have seen some of the problems that led to Populist defeats. Democratic control of the election machinery, Democratic control of a great majority of the state's newspapers, and Democrats' claim of white voters' support in return for the party's having ending Reconstruction rule helped insure that most Populist candidates were defeated. One more possible explanation for the failure of Populism during the first half of the 1890s is the reduced electorate that resulted from the constitution of 1890.

In his study of the motivations of the framers of southern disfranchising laws, J. Morgan Kousser found that partisanship was of central importance. That is, Democrats framed the disfranchising laws to prevent any resurgence of the Republican party and to keep any agrarian third parties in check. Kousser noted that Democratic leaders tended to favor the constitutional conventions or referenda, while Republicans and third party members opposed them. In the southern constitutional conventions themselves, Kousser found that a majority of Democrats favored disfranchisement, while non-Democratic delegates fought such measures. After passage of the new laws or constitutions, Professor Kousser argued, the position of the Democratic party was more secure, and Republicans, Populists, and Independents rarely were able to win any victories.[64]

Kousser's scenario for the typical southern state does not always correspond to what happened in Mississippi. While it is true that all five Republican legislators who voted on the calling of the constitutional convention voted no, it was not true that the Republican party continued to fight disfranchisement. The party was singularly inactive in the delegate elections, offering only one candidate outside the Delta. Of the three Republicans who served in the convention, all of whom were longtime party leaders, Isaiah T. Montgomery spoke in favor of the new laws, while James Lusk Alcorn and Horatio F. Simrall eagerly contributed their own ideas on how to reduce the influence of black citizens on the electoral process. All three Republicans voted in favor of one or more disfranchising proposals, and all voted for the constitution in its final form. Of the three

delegates who called themselves Democrats but had demonstrated their insurgency by running against and defeating Democratic nominees, all voted to pass the constitution. Of all the non-Democrats in the convention, only Greenbacker John E. Gore opposed the revised suffrage rules, voting against both the disfranchising section and the constitution itself. Yet Gore's party no longer existed, except in his own county. The most consistent opponents of the new suffrage provisions were a small bloc of Democratic delegates and a large group of Democratic newspapers.[65]

As for the effect of the constitution on partisan politics in the state, it is surprising to note that in at least one important sense, the new document actually aided the People's party. Thanks to the new constitution, one overwhelming problem experienced by the Populist parties of *other* southern states was not an obstacle for the Mississippi party. In other areas of the South, Democrats accused Populists of being Republicans in disguise and of seeking black votes. Indeed, in a number of states, including North Carolina and Alabama, Populists and Republicans *had* cooperated, and Populists had sought black support. By constantly linking the Populist party with black voting, Democrats across the South were able plant the idea in white voters' minds that in order to preserve white supremacy, voters must vote Democratic. In Mississippi, on the other hand, the new constitution meant that Democrats seldom made these accusations. In fact, if Democrats raised the bugaboo of black voting, they left themselves open to the question, "Well, then wasn't the Democrat-led constitutional convention of 1890 a failure?" The Cumberland *Mississippi Populist* took it a step further: Democrats could no longer preach the necessity of one-party rule in the state, since white men now dominated the state's politics.[66]

Indeed, of all the opposition movements in Mississippi in the late nineteenth century, the Populists received the strongest white support. While it was true that Independent People's candidate Benjamin King won more votes in 1881 than Burkitt did in 1895 (40 percent versus 28 percent), King's supporters included tens of thousands of black voters. Similarly, white Republican John McGill built a municipal machine that governed Jackson for many years; his success rested largely on black voters. The problem was that this large base of black support repeatedly led white community leaders to vow that the candidate in question should not be permitted to take office, whatever the votes showed. Many intelligent observers of Mississippi politics believed King was actually elected governor in 1881 but was counted out by election officials. Few could doubt that

John McGill's Republican municipal ticket would have won in 1888 if not for severe threats of violence.

By building a party of white dissidents in an overwhelmingly white electorate, the Populists could hope to attract a very large group of supporters, since their platform was very popular among agrarians, and since Mississippi was an overwhelmingly agricultural state. Careful estimates of voting behavior for 1881 and 1895 show that *among those white voters who voted*, Populist Frank Burkitt won considerably more support than did Independent Benjamin King:

Of whites who voted, 22 percent voted for King in 1881
Of whites who voted, 35 percent voted for Burkitt in 1895[67]

Still, this is a measure of those white voters who voted. If one looks at the entire adult white male population, there was little change between 1881 and 1895:16 percent of adult white males voted for King, while 19 percent voted for Burkitt. The great drawback of the new constitution, for the Populists, was that a much larger percentage of whites were now failing to register or vote. The percentage of adult white males not voting rose from 26 percent in 1881 to 45 percent in 1895. Since the poll tax was the chief disfranchiser in Mississippi, we can assume that those from the lower end of the economic ladder were the ones who failed to register. Certainly the Populist party's program of the subtreasury, inflation, the slashing of government expenses, and government control of railroads appealed to poorer farmers. Had the new constitution disfranchised no whites, it is likely the Populists would have won a great many elections, at various levels. Had the constitution disfranchised no one at all, or had the constitution never been drafted, it is likely that racial issues would have played a much larger role, violence and intimidation would have been widespread, and Democrats would have drawn the color line quite successfully.[68]

A few Republicans and a few Populists made feeble challenges to the constitution of 1890. After the 1894 election, W. P. Ratliff and two of his Populist colleagues contested the results before the U.S. House of Representatives. The three Populists did not even present evidence that Democrats had practiced fraud against them. For once an investigation of a Mississippi election did not bring out lurid detail of shootings, threats, and ballot box stuffing. The three contestants simply charged that the Mississippi constitution of 1890 was contrary to the provisions of the U.S. Constitution. But an uninterested House committee noted that while this

might be true, it did not mean that the three Populists had been elected. Several years later the U.S. Supreme Court ruled favorably on the validity of the suffrage provisions of Mississippi's constitution, after a challenge by black Republican lawyer Cornelius J. Jones in the case of *Williams* v. *Mississippi*.[69]

What was the future of the two-party system in Mississippi? From Jackson, the *Clarion-Ledger* editor in November, 1895 announced that "The Populist party in Mississippi is too dead to skin." In Webster County, on the other hand, the editor of the Eupora *Sun* came to the opposite conclusion. Given the Democratic party's horrendous defeats nationally in 1894 and 1895, he predicted that now the two-party system in the United States would be Republicans versus Populists. "The Democrats may keep up a local organization for a short time," he added, "but as a national organization Democracy has seen its day." Indeed, the state's Populists had every reason to be optimistic about the coming 1896 election. Democratic president Grover Cleveland was highly unpopular nationwide, and his failed policies would doom the Democrats to losing the White House in the coming election. Meanwhile, Republicans were sure to nominate a gold standard candidate. Since silver was the most popular issue in the nation, Populists reasoned, their candidate was sure to win, carrying along on his coattails many of the party's congressional candidates. Even in the wake of the defeats of 1895, Mississippi's Populists smiled as they thought about the next election.[70]

SIX

The Decline of All Opposition

Mississippians were feverish with excitement as the day of the 1896 presidential election approached. Both the Democratic and Populist parties had nominated William Jennings Bryan, who, according to the *Yazoo City Herald*, was "the greatest American statesman since the days of George Washington." Opposing Bryan was Senator William McKinley of Ohio, the Republican nominee. Democratic editors in Mississippi predicted that if McKinley were the victor, tariffs would be high, European nations would dominate the world's economy, monopolies would wield extraordinary power, "and American independence will be at an end." The *Gulf Coast Progress* worried that if McKinley won the White House, Republicans again would try to control southern elections, which would require Democratic resistance. Thus the election of McKinley would mean "the shedding of rivers of our best Southern blood." For the first time in a presidential campaign, voters sported celluloid buttons emblazoned with the candidates' photographs; replacing the earlier campaign jewelry made of tin or bronze, political buttons were soon seen on the silk lapels of Mississippi bankers and on the cotton shirt-fronts of the state's farmers.[1]

Finally the day of the election arrived. In the state's cities, voters turned out at fire houses and city halls; in the rural precincts they rode to country schoolhouses to cast their ballots. By evening, tens of thousands of Missis-

sippians were anxiously awaiting the early returns. In Jackson the returns were received, read, and posted at a number of locations, including the senate chamber, the federal building, the Stag Club, and a tavern in one of the black neighborhoods. The biggest crowd assembled on the third floor of the Clarion-Ledger Building, where citizens listened to returns until 4:00 a.m. Much to the crowd's dismay, the national returns showed great McKinley strength from the beginning. In Grenada, the crowds listening to the returns refused to believe them, suspecting the Republican party of manipulating the telegraph reports.[2]

At a small crossroads named Harrisville in Simpson County, several farmers were discussing what little news they had received—all of which was bad, from their standpoint. Like their fellow Mississippians in Grenada, they refused to believe that William Jennings Bryan was defeated. Finally they selected one of their number, T. N. Touchstone, to go in search of reliable information. Touchstone saddled his mule and rode twenty-seven miles to the state capital. After spending the night in Jackson, he visited the *Clarion-Ledger* office for the most up-to-date returns. But Touchstone and farmers like him were doomed to disappointment. McKinley was the clear choice of a majority of the nation's voters.[3]

Mississippi's Populists, in particular, found the 1896 election to be a nightmare from which they wished they could awaken. They had certainly felt high hopes earlier, as they had looked forward to the race. In Attala County, one Democrat complained late in 1895 that the Populists had become "walking question marks." For everyone they met, they had the same question: What will you do if the Democratic national convention chooses a gold supporter for president and writes a gold platform? This is exactly what the Populists expected would happen. For four years Grover Cleveland, a "sound money" Democrat, had occupied the White House; Populists had every expectation that another sound money Democrat would be nominated to succeed him, on yet another sound money platform. Since the Republicans undoubtedly would choose a gold candidate too, the Populists should have little trouble winning the presidency, since the inflationary policy of "free silver" was popular with voters both in Mississippi and in the country at large. The first Populist disaster of 1896 would come when the Democrats abandoned their gold standard president, forsook their sound money platform, and nominated young William Jennings Bryan, a champion of free silver, for the presidency.[4]

The state People's party convention met in Jackson in February, choos-

ing delegates to the national convention and writing a state platform. The platform stressed the need for a larger money supply based on silver as well as gold; it urged the abolition of national banks and argued that no U.S. bonds should be issued in peacetime. The document called once again for a free ballot and a fair count, accusing the state's Democrats of "intolerance and fraud in elections." The delegates tapped sixteen Populists to attend the national convention; among these were Frank Burkitt and the two People's party legislators, Rufus K. Prewitt and Scott Hathorn. As the date of the national convention approached the editor of the Pontotoc *People's Banner* noted that many Populists urged endorsement of the Democratic nominee Bryan, but he implored Populists to maintain their own identity, and make a "straight, unwavering fight."[5]

At the national convention in St. Louis, Mississippi's Populists were vocal leaders of the "middle-of-the-road" faction that opposed nominating the Democrat Bryan; at one point they helped organize a boisterous demonstration that blocked the aisles. Later, Frank Burkitt rose and begged the convention not to abandon southern Populists to the Democratic party. "I am not willing to be chained to a Democratic bandwagon," Burkitt declared. For most Populists, the choosing of a presidential nominee presented a painful dilemma. Endorse the Democratic nominee Bryan, and the Populist party could lose its own individual identity. Nominate someone other than Bryan, and silver votes would be split between two candidates, assuring the election of a sound money Republican.[6]

When it was clear that the convention's endorsement of Bryan was inevitable, the middle-of-the-roaders made an unusual parliamentary maneuver. They succeeded in getting the convention to select a vice-presidential nominee first. By choosing a vice-presidential nominee different from the man already chosen by the Democrats, the Populists could maintain some of their independent identity as a party. Besides, Bryan's Democratic running mate was Arthur Sewall, a banker from Maine whom Populists regarded as weak on silver. As the chair opened the floor for nominations for vice-president, Frank Burkitt's name was one of the first suggested. The convention finally settled upon Tom Watson of Georgia, while Burkitt placed third in the balloting. Watson accepted the vice-presidential nomination, he later explained, only after the Democrats promised that Sewall would step down in his favor. The convention nominated Bryan for president and then adjourned.[7]

Back in Mississippi, the Populists had to sort out their feelings. Although the *People's Banner* had opposed the nomination of Bryan, it now

| raged. The paper dying 'ticket. | | priviliges to nor It was he wl submitting the r |

Column 1

raged. The paper dying
'ticket.

aything on subscription
oxi. It will help us pay

at THE SUN is a paying
you take it, run a few
fortune?

who have not announ-
ou are not true Populists
'eated.

whose love for party
nough to cause him to
aonths on wind, when
ositions are being of-
k? Point him out.

the county last fall we
with Miss Edgeworth
l not make expenses and
ing by seeking bettter
formed a partnership
and he too became con-
as not a living in the
oned the sinking vessel,
iise, true to our princi-
party we have fought
iave won the battle with
and can leave Webster
ubt that we have per-
ll.

LATEST.

ntial Populists have the

Column 2

HON. FRANK BURKITT.

A Short Sketch of the Life and Service of the Populist Candidate for Gonernor of Mississippi.

Hon. Frank Burkitt, Populist nominee for Governor of Mississippi, was born in Lawrence county Tenn·, in 1843, conse- quently is now fifty two years of age. He received a practical education in the com- mon schools and accademies of his native state. The war coming on before he was 18 years of age, Mr. Burkitt enlisted in the Confederate army in June 1861, where he served as a private in the line until 1863, when he was promoted to the rank of Lieu- tenant. and at the close of the war in 1865 he held a Captain's commission.

The war ended the subject of this sketch engaged in school teaching and farming in Alabama and Mississippi until 1872, when

HON. FRANK BURKITT.

he became connected with the press of Mis- sissippi, and is to-day perhaps as well known as a newspaper writer as any man in the state.

Captain Burkitt has always evinced a

Column 3

priviliges to nor
It was he wl
submitting the r
ple for ratificati
being defeated,
the presence of
delegates and as
prives many poi
one of whom wi
and my mess n
faithful man co
believed to be j
and kept me fro
enemy at anothe
ment if you plei
fall palsied by i
signature to suc
Endowed witl
viction, taking t
the uplifting of
object in life, F
thousand battle
ple of this coun
them.

Such is the
Populists offer j
Mississippi. E
ticket nominate
guage of our sta
elected an "ad
by the strictest l
gality and devot
improvement on

Our

First. We der
safe, sound and
eral government
all debts, public
out the use of b
equitable and eff
direct to the peop
per cent. per an
forth in the sub-
er's Alliance, or

Frank Burkitt was Mississippi's most well-known Populist. At the 1896 People's party national convention, his name was placed in nomination for the vice-presidency. (From the *Eupora Sun*, September 7, 1895)

noted that the nomination provided the surest route to victory for the principles of Populism. Anyway, the only way to prevent election of the Republican's gold standard candidate was "united opposition." The national Populist chairman tried to soothe any dissatisfaction by pointing out that in fusing with the Democrats, southern Populists were assured of an honest election; the compact would mean that "ballot-box stuffing and 'counting out' won't go." Still, many Mississippi Populists suspected that any new honesty in the state's elections would last just long enough to get Bryan elected and no longer. A letter from "Populist," published in the *People's Banner*, pointed out that "the burnt child dreads the fire," yet once again reformers were cozying up to the Democrats, "believing the same old lies, and trusting the same liars."[8]

The situation worsened when Sewall refused to step down in Watson's favor, when Bryan continued to back Sewall, and when Bryan neglected to publicly accept the Populist nomination. Populist editor W. P. Ratliff, writing from Kosciusko, noted that it was bad enough the Democrats hadn't accepted Watson; now they were subjecting him to a barrage of attacks. If the Democrats were not going to acknowledge Populist help gratefully, "this writer prefers anything to licking the feet of Dems who have nothing to commend them but . . . a platform stolen from us." Another Populist editor believed that if the Democrats did not have the "courage" to acknowledge their People's party allies, then they would not have the courage to initiate their promised policies. In that case it might even be better to have McKinley as president, since McKinley at least was honest about his intentions. Democratic editors, on the other hand, urged the Populist rank and file to realize that the best way to win silver coinage and other reforms was to support Bryan wholeheartedly.[9]

Bryan's national campaign managers realized there was one great danger in their candidate running on both Bryan-Sewall and Bryan-Watson tickets. Take a hypothetical case, where Bryan-Sewall won 30 percent in a state, Bryan-Watson won 30 percent, and McKinley won 40 percent. In this case McKinley would win the state's electoral votes, even though 60 percent of the voters wanted Bryan. Accordingly, the national chair of the Democratic party urged that fusion elector slates be set up, where some of the electors on the slate were for Bryan-Sewall and some for Bryan-Watson. By election day, Bryan's managers had arranged fusion slates in twenty-eight of the forty-four states.[10]

Mississippi's Democrats were reluctant to sponsor a fusion slate. When the subject first came up at a meeting in September, the Democratic state

executive committee refused to allow any Populists onto their ticket, explaining that the Democratic electors had already been named, and that the committee did not have the power to remove electors from the ticket. The Democrats' explanation was not convincing. At this same meeting, two electors resigned from the ticket (one was too busy, and one was ill). Certainly these two electors could have been replaced with Populists, and the committee could have asked other Democratic electors to step down. A more likely explanation for Democrats' refusal to fuse was that they knew it was not necessary. In Mississippi, the Bryan-Sewall slate could be assured of victory.[11]

The national Democratic chair continued to press the Mississippians, and finally the state executive committee invited the Populist executive committee to meet with them in October. The state's Democratic journalists had a field day when only one Populist showed up at the meeting. The general conclusion was that the Populists must not have wanted fusion very badly. The Democratic executive committee ruled that, in the absence of the Populist committee, a fusion slate was impossible. Only a few Democratic newspapers bothered to print the Populist side of the story as explained by state People's party chair Rufus K. Prewitt. Prewitt was livid because the Democrats had invited the Populists to come to Jackson on October 23, while they had actually met on October 19. Since the Populist and Democratic press give differing accounts, it is not really clear what happened in this disagreement. It is possible the Democrats changed the date hoping the keep the Populists from attending; it is possible there was a genuine misunderstanding; it is possible the Populists haughtily refused to notice a last-minute change of dates by the Democrats.[12]

What is important about the flap over the electoral slate is that it made Mississippi's Populists even less enthusiastic about this presidential election than they had been before. Nearly all Mississippi Democrats rejoiced that fusion had not occurred. As the *Greenwood Enterprise* put it, the very idea of voting for electors pledged to the radical agrarian Tom Watson "is nauseating to say the least of it." The state's Populist leaders had to push hard to convince the rank and file to support Bryan. Former Populist congressional candidate Nat Jackson urged his fellow partisans not to "sulk in your tents"; after all, Bryan did represent the reforms the Populists had so long sought.[13]

Not all Populists were conciliatory, however. Frank Burkitt's *People's Messenger* proclaimed the newspaper's new motto: "No Watson, no Bryan." Another People's party editor advised a friend to take his ballot on elec-

tion day, mark an X by the Populist congressional nominee's name, "and let her go. The jig's up, anyway." The Leake County Populist executive committee passed a resolution informing Bryan that "We cannot support a man for president who would not accept the nomination when tendered." It may not have been the Leake County resolution that made him act, but about a month before the election Bryan did officially accept the Populist nomination for president, although he persisted in sticking by Sewall. Burkitt continued to use the *Messenger* to urge the state's Populists to abstain from the presidential race and to vote for the Populist congressional candidates only. To those who worried that Bryan might fail to carry the state if the Populists abstained, Burkitt responded that this was unlikely; anyway, he said, the Democrats would undoubtedly stuff the ballot boxes if needed to assure Bryan's victory.[14]

In addition to battling the Republicans and Populists in 1896, Democrats also faced dissension within. In August, the nation's disgruntled Democrats met in Indianapolis; Meridian insurance agent H. M. Street attended as the Mississippi delegate. These so-called National Democrats were angry that the party had abandoned President Grover Cleveland and forsaken the gold standard. The *Choctaw Plaindealer* called the convention "small potatoes . . . and few in the hill," but the meeting did nominate John M. Palmer for president and Simon Bolivar Buckner for vice-president. The Mississippi press pointed out that Palmer was a former Union general who had been a carpetbag governor in Kentucky; Buckner was only a recent convert to sound money. Surely there was little to worry about, nationally or in Mississippi, because loyalty to the party was a widespread trait of Democrats everywhere.[15]

Then the defections began. Harrison County legislator A. M. Dahlgreen was one of the first to endorse the Palmer-Buckner slate. Next came an endorsement from former state attorney general Thomas S. Ford of Marion County. Former speaker of the state house of representatives H. M. Street was the most visible leader of the new movement. In Warren County three prominent lawyers, two jewelers, and the president of the First National Bank endorsed the so-called National Democrats. A number of Democratic papers began to trumpet the cause of Palmer and Buckner; among these were the Poplarville *Free Press*, the Senatobia *North Mississippi Democrat*, the *Brookhaven Citizen*, and one of the state's largest and most respected papers, the *Vicksburg Evening Post*. The defections were frightening to state Democratic leaders, being reminiscent of the

wholesale defections to the new Greenback party in 1878, or the defection of twenty-two legislators to the Populists in 1894. One never knew how long the period of defections might last or how badly riddled it would leave the party ranks. For the rest of the campaign, the state's Democrat press paid scant attention to McKinley and to the Populists' Bryan-Watson movement. The most important goal for the Democratic campaign was to put down this uprising of the gold Democrats.[16]

The gold Democrat revolt was strongest in Mississippi's larger towns and cities; it was also stronger in the Delta and along the Gulf Coast than elsewhere. Soon "sound money clubs" were being organized in Biloxi and Brookhaven, in Port Gibson and Vicksburg; mainstream Democratic editors were aghast that formerly loyal Democrats were treading "that dangerous path that leads to the Republican camp." After all, McKinley was the chief candidate of the nation's gold standard supporters. The *Grenada Sentinel* warned that a vote for Palmer and Buckner was a vote against silver and therefore helped McKinley and all that he represented: "free niggerism, carpetbagism, force bills, trusts, monopolies, and plutocracies." The mainstream press developed a series of labels to pin on Street's followers, including "boltercrats" and "the McKinley aid society."[17]

Meanwhile, H. M. Street laid plans for a state sound money convention in Jackson. From Vicksburg, delegates boarded a special railroad car, provisioned with ham and cheese sandwiches and ice-cold beer, and set off for the convention. In the house chamber of the state capitol, Street called the convention to order, noting that really this group was not comprised of "bolters"; actually, since the state Democratic convention, "three-fourths of the party have left us," taking the organization and the name, and "leaving us the principles to uphold." The meeting adopted a platform that praised President Cleveland and the gold standard and denounced Bryan and the cause of silver. To those who accused them of disloyalty to their party, the platform explained that party loyalty was for "routine matters"; it was less important for "questions of fundamental truth or vital principle." To those who warned the Palmer men that they would not be allowed back into the Democracy, the platform asserted, "We remain in our father's house."[18]

After the convention, the *Vicksburg Post* explained why the Palmer Democrats had broken with the main branch of the party. The chief problem was that the Democrats had nominated a man who was really a Populist and they had adopted what was really a Populist platform. Mississippi's Palmerites would keep true Democratic principles alive until, on elec-

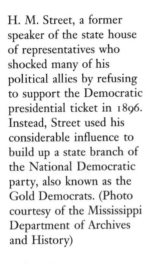

H. M. Street, a former speaker of the state house of representatives who shocked many of his political allies by refusing to support the Democratic presidential ticket in 1896. Instead, Street used his considerable influence to build up a state branch of the National Democratic party, also known as the Gold Democrats. (Photo courtesy of the Mississippi Department of Archives and History)

tion day, Bryanism would be killed as dead as "Greenbackism and Sub-treasuryism." To those who accused these sound money Democrats of betraying their party, the *Post* was sure it was the larger branch of the party that had been disloyal, abandoning all their principles to mollify "the cranky populists." Finally, the Vicksburg newspaper noted that northern investors would never come to Mississippi if there was only one party active there—the Democratic party controlled by wild-eyed Populists. If the state were to reject Bryanism, the *Post* promised, it would see thousands of new residents from the north arriving and millions of dollars of new investments.[19]

Mississippi's National Democrats played host to their two standard-bearers, as the candidates visited briefly Biloxi, Canton, and Jackson. At Jackson, Palmer appeared on the rear platform of his train; he noted that since it was Sunday he should not speak. Buckner appeared next, very well-dressed but clenching a corn cob pipe in his mouth. Buckner showed a knowledge of state issues, as he asked when Mississippi was going to

build a new capitol to replace the dilapidated one then in use. A man in the crowd answered that Jackson would get a new capitol at about the same time Buckner took the oath as vice-president. Buckner took this ribbing good naturedly. At Canton, however, his patience was tested, as a knot of men cheering for Bryan kept the two candidates from even being introduced. As attacks on the Palmer-Buckner movement intensified, its backers in Mississippi brought out one of the big guns: Thomas Jefferson. In a quotation of highly doubtful authenticity, the *Vicksburg Post* had Jefferson saying, "When your party is right, sustain the party. . . . When it is wrong, do your best to set it right, and if you fail in that, bolt your party and try to beat it."[20]

In meeting this party schism, a number of mainstream Democrats tried to conciliate and to avoid angry denunciation of the gold Democrats. A letter from a Democrat printed in the *Magnolia Gazette* admitted that the Palmerites were acting from "the courage of their convictions." The *Jackson News* announced that it had "no word of censure for the gentlemen who have dared to proclaim their fidelity to principle rather than party" and added that the citizens who attended the Street convention were "the peers of any in Mississippi." The *Clarion-Ledger* admired the courage of Palmer's followers but warned that they could help elect McKinley by denying Bryan needed votes. "This may not be their object," intoned the *Clarion-Ledger*, "but this will be the effect." Besides, while they might be fighting for a principle, it was the principle of Wall Street and the Bank of England, not the rights of the people. The *Eupora Progress* was one of several papers favoring sound money that remained loyal to the main branch of the Democratic party. "A bolter in Mississippi is a courageous oddity," wrote the *Progress* editor, but "such courage is not to be admired at this particular time."[21]

As if the race between Bryan-Sewall, Bryan-Watson, and Palmer-Buckner did not offer choices enough, Mississippi voters had the opportunity to consider several other elector slates. The state's Republican party continued to be badly split between a faction led by John R. Lynch and one headed by James Hill; each of the two factions offered a full slate of electors pledged to McKinley. The Prohibition party offered an elector slate too, and its presidential candidate Joshua Levering visited Jackson and addressed a large crowd in the house of representatives chamber. Levering told the voters that if they believed silver was the most important issue, they should vote for Bryan. If they believed sound money was the most important cause they should support McKinley. But if they believed

protecting homes and communities was most important, they should vote the Prohibition ticket. Levering warned that if either the Democrats or Republicans won, drunkards would continue to die and be buried in drunkards' graves, adding to a death toll higher than that of the Civil War.[22]

Along the Gulf Coast, a band of settlers from the northern states had recently taken up residence; most were Populists and believers in farmers' and workers' cooperatives. Led by Sumner W. Rose of Greensburg, Indiana, the group built homes, a store, and a print shop, and planned to farm, raise fruit, and engage in light manufacturing. Rose called his colony Coopolis, and in the mid-1890s he began publishing a newspaper there called the *Grander Age*. The paper was national in its circulation and Populist in politics. Rose was so disgusted at the Populist decision to nominate Bryan, however, that he endorsed instead the candidate of the Socialist Labor Party. Yet while Rose enthusiastically drummed up support for this candidate, carpenter Charles H. Matchett, there were no Matchett electors on the ballot in Mississippi. Still, the state's voters did have six choices: Bryan-Sewall, Bryan-Watson, gold Democrat, Prohibition, and two Republican slates.[23]

When the presidential returns began to filter in, there were many surprises. Most Mississippians believed a groundswell of popular support would sweep Bryan into the White House. While Bryan did receive more votes than any previous presidential candidate in history, McKinley did too, and won about half a million votes more than Bryan. Moreover, while Bryan carried more states than McKinley, McKinley trounced his opponent in the electoral college by winning the more populous states. Pundits had expected that the gold Democrats would win a sizeable chunk of Mississippi's vote. This did not happen; it turned out that Palmer's support in the state was deceptively shallow. Some respected Democrats and some important newspapers had defected, but the movement attracted urban commercial elites and few others. The *Vicksburg Evening Post* explained the small Palmer vote by saying that many gold Democrats had simply voted for McKinley, believing that he was more likely to win and continue the nation's sound money policies. Indeed, as the twentieth century dawned, what support white Mississippians gave the national Republican party was centered in the areas where the Palmer movement had been prominent: towns and cities in the Delta and on the Gulf Coast.[24]

A great many Populists heeded Frank Burkitt's counsel and abstained from the presidential race. In Burkitt's county of Chickasaw, where about

half the voters were Populists, only 13 percent of votes went to the Bryan-Watson ticket. Some of the Mississippi Populists apparently returned to the Democratic fold, seeing their own party in disarray and noting that both the platform and candidate of the Democrats were now acceptable. All told, the Bryan-Watson ticket won only 11 percent of the vote in Mississippi; the two McKinley slates taken together won 7 percent; Palmer won about 1.5 percent; and Prohibitionist Joshua Levering garnered only 390 votes, or 0.5 percent of the total. The state's Democrats were pleased that despite being opposed by five other elector slates, they had managed to win 80 percent of the presidential vote. Still, Bryan had lost, and the country faced four years under Republican rule.[25]

Given the confusion, mixed signals, and disappointments of their involvement in the 1896 presidential race, Mississippi's Populists hoped desperately for some good news from the congressional races that same year. The party had done tolerably well in the 1892 races, then had improved their performance in 1894, carrying seven counties. In the first (northeast) and fifth (east-central) district, the Populists hoped to win by championing prohibition. From Kosciusko, the Populist *Alliance Vindicator* denounced first district congressman "Private" John Allen as one of several "old drunk debauchees" that the Democrats continued to send to Congress. In the fifth district, Populist candidate W. H. Stinson spoke for temperance, while the Populist press reminded voters that Stinson's opponent, Congressman John Sharp Williams, "got drunk and sang songs" at the last state Democratic convention.[26]

The fourth district contained many Populist centers of strength including Chickasaw, Choctaw, Pontotoc, and Webster counties; here Frank Burkitt had won just under 40 percent of the congressional vote in 1892, while People's party candidate J. H. Jamison won 42 percent two years later. The Populist candidate this time was the respected physician and editor Rufus K. Prewitt, who was an incumbent state legislator. Prewitt took heart from the fact that the entrenched incumbent Hernando D. Money was not running; instead, Prewitt faced a newcomer named A. Fuller Fox. In their joint campaign appearances, Prewitt stressed the fact that the Populist party had been working for several years on a host of reforms that the Democrats were only beginning to support. He told how his bill allowing the state's citizens to use silver money to satisfy any contract had met determined Democratic opposition in the legislature. Fox, though, spent his entire time praising silver, promising that the Democrats would successfully inflate the money supply. He sounded very

much like a Populist candidate as he denounced President Cleveland, and given two candidates that seemed identical on the issues, many undecided farmers decided to vote Democratic rather than risk a vote on a party that had not yet won a congressional race in Mississippi.[27]

The race in the sixth (southern) district followed a similar pattern. Here the People's party candidate was the popular farmer Scott Hathorn, who like Prewitt was an incumbent state legislator. Yet once again the joint meetings between Hathorn and his Democratic opponent showed the voters two men who were almost perfect reflections of each other. Both denounced President Cleveland, both praised the free coinage of silver, and both heartily endorsed Bryan. Hathorn's opponent tried to maneuver him into criticizing Bryan for ignoring Watson, but Hathorn refused to say anything that might harm Bryan's candidacy. Again, voters who were not strong Populists saw little reason to go outside the dominant Democratic party when both candidates seemed the same and the Democrats were more likely to wield power locally and nationally.[28]

Voters in the second (north-central) district did have more of a choice than their neighbors to the south. Here four candidates tried for Congress and campaigned actively. The Democratic nominee was William V. Sullivan, but many Democrats argued that his nomination was invalid for technical reasons. These Democrats supported the Independent candidacy of W. D. Miller, who like Sullivan was an attorney. Republicans offered candidate W. A. Montgomery, also an attorney. The Populists rounded out this "quadrangular contest" by naming farmer Frank E. Ray to be their candidate. All across the second district, the four candidates met the voters in joint appearances. Typically, Independent Democrat Miller spent his time arguing that Sullivan's nomination had been irregular. Sullivan would then respond with his defenses, ending his presentation by praising free silver if there was time. Populist Frank E. Ray spoke with Bible in hand, reading scriptures to prove "the heinousness of the gold standard." Republican Montgomery closed out the meeting by using a chalkboard and proving to the voters that silver money would hurt the farmers. He warned that their contracts with creditors would undoubtedly call for payment in gold, while cotton buyers would seek to pay them in depreciated silver money. The Palmerite *North Mississippi Democrat* praised Montgomery's presentation but added that he ruined it by advocating a high tariff at the end.[29]

The third (Delta) district provided plenty of action for the citizens to watch and consider. Here incumbent congressman Thomas C. Catchings

was considered at some risk because he was well known as a sound money man. Although he was the regular Democratic nominee, he had the dubious distinction of being endorsed by the Palmerite *Vicksburg Evening Post.* Further, residents of a number of localities complained that while Catchings *had* won levee appropriations, the levees had not been built in their communities. At a campaign appearance in Coahoma County, Catchings said he would support free silver in the future because his constituents demanded it; "if evil came of it," he personally would not be responsible, but the people would. As for the levee appropriations, he explained, it was not a congressman's job to decide precisely where the levees would be built.[30]

Some citizens continued to voice dissatisfaction with Catchings, and at court week in Quitman County a new candidate tossed his hat in the ring. This was James R. Chalmers, former Democrat, Greenbacker, Independent, and Republican. Now, he explained, he was a free silver Republican candidate, supported mostly by free silver Democrats. He praised the Bryan and Sewall ticket but blasted Catchings's past support of the gold standard. The *Vicksburg Evening Post* noted that if Chalmers was going to call himself both a free silver Republican and a free silver Democrat, he might as well call himself a free silver Populist too, just to keep his hand in. From outside the district, the *Choctaw Plaindealer* said it was ludicrous that a Republican candidate should endorse free silver, and commented that "that kind of bird is seldom seen and is of very rare plumage." Of course, Chalmers's plumage was no rarer than that of Catchings, a Democrat who personally favored the gold standard in this year of a Democratic silver platform. But many Democratic editors felt Chalmers had disrupted the state's politics long enough; "His political neck should be placed on the block," and the people should "bring down the blade with a deep, sickening thud."[31]

The third district campaign soon deteriorated into a welter of lawsuits and administrative reviews as the candidates attacked each other. Governor Anselm McLaurin announced that he believed Chalmers should be denied a place on the ballot because he was not really a state resident. Although he owned property in north Mississippi, Chalmers was a practicing attorney in Memphis. McLaurin made the same point about John R. Lynch, who was running for presidential elector and claimed to be a resident of Adams County. McLaurin pointed out that Lynch was a federal official and actually lived in Washington, D.C. Both men labored to prove to each county election commission that they were residents and

should be placed on the ballot. Lynch won one breakthrough when he was admitted to practice law before the state supreme court; state residence was required for such practice. Several newspapers came to the aid of Chalmers and Lynch. The *Vicksburg Evening Post* said it was clear Lynch was a Mississippi resident; sojourn in Washington, D.C., was required of many politically active men, but this did not negate their state residence. The *Greenwood Enterprise* declared that Governor McLaurin's opinion was the "silliest" aspect of the 1896 campaign, and that he seemed to be inviting a congressional investigation.[32]

Meanwhile Chalmers retaliated against the Democrats by filing suit to get his Democratic opponent thrown off the ballot, alleging that Catchings's nomination was technically flawed. Specifically, Chalmers argued that the date of Catchings's nomination was outside the permissible range of dates set by statute. Since each county's ballot was prepared separately, Chalmers had to file suit in each county of the district. Democrats denounced Chalmers's "puny efforts" to "subvert the will of the people" by taking away Catchings's candidacy. Others laughed and said Chalmers was just after the two thousand dollar stipend given to candidates who file an election contest before the U.S. House of Representatives. Chalmers failed in his attempts to disqualify Catchings; he himself was denied a place on the ballot in the largest county of the district, Warren.[33]

Taken as a whole, the congressional races proved disastrous for the various opposition candidates. The total Populist congressional vote statewide was about 17 percent of the total, down from the 1892 and 1894 figures of 25 and 31 percent, respectively. The two strongest Populists, Prewitt and Hathorn, each received just over 25 percent. The non-Populist opposition proved even weaker. Independent Democrat W. D. Miller won 8 percent, free silver Republican Chalmers won 13 percent, and the top regular Republican vote-getter was Henry C. Griffin, who won 10 percent in the sixth district. Amazingly, the Democrats carried all but two counties in the state. Chalmers carried Quitman County, while Hathorn once again carried his home county of Marion. Despite the three- and four-way races, Democrats won with a majority (not a mere plurality) in all but Quitman, Marion, and Panola counties.[34]

Given the low Populist congressional vote, and the Populists' divisions, confusion, and defections over Bryan's candidacy, there seemed to be no cause for optimism about the future. Under the old constitution, races for the legislature and for county offices would have occurred in 1897, allowing the Populists to follow up their 1895 victories of some offices in

twenty-four counties. Surely the party could capitalize on dissatisfaction over high taxes during a persistent depression and win a good number of additional county offices. But under the constitution of 1890, county elections were held every four years instead of biennially, and so the Mississippi Populists followed the 1896 election by entering a period of relative inactivity.

The deaths of three Mississippi statesmen in late 1897 and early 1898 signaled the end of an era. The state's newspapers were filled with obituaries of Senator Edward Cary Walthall, Senator James Z. George, and former congressman James R. Chalmers. The obituaries of Chalmers were kind enough to omit the fact that he had abandoned the Democratic party; these notices simply described his role as a Confederate cavalry officer during the Civil War. Meanwhile, international events provided a new focus for U.S. politicians. The battleship *Maine* was sunk in Havana harbor during Cuba's fight for independence from Spain, and soon the United States declared war on Spain and began raising troops to send to Cuba. Former Populist legislator A. M. Newman raised a unit in south Mississippi and himself served as an officer. When the war resulted in Spain's cession of Puerto Rico, Guam, and the Philippines to the United States, Mississippi Democrats found a new issue. Arguing against U.S. imperialism, the *Clarion-Ledger* warned that the new territories would only cause problems for the nation, and besides, "We have . . . too many dark races already." Populists tended to ignore the imperialism question, and accused the Democrats of forgetting the silver issue.[35]

Several special elections in 1897 ended in disappointment for the People's party. While the Populists did win an election for justice of the peace in Franklin County with an impressive 94 percent of the vote, the officer who had resigned was a Populist too. The sheriff in Franklin County was Populist J. L. Calcote, who according to the grand jury was doing an excellent job of insuring law and order. In August 1897, however, Calcote resigned, giving as his reason the need to keep up with his own business affairs, which were in a rural area distant from the county seat. The night of Calcote's resignation Meadville filled with farmers and would-be politicians, who clustered in small knots, discussing who his successor should be. Two or three men made "fence corner speeches" while the farmers and townspeople looked on. The Populists finally nominated A. M. Newman in mass meeting, while Democrats settled on J. P. Jones. The *Franklin Advocate* declared that both candidates were fine men,

and that if Franklin County must have a non-Democratic sheriff then Newman would be a "fortunate choice."[36]

When the special election was held, Newman carried over half the precincts in the county, but the official returns showed him losing by twelve votes. Newman made it clear that he believed he had lost votes in beat three "in part to chicanery, in part to fraud, in part to whiskey and in part to lies"; in beat one the problems were "intimidation and fraud." Two weeks later Newman filed an official contest suit in the chancery court, focusing on four precincts where fraud, intimidation, and other irregularities had cost him the election. "I do not intend to sit quietly by," Newman declared, "and let the desire of the majority be trampled under foot." The jury did find that there were "irregularities" at the four precincts in question, but noted that Newman had not proved that the irregularities hurt his candidacy in particular. The Populist candidate appealed the decision, but without effect.[37]

A second special election was held in Chickasaw County, home of Frank Burkitt and reputed to be one of the stronger counties for the People's party. Although the Populists had lost the 1895 county elections, many observers attributed the loss to gross fraud on the part of the Democrats. In this 1897 race to fill a vacancy in the chancery clerk's office, the two candidates stressed the prohibition issue, with the Populist advocating county prohibition, while the Democrat was a "wet." Burkitt was disgusted that other issues were ignored, and in fact he himself did not favor prohibition. When the Populist lost, with 48 percent of the vote, Burkitt admitted the election had been an honest one. His friends reported that he was losing faith in the People's party and was considering turning his *Messenger* into an independent publication. Burkitt, though, denied he was ready to give up on the party, urging instead one great organizational push. The party did form a committee made up of the state's most prominent Populists and charged with sponsoring the new drive for party organization.[38]

Entering the 1898 congressional races, the People's party expected to benefit from an economic downturn. In 1895 the economy had improved dramatically just in time to dash the Populists' hopes; now, gloomy news for the farmers could help propel a protest vehicle like the People's party. Cotton prices in 1898 reached 4.75 cents per pound, more than 2 cents below the cost of production. Furthermore, in many counties the 1898 crop was 20 percent smaller than in previous years because of "boll worms, rain, shedding, and rust and rot." Democratic editors probably won few

votes for their party as they told the state's farmers that things weren't so bad. "It is astonishing how well a farmer can 'get along,'" urged one editor, "when he has made up his mind to buy only the absolute necessities of life." But the planned organizational drive for the People's party was seriously hampered by a new wave of yellow fever, which led to local quarantines prohibiting travel from county to county. In some cases the congressional candidates had to cancel dozens of appearances.[39]

Populists continued to suffer from an inadequate party press, and in 1898, more than in any previous year, the Democratic press began simply to ignore the opposition. Rather than attack the Republican and People's party candidates, Democratic editors said nothing at all. Perhaps they believed the opposition candidates were too weak to merit notice, yet given the amount of space dedicated to church suppers and children's parties, it is hard to believe that opposition candidates' rallies were not at all newsworthy. The district where the People's party was strongest was the fourth, the residence of influential party leaders including Burkitt, Prewitt, John E. Gore, and others. But in this district the *Pontotoc Sentinel* carried only two tiny "filler" articles covering the campaign in the five weeks before the election. The Populist newspapers provided some coverage, but these reached only a fraction of the district's voters. When the Democratic editors did notice the Populists, they often chose to cover events in North Carolina, where Populists and black Republicans were working together and a race war seemed to be brewing. While Mississippi's Populists had scant interest in black voting, the North Carolina situation waved red flags in the minds of many Magnolia State voters.[40]

The only congressional race that attracted much attention in 1898 was the race in the sixth district, where People's party legislator Scott Hathorn was making a third try for the halls of Congress. In late October Hathorn's Democratic opponent, the incumbent William F. Love, died, and eight Democrats announced their intention to run. From Columbia, the *Pearl River News* warned that unless the Democratic candidates agreed "to chip down to one man," it was almost certain Scott Hathorn would be the next congressman. A week later the number of Democrats had been reduced to five, and just before election day a Democratic conference settled on Frank A. McLain to be the standard-bearer. One other Democrat, M. M. Evans, refused to drop out, saying the Democratic conference had had no official party standing. Democratic leaders accused Evans of saying, in effect, "I will stay in the race [even] if it means the election of a populite." But the Democratic voters rallied behind McLain, and he won

54 percent of the vote over Evans, Hathorn, and Republican Henry C. Turley. Hathorn carried his home county of Marion with an impressive 66 percent of the vote over his three opponents; he tied another candidate for first place in Covington County. But in the district he won only 998 votes, while in his previous runs for Congress he had never won less than 2,000.[41]

In other districts the Populists also lost ground from previous elections. In the fourth district Raleigh Brewer won 23 percent, while the Populist candidate in the second district barely topped 5 percent. In several districts Republicans furnished the opposition, but in no county did a Republican candidate win even one hundred votes. The highest percentage won by a Republican was the 15 percent garnered by black lawyer Cornelius J. Jones, a former legislator running in the third (Delta) district. The *Clarion-Ledger* pointed out that the statewide turnout was very low; "It seems that everyone knew the inevitable result," and many simply stayed home. Not only Democratic voters who felt certain of the outcome but Republicans and Populists too were failing to vote. It now seemed clear that no opposition candidate could hope to win a state or district race in Mississippi.[42]

There remained, however, the possibility of victories at the county level. There were a number of counties where in the past a majority had voted for one Populist candidate or another. As the 1899 races approached, it seemed plausible that Populists could win legislative seats or county offices in Attala, Carroll, Chickasaw, Choctaw, Franklin, Marion, Pontotoc, and Webster Counties, and perhaps others. The Populists were also determined to run a slate of candidates for statewide offices to maintain their party organization, if not to win.

The 1899 state convention met in Jackson in August, with about sixty-five Populists attending; the delegates elected Frank Burkitt chair. The platform called for voter participation in legislation through the referendum; for regulation of trusts; for an economical state government coupled with lower taxes; and for an elective judiciary. The document also denounced Democrats' use of fraud in elections, as they attempted to force a "corrupt political ring" on the state. The convention selected Rufus K. Prewitt of Choctaw County to be the gubernatorial nominee. Prewitt was a former Confederate officer and former Greenbacker; he was a physician and druggist, former editor of the Ackerman *Phagocyte*, and one of the two Populist state legislators. He had been state chairman of the party since 1895 and had been the strongest People's party congressional candidate of

1896. Prewitt was popular with many voters because of a bill he had written in the legislature that would have allowed payment of all contracts in silver.[43]

Prewitt invited Democratic standard-bearer Andrew H. Longino to a series of joint campaign meetings; Longino, however, declined. The state's Democratic editors applauded their candidate's decision, accusing Prewitt of seeking to use Longino to attract an audience. A *Clarion-Ledger* journalist felt the Populists had too few followers to justify Longino spending money and energy following Prewitt "in his wild goose chase." Besides, if Longino entered a joint campaign it might lead some voters to believe the Populist party still had some vitality, when in fact it did not. From north Mississippi the *Sardis Reporter* was sure Prewitt had no more chance of election "than he has of going to heaven on a corn stalk horse." The *North Mississippi Democrat* agreed: Prewitt was simply on a "time killing tour." Longino was so certain of his election that he made only a handful of speeches after his nomination, all in the two Populist strongholds of Chickasaw and Pontotoc counties. Even there, he explained that the speeches were only for the purpose of preventing a light turnout in those counties; he did not need to win converts.[44]

The were two important issues before the state in 1899. One was the debate over building a new capitol; many legislators argued that the old one was about to fall in, while a number of agrarians argued that the million dollar expenditure was unnecessary. The Populist *People's Banner* did not believe the architects' reports of eminent disaster and argued that the legislators should simply hire a few masons and carpenters rather than build themselves a palatial new workplace. The People's party platform firmly opposed spending money on a new building, although unfortunately for the sake of consistency, candidate Prewitt had supported a new capitol in the last legislative session.[45]

The other key issue of the campaign was a proposed change to the state constitution, the Noel Amendment, which was on the 1899 ballot for the voters' ratification. The Noel Amendment called for an elective judiciary, which had long been a goal of the Populists and of the Greenbackers before them. But the Populist platform opposed the Noel Amendment because of certain provisions inserted by the amendment's author, legislator Edmund F. Noel. Noel called for nominations for judges to be made at the district level (as they had been before the Civil War); then, however, all of the district candidates would appear on the statewide ballot. Noel

explained that his plan was designed to prevent Republican judges in some of the black-majority districts; if the general election were held at the district level, Republicans might win in the Delta.[46]

To most Populists, however, this explanation was not convincing. After all, prosecuting attorneys were elected at the district level, and there were no Republican district attorneys. Nor were there any Republican members of the state senate or house, despite the majority of black citizens in many counties. Noel's plan seemed designed to ensure that no locally strong opposition party or Independent movement of any kind could ever win a judicial election in Mississippi. For that reason, People's party leaders opposed the plan. Once again, Prewitt had to admit that he had supported the Noel plan in the legislature. (Only sixteen lawmakers had voted against it.) He now announced that he had changed his mind and opposed the Noel plan, but his flipflop on the issue won him few new friends.[47]

At his many campaign stops, Prewitt would typically open by denouncing the trusts and saying that Democratic governments in states like New Jersey were allowing monopoly to run rampant. He denounced the state debt contracted under the Democrats, but unlike Frank Burkitt in 1895 he did not compare the Democratic expenditures with spending under the Republican Reconstruction governments. Instead, Prewitt compared the state debt in 1880 with the 1899 debt and found it had grown from less than one million dollars to three million. He spoke in favor of government ownership of railroads, pointing out that the world's most modern nations already had this system. When he addressed the race issue at all, Prewitt said simply that those blacks who paid their taxes should be permitted to vote. A forerunner of the political styles of Jimmy Carter and Jerry Brown, Prewitt stayed with his supporters in each town as he traveled rather than relying on hotels and restaurants.[48]

Meanwhile the Democratic press kept up an incessant stream of invitations to the Populists to come back to the Democratic party. The People's party was nearly without influence, argued the *Choctaw Plaindealer*. It had only two Mississippi legislators and no members of Congress except a handful of fusionists. How could such a weak party hope to fight the high tariff, the gold standard, and monopolies? Populists should come back to "the house of their fathers," the Democratic party. More darkly, the *Walthall Warden* in Webster County warned Populists that "There is nothing to be gained but everything to be lost to you by longer protesting" against Democratic rule. Yet even if the Democrats had begun to champi-

on many of the Populists' most important issues, the two parties' disagreements at the county level continued unabated.[49]

The issues debated in late-nineteenth-century county politics receive scant attention from historians yet often excited very strong feelings among the voters. Even something as seemingly noncontroversial as the yellow fever quarantines could lead to fierce debates. The hottest issue in Quitman County revolved around the quarantine. Were state and county health officers subject to "severe attacks of 'hysterics' " when rumors of the fever appeared? An editor writing in the *Quitman Quill* complained that unnecessary quarantines were often set up, "travel rendered impossible, [and] business paralyzed." In Chickasaw, as we have seen, the most divisive issue was county prohibition, with Populists advocating the policy and Democrats opposing it. In Choctaw County many citizens charged the Democrats with allowing the American Book Company—a publishing trust—to monopolize the sale of textbooks to area school children. The power of all monopolies must be curbed, these citizens argued.[50]

In Marion County the 1899 races were between "the bridge builders" (Democrats) and those who wanted to slash county expenditures (Populists and agrarian Independents). Pontotoc County Populists accused the Democrats of enriching themselves by working county convicts for their own profit. Whatever the issues in each county, Populist and Independent candidates began cropping up across Mississippi in the fall of 1899. From Webster County, one Democrat complained that the village of Mantee was full of washing machine salesmen and political candidates. It was difficult to tell the difference: "They all have bright faces and sweet smiles for everybody."[51]

Franklin County Populists hoped to sweep the offices in the 1899 elections. The county had long been a hotbed of agrarianism; home to a strong Farmers' Alliance, the county had also seen instances of "whitecappers" in the early 1890s. Whitecappers were white small farmers who banded together after merchants had foreclosed on their farms (or those of their neighbors); the merchants used black labor to work the farms. The whitecaps employed intimidation or violence to drive blacks from these and other farms. At about the same time whitecapping was dying out, the Populist party was rising in the county, providing a new and more respectable outlet for agrarian discontent. The People's party in Franklin was led by several substantial farmers and two of the county's

physicians. In 1895 the Populists had won two countywide offices and several at the beat level.[52]

A number of issues were dividing the county in 1899, and Populists hoped to use some of these to win control of Franklin County. One accusation, made in a letter to the *Franklin Advocate*, was that members of the Democratic board of supervisors were awarding county contracts for road and bridge work to their friends and relatives. While state law required the board to publicly solicit bids for projects estimated to cost more than fifty dollars, Populists accused the board of various forms of subterfuge, such as dividing one project into several smaller ones to keep the estimates below fifty dollars. Populist leaders denounced the Democratic leaders for giving special privileges to a closed clique instead of seeking to minimize county expenditures.[53]

Like Quitman County, Franklin County was also torn apart over the quarantine issue. While all agreed that the 1898 county quarantine had been justified, the Democratic board of supervisors made a number of enemies by paying some quarantine guards less than they had been promised and refusing to pay the guards at Meadville anything at all. While the board of supervisors had explanations, many politically active citizens believed they had been cheated, and threw their support to the Populists. In several other ways the Democrats hurt their own chances. In their primary election to choose the county nominees, Democrats had defrauded each other, and everyone agreed that liquor had been used to win votes. The Democratic editor of the *Franklin Advocate* said that he hadn't actually seen the whiskey, but that he had seen men at the polls who could not have marked an X on the side of a building. Meanwhile, the Democratic chancery clerk announced that robbers had stolen the county's funds after he forgot to shut the inner doors of the safe. Many voters suspected the clerk had lost the money through dishonesty or incompetence and had manufactured the story of the robbery.[54]

In November, the Franklin County voters turned the robbery victim out of office and put a Populist in his place. The voters also chose to send a Populist to the legislature. This was Thomas K. Magee, a thirty-five-year-old physician. The Populists elected three beat officers but were disappointed to see the Democrats again win all five seats on the board of supervisors.[55]

In Pontotoc County, Populists decided to sponsor a "Citizens' Ticket" and to seek some new faces as they filled out their candidate slate. The Citizens' platform called for honest elections, honest government, and

lower taxes. They also charged that the county was under the control of a town "ring," or political machine, and urged voters to end the ring's long-standing control. While a few men on the Citizens' slate were new to politics, most were Populists, and most of the ticket's rank-and-file supporters were long-time Populists too. One of the new faces was W. B. Pinson, who was running for the state senate. His letter of acceptance betrayed the Citizens' fears that Democrats would resort to fraud or intimidation. Most of Pinson's letter was devoted to urging Pontotoc residents to "go to the polls, exercise your franchise as true Americans, courteously, yet firmly and bravely."[56]

Among county issues, the Citizens protested exorbitant expenditures by the Democratic board of supervisors. Editor E. T. Winston of the *People's Banner* accused the board of arranging for the building of a schoolhouse worth $2,000, then charging the county $3,500. It is not clear whether Winston was accusing the board of dishonesty and graft or simply of extravagance. Several county Populists won a court injunction forbidding the board to sell bonds to finance the building, on the grounds that the bond proposal featured a rate of interest higher than that allowed by law. Winston and the other county Populists complained that the schoolhouse episode was just one example of the perils of "ring rule." The Citizens candidates promised to bring fresh ideas to the county's government; they would not form any new ring, because they pledged to serve only one term. The Citizens urged that national issues such as free silver be ignored during the campaign; the election was simply "the people against ring politics."[57]

When the voters spoke in Pontotoc in 1899, they spoke with an unmistakable voice. The Democrats won a clear victory for every countywide office except that of surveyor; for that office there was a tie, but the Democratic candidate won the tie-breaking drawing of straws. Further, the Populists and Independents had to admit that the election had been fair and the votes counted honestly. Yet the only Citizens' party victor was a justice of the peace candidate in beat two.[58]

E. T. Winston responded with a frank editorial in the pages of the *People's Banner*. He admitted that the thought had crossed his mind that perhaps the Populists should have run a straight People's party slate rather than experiment with attracting Democratic voters via the Citizens' label. But Winston knew it made little difference; "If it had not been a beat out, it would have been the same old steal out." Winston must have taken a deep breath before he penned the next words. "As to the future, we are

bound to confess that the Populist organization is 'done for.'" Winston believed the fatal moment had come three years earlier, with the "miserable sell-out in St. Louis" when Bryan was nominated. At any rate, the Mississippi Populists who had long labored to "infuse new life into the corpse" might as well invest their energies in more productive causes. The Populist editor closed by noting that the Populist party was worth about as much as a Confederate bond; it was now time to abandon this lost cause.[59]

The results of the 1899 gubernatorial race only strengthened Winston's assessment. Rufus K. Prewitt won just over 6,100 votes, less than one third of the votes won by the previous Populist gubernatorial nominee, Frank Burkitt. Prewitt's votes comprised only 13 percent of the total, and he did not carry a single county. The Populist standard-bearer did best in Choctaw County, where he won 44 percent of the vote, and in Franklin County, where he won 41 percent.[60]

In the county races, the Populists won about thirty offices across the state, mostly at the beat level. These Populist minor victories came in Carroll, Chickasaw, Choctaw, Franklin, Lauderdale, Lee, Marion, Panola, Pike, Pontotoc, Tippah, and Webster counties. Independent candidates won an additional ten or so beat offices. At the countywide level, Populists took control of the chancery clerk's office in Chickasaw County, the circuit clerk position in Choctaw and in Franklin counties, and won the race for cotton weigher in Choctaw. Also, as in 1895, two members of the new legislature were Populists. The People's party legislative victors this time were Thomas K. Magee of Franklin County and Scott Hathorn of Marion County. Several of the Populist winners in 1899 were incumbents who had served well, and voters in otherwise-Democratic counties declined to turn them out.[61]

A small band of the party faithful met in Jackson in August for the 1900 Populist convention. With less than twenty delegates in attendance, the Populists framed a platform reaffirming the previous platforms, and calling for government ownership of utilities. The Mississippi Populists accused the nation's Democrats of trying to bury the divisive silver issue, by stressing instead anti-imperialism. Silver was still the main issue, the People's party platform asserted, and when Democrats pretended it was not they were guilty of "the rankest deceit and treachery." The delegates affirmed the party's endorsement of Populist presidential candidate Wharton Barker, disdaining any possible support of William Jennings Bryan, who again was the Democrats' choice to do battle with President

William McKinley. The delegates passed the hat and raised about five dollars for expenses of the state campaign.[62]

In congressional races, Populists offered their candidacy only in two districts. In the fourth, Raleigh Brewer tried a second time to defeat Congressman A. Fuller Fox; also opposing Fox was long-time white Republican leader William D. Frazee. In the seventh (southwest) district, Populists named Hinds County farmer N. M. Hollingsworth to be their candidate. In three other districts the Republicans nominated candidates. Yet despite the efforts of Populists and Republicans to wage an active campaign, the Democratic press ignored them, and few Mississippians knew they were running. When the editors did give notice to the opposition candidates, it was not useful coverage. When Frazee spoke at the Choctaw County courthouse, the *Plaindealer* wrote that the speech "was entirely satisfactory to the few Republicans present"; no indication of contents of the speech was provided. In one of the rare notices of Raleigh Brewer's Populist candidacy, a Democratic newspaper charged that the only reason Brewer was running was that he wanted to delude Populist voters into thinking their party was still alive.[63]

Mississippians did show some interest in the 1900 presidential election, since the popular Bryan was running again; the *Clarion-Ledger* noted that many men were betting their hats on the results of the election. As an added bit of interest, several Democratic papers refused to endorse Bryan; these included the venerable *Vicksburg Herald*. Most Democratic newspapers denounced McKinley's imperialistic policies and complained that now Filipinos would be subject to American taxation without representation. Above all, the state's editors focused on getting out the vote. Mississippians should show the world that they still took some interest in elections, the editor of the *Clarion-Ledger* urged. Nevertheless, a small turnout was what Mississippi got. The total number of votes cast was 59,055, down by nearly 11,000 from the last presidential race. Mississippi's electorate was less than half its 1888 size.[64]

The results of the 1900 election made it clear that the Republicans had now surpassed the Populists as the state's chief opposition party. William McKinley won 10 percent of the vote in the state, while Wharton Barker's Populist ticket won less than 3 percent. The four Republican congressional candidates won about twice as many votes, taken together, as the two Populist nominees. Yet the congressional races furnished good news to neither the People's party nor the Republicans. Only Republican Henry C. Turley of Natchez topped one thousand votes, and in only nine coun-

ties did an opposition candidate win more than one hundred votes. Interestingly, several of the old Populist counties showed a new interest in voting Republican; apparently some of the old anti-Democratic feeling was now translating into Republican rather than Populist votes. In Webster and Pontotoc, formerly two of the strongest counties for the Populists, Republican Frazee won 14 and 19 percent respectively, and in fact these were his two strongest counties.[65]

The poor showings of Wharton Barker, Raleigh Brewer, and N. M. Hollingsworth in 1900 reinforced the clear message of 1899: that the People's party had no real future in the state. After 1900 the party never held another state convention and never sponsored another congressional candidate. A few diehards did put together an electoral slate pledged to Populist presidential nominee Tom Watson in 1904 and 1908, and in fact these slates won almost as many votes in Mississippi as had the Wharton Barker ticket of 1900. But 1,300 to 1,600 votes in a statewide race was an extremely disappointing showing for a party that had won eight times as many votes in the 1894 congressional races.[66]

At the county level, a few remnant Populists ran in 1903 using Independent labels. John E. Gore, the old Greenbacker and Populist from Webster County, won 38 percent of the vote in his bid for the legislature; Populist Thomas K. Magee of Franklin believed himself reelected to the legislature but was denied the certificate of election. He contested the seat before a legislative committee but lost the contest. It became clearer and clearer that, outside of the Democratic party, there was virtually no electoral politics in Mississippi. Nothing symbolized the new political era better than the convening of the new legislature in 1904. Meeting at last in the new capitol, the legislature for the first time had no non-Democrat members. For the next six decades, no one elected on a Republican or third-party ticket would sit in the legislature of the state of Mississippi.[67]

Mississippi, like several other Deep South states, was in the process of evolving a novel political system. A new saying began to be heard, that winning the Democratic nomination was "tantamount to election." A person who won the Democratic nomination was not, as might be expected, referred to as the Democratic nominee. Instead, such a person was called the "sheriff-elect," or the "legislator-elect." Candidates for Congress, after winning the Democratic nomination, usually spent the fall campaigning in the northern states, helping their colleagues who did have opposition. Under this new political system, Mississippi's secretary of state issued the roster of the new legislature in September—two months

before the general election was to take place. Typically the state's newspapers would print the chart, adding words of thanks to the secretary of state for providing the official roster of the legislature "which will be elected in November."[68]

General elections were still necessary, but in the vast majority of cases in the first half of the twentieth century, the voter's ballot would have only one name listed for each office. Predictably, this led to extremely low voter turnout in these November elections. Even as early as 1899, the *Natchez Democrat* marveled on election day that "A stranger would not have known an election was taking place in this city yesterday, so quietly did the day pass." In a county of thirty thousand residents, less than five hundred people voted in Adams County that day. Nor was the low turnout confined to black-majority counties. In Biloxi, a bustling coastal town with few black residents, an early twentieth century general election for two city council seats attracted only five voters. In some cases elections were held at only a few polling places in a given county. In the report of a congressional election in Quitman County, the *Quitman Quill* gave the election returns (fifty-nine voters turned out in the county), then noted without comment that "No election was held in Beats 3, 4, and 5."[69]

In Hinds County, a thoughtful editor writing in the *Terry Headlight* noted that "indifference" and low turnout was beginning to characterize not only the general elections but Democratic primaries as well. The editor contrasted the 1898 election (and its low voter participation) with the exciting 1878 race, in which Democrats had battled the Greenbackers. As long as voters remained uninterested in politics, Mississippi faced "an awful condition." This awful condition, according to the Hinds County journalist, was a political system in which candidates only wanted the spoils of office. When two parties were battling each other, issues were discussed; now, with Mississippi's emerging one-party system, politics was nothing more than "a scramble for pie." On the other hand, some editorials in Mississippi celebrated the monolithic rule of the Democrats. An editor in Meadville argued that Franklin County needed only one party; "our interests are one." He believed that inter-party battles only led to hard feelings and a lack of cooperation between the county's best citizens.[70]

Nothing showed the emerging one-party system better than the congressional races of 1902. Simply put, every Democrat won 100 percent of the vote in every district. The numbers in table 6.1 show graphically the decline in vote of the opposition candidates from the last congressional

TABLE 6.1

Percentage of Votes Won by Congressional Candidates, 1890–1902

Year	Opposition candidates	Democrats
1890	21.6	78.4
1892	25.7	74.3
1894	32.1	67.9
1896	24.5	73.5
1898	12.8	87.2
1900	7.1	92.9
1902	0.0	100.0

SOURCES: "Old Elections Returns Book," Mississippi Secretary of State Papers, Record Group 28, Department of Archives and History, Jackson; *Congressional Quarterly's Guide to U.S. Elections*, 2nd ed. (Washington, 1985), 815–49. Note that the total votes (for all the opposition candidates combined) ranged from 12,000 to 16,000 in the elections of 1890–1896, then fell sharply to about 3,500 in 1898 and 1900.

election before the new constitution took effect (held in 1890) to the end of all opposition (in the races of 1902). Note that the new constitution did not immediately crush the opposition; coincident with the new constitution was the rise of a new political party, the Populists. But as the 1890s wore on, the Populists and Republicans lost hope, and opposition within the Magnolia State dwindled to nothing.

As for the Republican party, while it did surpass the Populists by 1900, it was nevertheless a party that harbored little hope for future success in the state. The occasional Republican congressional candidates secured places on the ballot, but admitted to journalists that they were "leading a forlorn hope" and "willing to make the sacrifice" for love of party. Some of the Republican candidates seemed a bit out of touch with reality. Running for Congress in the seventh district in 1898, E. F. Brennan published a leaflet in which he told the voters, "I am vain enough to believe I can secure for the citizens of this district the honest claims against the government for destruction of their property in the late war between the states." If a Republican candidate began to show any strength, Democratic speakers would quickly attack the Grand Old Party for embodying hatred of "everything that has a white skin south of the Potomac."[71]

As if the Mississippi Republicans were not weak enough, they further divided their influence by engaging in constant factional struggles. For many years, the state party had two chief factions, one led by John R. Lynch, and the other by James Hill. Both wings had white as well as black members. In 1896 the Republicans held two state conventions, named two sets of delegates to the national convention, fielded two presidential elector slates, and nominated two congressional candidates in a number of districts. That year the national committee made it known that the Hill faction was the officially recognized one, but most of Lynch's followers refused to disown him.[72]

Three years later, in 1899, Jackson witnessed a "red hot" Republican mass meeting supported by the black Republican newspaper *The People's Defender*. The meeting was very well attended and denounced both Lynch and Hill for providing only "indifferent and lethargic leadership." The chief complaint was that the Republican president was appointing fewer and fewer blacks to federal jobs in Mississippi. What was interesting about the 1899 "red hot meeting" was the emphasis on federally appointed jobs with no mention whatever of elections. In fact, many Democrats believed the Mississippi Republicans were no longer very interested in participating in elections; they spent their time "busily engaged in discussing the pie question." The *Greenwood Enterprise* dismissed the congressional candidacy of black lawyer S. A. Beadles by saying that Beadles had absolutely no expectation of winning but that he would "stand a mighty good show at the pie counter, where Jim Hill will preside."[73]

Black Republicans would experience new difficulties, though, in winning the federal patronage plums. When President McKinley named a new black postmaster for a Claiborne County town, white citizens of the community informed the appointee that "his services were not needed." The would-be postmaster then declined his commission, saying politely that he did not want to be an "uninvited guest." The president even began giving some lucrative jobs to Democrats at the request of Mississippi's congressional delegation. After all, McKinley never knew when he might need some Democratic friends in Congress.[74]

Race was still a key issue for the Republican party. Hundreds of blacks were still voting in each of several Delta counties, and in some southern counties such as Covington and Marion. Black voters were fewer in number in other areas, but still could hold the balance of power in very close elections. This meant that in the late 1890s, some Democrats encouraged blacks to vote in Democratic primaries, much to the disgust of many other

white citizens. Democrats sought black votes in many general elections too, just as an added insurance of victory. The *Greenville Spirit* in 1898 encouraged Delta blacks to notice the "tall, useful levees," then vote in the general election for Congressman Catchings, who had helped secure the levee appropriation.[75]

When the city of Natchez in 1899 decided to choose its city officers in a whites-only Democratic primary, thus denying any real voice to the city's blacks, the Natchez *Evening Bulletin* objected. While the *Bulletin* did not favor mass voting by blacks, it did name a number of substantial black businessmen in the city who should not be shut out of the political process. Yet the *Bulletin's* arguments went unheeded. In Jackson, members of the city council divided the city into four wards, making sure that the vast majority of blacks were crowded into one ward, the fourth. During the late 1890s white Jacksonians had no objection to the fourth ward voters voting and choosing one black and one white councilman. Still, black councilman Smith Robertson was in a state of limbo—he considered himself a loyal Republican, but was elected to council in a Democratic primary, as were all his colleagues. The one town in Mississippi with a Republican mayor was Mound Bayou, an all-black town in the Delta. Yet while there was no doubt Mayor Isaiah T. Montgomery was a Republican, Mound Bayou was not home to two party politics; it had a one-party system of its own, lacking Democrats.[76]

During the 1890s, two-party politics was given a new breath of life in Mississippi, though a short-lived one. For the first time in many years, most counties featured an opposition ticket for the legislature and for county offices. Twenty-two Populists sat in the legislative session of 1894. Populists won at least some of the offices in two dozen counties, controlled the boards of supervisors in Amite, Carroll, Webster, and Marion counties, and ran the municipal governments in a number of small towns such as Cumberland, Houston, Troy, and Walthall. And yet the question is inescapable: Why did the Mississippi Populists not do better than they did? In neighboring Alabama, Populists several times carried one third to one half of the counties, while in Mississippi the People's party carried only seven counties in their best statewide race. In Alabama the Populists won two congressional seats in 1894, while in Mississippi that year no People's party candidate topped 42 percent.[77]

There were abundant reasons to expect that a protest party like the Populists could win some real power in Mississippi by offering change to a

state that had a number of serious problems. As Mississippi's small farmers left their antebellum subsistence traditions and entered more exclusively the commercial world of cash crop farming, they encountered a number of problems, including indebtedness, high transportation costs, and exorbitant interest rates charged by storekeepers. Declining soils and high taxation were two other recurring problems. Meanwhile, two well-publicized cases of embezzlement in the state government gave the Democratic party two black eyes. Yet a number of obstacles for the People's party proved insurmountable.[78]

First of all, there were large areas of the state where the party never won any support whatever. In the Delta, the whites were vastly outnumbered by the blacks; whites were governing through the Democratic party and wanted no new divisive politics. The politically powerful men in the Delta counties were generally well-to-do white planters and merchants and they had little sympathy with the Populists' championing of small farmers. They tended to be creditors and were not pleased at the Populists' promise to help the indebted by bringing inflationary silver coinage. When gubernatorial candidate Rufus K. Prewitt visited the Delta county of Leflore in 1899, political pundits remarked that it was "inconceivable" why a Populist would waste his time there. If Prewitt believed he would win a single vote in Leflore, they added, he was clearly guilty of a gross lack of discernment. Actually Prewitt proved his critics wrong. He won exactly one vote in Leflore (one of the state's larger counties) in 1899.[79]

Populists were also victims of the whims of cotton prices. Low cotton prices in 1894 led to agrarian discontent and the high water mark of Populist vote-getting in Mississippi. But in 1895 and 1899, just in time for the legislative and county elections, cotton prices advanced sharply, making Mississippi farmers less distressed by the status quo and less likely to vote Populist.[80]

One of the most serious problems confronting the state People's party was the Democrats' co-opting their issues. The Populists made a promising beginning in the 1892 presidential and congressional elections, as they advocated free silver, railroad regulation, an income tax on larger incomes, and the ending of the U.S. government's indebtedness. The Democrats for their part denounced the Populist platform as radical and the Populists themselves as cranks. But in 1894 and 1896 the Democrats moved to support precisely the same issues as the Populists, leading one Mississippi Populist to note wryly that the People's party should have copyrighted its platform. E. T. Winston of the *People's Banner* called the Democrats "po-

litical prostitutes" who were even willing to steal platforms to win elections. A Populist citizen in Union County did not understand how Democrats could support silver, an income tax, and prohibition of U.S. bonds in peacetime when they had called the Populists "traitors, agitators, and anarchists" for advocating these same principles four years earlier.[81]

Throughout its history, the Mississippi People's party suffered from an inadequate press. More than thirty-five of the state's newspapers supported the Populists, but never more than about eighteen were operating at any one time. The party lacked any sort of flagship newspaper; the Democrats had their *Clarion-Ledger*, which supplied news and editorials that were freely copied by the Democratic weeklies in the hinterlands. All the Populist newspapers fit the mold of a small-town weekly, typically with a circulation of about five hundred. The party's two largest newspapers were the *Alliance Vindicator*, published at Kosciusko, and Burkitt's *People's Messenger*, each of which sold about thirteen hundred copies weekly.[82]

Many of the Populist newspapers faced resistance within their communities; the *Messenger* was burned in the early 1890s as the agrarians were just beginning to turn to independent political action, while the *Neshoba Press* was destroyed by a fire "of incendiary origin" just after the 1895 election. All across the state, many newspapers of all kinds folded each year as the price of ink, paper, and type advanced steadily in the late 1890s. But the Populist papers had the added problem of merchants who declined to advertise in a People's party sheet. "It is a boycott, pure and simple," asserted the *People's Banner* editor as a lack of advertisers forced him to cut off delinquent subscribers. Farmers were often behind in paying for their subscription, typically catching up with the editor only once a year. So when editor Winston cut off his delinquents, he cut his circulation in half.[83]

The fact remained that the state's voters would get most of their news about the People's party from the Democratic press. Misrepresentations were a constant problem. According to the Democratic papers, the Populist rallies had very few people attending, and those who were present were mostly curious Democrats. During the 1895 election the Democratic papers circulated the false rumor that the Populist-dominated North Carolina legislature had adjourned to mourn the death of black Republican Frederick Douglass but had refused to honor the birthday of Robert E. Lee. In a very serious misrepresentation that same year the Democratic press claimed that Frank Burkitt had attacked the constitution of 1890 for

disfranchising thousands of blacks; actually, Burkitt had complained about white disfranchisement. Whenever the Democrats' newspapers misquoted or misrepresented the People's party, the Populists had a difficult time getting their version of the facts before the people.[84]

Of course, distorting facts in the partisan press is a typical act in any political campaign. More seriously, in a number of cases it seems clear the Populists were denied victories through ballot box stuffing and fraudulent counting. Among the most notorious cases were the Chickasaw County and Pontotoc County elections of 1895 and the 1897 special election in Franklin County. In all three instances, a fairer election almost certainly would have resulted in a Populist victory. But the Democrats controlled the election machinery, and it was difficult for Populists to insure fairness.[85]

It was possible to contest elections in the state courts, and the Populists tried this in the Chickasaw case and in the Franklin special election. In the Chickasaw case the Democrats delayed the suit as long as possible and made the costs mount up; in neither case did the Populists win. In the Franklin case, at least, it seemed clear that Democratic control of the judicial system helped insure a defeat for the People's party in court.[86]

The newly enacted constitution of 1890 provided a certain amount of aid to the People's party, but offered even larger obstacles. By creating a Mississippi electorate that was overwhelmingly white, the new constitution did help prevent any credible Democratic allegations that Populist victories would mean a return to extensive black voting. While the state's Democratic newspapers did occasionally report on black involvement in Populism in North Carolina and in Alabama, they could not seriously assert that such black involvement was present in Mississippi. If they had made such an assertion, they would have weakened their own claim that the Democratic party deserved credit for ending widespread black participation in the Magnolia State. Since the state's Populists did not have to worry about voters linking their party with a black political resurgence, they were able to make greater inroads with white residents than had the earlier Greenbackers, Republicans, or Independents.[87]

On the other hand, the poll tax did pose a very serious obstacle to Populist success. In the depths of a long agricultural depression, fewer and fewer residents were willing to pay the poll tax for two consecutive years as required by law for voters. There can be little doubt that it was those at the lower end of the economic ladder who fell away from political involvement. One reliable estimate says that in the 1895 race for the governor's

office, 45 percent of the white male citizens did not vote, forming a larger group of voters than voted for the Democratic victor. It is certainly plausible that if these white men who failed to pay the poll tax had voted, they would have elected Frank Burkitt governor, and elected a respectable number of Populist legislators.[88]

An additional piece of evidence backs up the notion that would-be Populist voters were more likely to fail to pay the poll tax than were would-be Democrats. Choctaw County was home to a strong Populist party, which won about half the county offices in 1895. The *Choctaw Plaindealer* in 1901 published a list of the county's poll tax delinquents. On this list are four of the county's 1895 Populist candidates; none of the 1895 Democratic candidates had become delinquent. If four of the Populist candidates had lost their right to vote, it undoubtedly was true that many Populist voters or would-be voters failed to pay the tax as well. The reason Mississippi Populists failed to match the performance of their colleagues across the state line in Alabama was that Alabama had not yet framed its disfranchising constitution. Alabama still had a large number of black voters in the mid-1890s, and Alabama Populists (unlike their counterparts in Mississippi) sought black support.[89]

Before assessing the importance of Populism in Mississippi, it is necessary to determine more clearly just who the state's Populists were.[90] The previous chapter featured a comparison of People's party and Democratic legislators in the 1894 session; this comparison showed that the Populist legislators were almost unanimously farmers, while less than half of the Democrats were. Thirty-five percent of the Democratic legislators were lawyers, while none of the Populists were.

Yet legislators tended to be an elite group of politicians in both parties; a fuller picture will emerge by looking also at candidates for county office. If we examine the 1895 candidates of both parties from Amite, Attala, Choctaw, Lauderdale, and Webster counties (all Populist centers of influence), we have a list of 101 names. Checking these names against the 1900 census yields information about nativity, age, home ownership, and occupation; data on occupation was also gleaned from newspapers. Table 6.2 gives a comparison between Democrats and Populists in the five-county sample.

Table 6.2 shows that the Populists were more likely than their opponents to be farmers and had three times as many individuals in the "other professional" category (school teachers and doctors). The Populists also had a small core of craftsmen and railroad workers, while the Democrats

TABLE 6.2
Characteristics of Candidates for County Offices, 1895
Amite, Attala, Choctaw, Lauderdale, and Webster Counties

	Populists	*Democrats*
Occupation		
Farmers	61%	51%
Lawyers	2	13
Other professionals	16	5
Merchants, salesmen, clerks	9	15
Craftsmen, railroad employees	7	0
County officers	5	13
Planters	0	3
Median Age	40.5	45.0
Nativity		
Mississippi	71%	73%
Other southern states	29	27
Home Ownership		
Owns home or farm	81%	95%
Rents home or farm	14	3
Boards	6	3

SOURCES: Twelfth Census of the United States, Records of the Bureau of the Census, Record Group 29, National Archives.

NOTE: Occasional failure of the columns to add up to 100 percent resulted from the rounding of decimal numbers. Figures on occupation are based on data for 44 Populists and 39 Democrats. In addition to these individuals, 3 Democrats had no occupation listed on their census entries (in two cases these were men past age 65). An additional 10 Populists and 9 Democrats could not be located on the census. Occupation data for some of these were added based on newspaper accounts.

did not. The Democrats were more likely to be lawyers than were the Populists, and were more likely to work in the commercial area. The Populists were a younger group of men, and (in a possibly related measure) they were less likely to own their home or farm. The differences between the parties are not as great among these county candidates as they were among legislators. This fact is not surprising, given that the legislators were from a wide geographical area, while these county candidates were

from a restricted group of five counties with a long history of agrarianism in politics.

Other sources of useful information about the sample are the personal property tax returns for these five counties, which assess various forms of wealth, including horses, mules, cattle, wagons, furniture, pianos, jewelry, securities, money at loan, and cash. The differences between the average assessment for the two groups of candidates is significant:

> Median Assessment of Democratic candidates: $208
> Median Assessment of Populist candidates: $110

These figures indicate that the Democrats enjoyed nearly twice the wealth of their Populist opponents. On the other hand, it should be noted that the average assessment of a random sample of 1,223 residents of these five counties was almost half as small as that of the Populist candidates.[91] Thus while the Populist candidates lagged well behind the Democrats in accumulating wealth, they were something of an economic elite when compared with all residents of the county. Taken together, the study of legislators and county candidates shows a People's party led by farmers, as well as a few doctors and teachers; they were generally a young group of men, southerners all, and most of them Mississippi natives. They owned far less personal property than their Democratic counterparts, and although most owned their house or farm, they had a lower rate of ownership than their Democratic opponents.[92]

Another important question about the Mississippi People's party was where its candidates did well.[93] What do their stronger counties have in common that might help explain the People's party appeal there? Table 6.3 offers a comparison between the ten strongest counties for Frank Burkitt's 1895 gubernatorial candidacy (labeled group 1) and Burkitt's ten weakest counties (labeled group 2). The table also includes the statewide averages for each characteristic.

Comparing group 1 with the statewide averages contained in table 6.3, a picture emerges of Mississippi counties that were above average in their support of the Populists. In these stronger Populist counties a significantly larger number of farm families owned their own farm compared with the state as a whole. The low number of bales per one hundred acres suggests soil quality poorer than the state average. The two strongest Populist counties devoted more acres to corn than they did to cotton, which was uncommon in Mississippi. Most of the Populist strongholds were white-

majority counties in this black-majority state; three of the top six Populist counties had populations that were over 70 percent white.

What all this suggests is that Populism was strongest in Mississippi where the commercial revolution was not yet in full flower, although it was underway. Unlike many commercializing counties nearby, in the group 1 counties a large percentage of farmers still owned their own farm, where they raised relatively less of the state's great cash crop and more corn (which could be used as meal for cooking and also as feed for livestock). The Populists in these counties undoubtedly hoped that railroad regulation, a cut in taxes, and other reforms would help prevent them from falling into debt slavery in a fully commercialized economy where town merchants and bankers held most of the power. While the People's party had a great potential appeal in white counties where tenancy rates were high, the poll tax limited the group's ability to win votes in those counties.[94]

Nine of the ten weakest counties for the Populists were located in the Delta (wholly or in part), while Lowndes was a black-belt county in east Mississippi. In none of these counties did the white residents comprise even 25 percent of the population. The ten counties in group 2 featured high rates of farm tenancy, high yields of cotton per acre, and relatively few acres of corn. Studies of other southern states have shown that the Populist party often did *well* in plantation counties, with their rich soil and large number of farm tenants; Mississippi offers a striking exception to this rule. The explanation for this difference is that most of the other southern states had not yet enacted disfranchisement, while in Mississippi the new system of voter qualifications preceded the founding of the People's party. In the Mississippi Delta, only a very small percentage of the population voted, and the elites who did vote were not likely to favor this party of small-scale farmers. In other states many blacks voted Populist, but in Mississippi relatively few blacks were registered voters, and the Populists generally ignored the state's black residents.[95]

We know, then, that the Mississippi Populists did best in counties with small owner-run farms, farms with low crop yields and poorer soil that was as suitable for corn as it was for cotton. The Populist leaders were more likely than their opponents to be farmers and tended to own less wealth. But it would be oversimplifying to say that the Mississippi People's party was a party of poorer farmers. Much of the direction and leadership came from physicians like Rufus K. Prewitt, A. M. Newman, and Thomas K.

TABLE 6.3
Comparison of Selected Characteristics,
Populism's Strong and Weak Counties

	Populist percentage of vote, 1895	Percent of farm families owning own farm, 1890	Bales per 100 acres planted in cotton, 1890	Percent of population white, 1890	Acres of cotton per acre of corn, 1890
Group 1: Burkitt's Strongest Counties in 1895					
Choctaw	50.6	70.1	27	75.7	0.91
Webster	48.6	60.2	25	75.3	0.88
Chickasaw	48.0	29.7	21	42.7	1.38
Carroll	46.2	62.6	30	43.5	2.00
Winston	45.8	65.9	31	57.9	1.13
Pontotoc	42.4	47.3	20	70.8	1.06
Franklin	42.4	41.9	49	52.6	1.56
Attala	41.1	57.8	33	57.4	1.35
Amite	39.7	39.1	46	41.8	1.58
Lawrence	39.5	66.6	42	50.7	1.00
Group 2: Burkitt's Weakest Counties in 1895					
Adams	6.3	11.7	59	23.5	4.04
Lowndes	6.2	23.1	24	22.2	1.74
Tunica	6.0	20.4	45	10.4	5.33
Madison	5.6	20.3	32	22.1	1.77
Coahoma	5.4	7.5	64	12.3	4.14
Bolivar	5.2	14.5	66	10.7	6.55
Claiborne	3.6	16.9	49	24.3	2.62
Leflore	2.6	4.9	62	15.4	3.06
Washington	2.4	8.1	68	12.0	5.14
Issaquena	1.0	6.4	69	6.0	5.04
Averages					
Group 1	44.4	54.1	32	56.8	1.28
State	27.1	37.7	40	42.3	1.68
Group 2	4.4	13.4	54	15.9	3.93

SOURCES: 1895 gubernatorial returns, Old Election Returns Book, Secretary of State Papers, Record Group 28, Mississippi Department of Archives and History,

TABLE 6.3 *(Continued)*

Jackson; *Report on Farms and Homes . . . in the United States at the Eleventh Census: 1890* (Washington, D.C.: G.P.O., 1896); *Census Reports, Volume V, Twelfth Census . . . Agriculture* (Washington, D.C.: United States Census Office, 1902); *Census Reports, Volume I, Twelfth Census . . . Agriculture* (Washington, D.C.: United States Census Office, 1901).

CORRELATION: Correlation of each county's Populist vote with the four measures: with percent of the population white, 0.63; with farm ownership, 0.56; with cotton to corn ratio, -0.58; with bales per acre of cotton, 0.46. These correlations are in the moderate to fairly strong range.

Magee, and from preacher-farmers like W. P. Ratliff and John E. Gore. A number of the Populist candidates at the county level were schoolteachers, and of course some of the most vocal leaders were journalists, including not only Prewitt and Ratliff but Frank Burkitt, E. T. Winston, and nearly three dozen others. Democrats who opposed the Populist candidates were much less likely to be doctors, ministers, and teachers. The Populist leaders in Mississippi, both farmers and professionals, worked together to craft a coherent set of goals for improving the Magnolia State.

At its heart, the Mississippi Populists' program was conservative. Members of the People's party looked backward to a golden era of independent yeomen farmers. The party promised to take power away from new-fangled political rings and give it back to the old custodians of power, the taxpayers. Like any true conservatives, the state's Populists wanted to conserve the good of the present, limit frightening change in the future, and restore the glories of the past. As the 1895 state platform put it, the Populist party sought to restore "the government of our fathers" to Mississippi. Specifically, the Populists wanted to restore the old antebellum system of the elected judiciary, in which taxpayers would have a larger voice in the judicial branch of the government. They wanted to return to an era when the legislative branch of government (the county board of supervisors as well as the legislature) refrained from bestowing special privileges upon certain elite groups; they disliked, for example, gifts and tax advantages for railroads and industries. The party sought to restore purity in elections, arguing that now that disfranchisement of blacks had taken place, there was no reason fair elections should not return to the state. Recalling an era when government spent little money on higher education, the Populists championed a cut in spending for the state col-

leges, viewing them as elite institutions where the students should pay the full expenses of an education.[96]

Of course, some of the conservative goals of the Populists involved novel, experimental techniques. The Populists believed that corporations and the wealthy had seized so much power in the United States that only the intervention of a strong U.S. government could restore power to the people. This brand of thinking was diametrically opposed to the Democrats' approach, which called for a weak central government, and warned of a return of federal "bayonet rule" in the South if national power were not kept in check. The greatest example of Populists' favoring strong federal government was the subtreasury plan. Never in its history had the U.S. government undertaken as expansive a project as was called for in the subtreasury system. Even so, the Populists explained that they wanted to return to an earlier time when not all money emanated from New York and Washington. Calls for inflation of the money supply were viewed as horribly radical by bankers, but Populists pointed out correctly that the money supply in the United States had been shrinking. They now sought to return to the earlier number of dollars per capita. In Mississippi, both Democrats and Populists claimed to be the true heirs of Thomas Jefferson and Andrew Jackson. The Democrats urged that true Jacksonianism meant limiting the size of government. Populists countered that cliques of elite merchants, creditors, and investors had won so much power and so many special privileges that only government action could redistribute some of this power to the people.[97]

Populist calls for national regulation or ownership of the railroads were a demand for a new federal power. On the other hand, government at various levels had long regulated, licensed, and even built and owned links of transportation, including steamboats, railroads, turnpikes, ferries, bridges, and county roads.Better that the government control the railroads for the good of the people, Populists believed, than allow investors in these monopolistic enterprises to grow wealthy off the sweat of the farmers' brow. The call of the Mississippi People's party for the initiative and referendum was also novel, but again sought to *restore* citizen involvement in government.

Of course, whether the Populists' golden era of the past ever really existed or not is an open question. Political rings and favors for the privileged have a long history in the United States at all levels of government. Yet certainly the Populists perceived that average citizens had lost power, had lost their formerly strong voice in government. The Mississippi

People's party sought to bring back the days of the citizen legislator, the elected judge, and the modest county tax bill. Clearly this was not a radical group of poor citizens who sought to overthrow capitalism. A majority of the Mississippi Populists ran their own businesses: owner-run farms especially, also physicians' practices, newspapers, and a few other small businesses. The party had no interest in toppling capitalism. It only sought fairer competition within capitalism—the regulation of railroads and prohibition of monopolies, for example.[98]

There is no denying that the Mississippi People's party did help move the Democratic party in an agrarian direction. Yet several historians of agrarianism in Mississippi have argued that the farmer's movement suffered "retardation" because of the division of Mississippi farmers between the Democratic and People's parties. The implication is that farmers could have accomplished more sooner by remaining in the Democratic party. But farmers had tried working within the Democratic party, for example when they hoped to win for Grange Master Putnam Darden the Democratic nomination for governor in 1885, and then in 1891, when they tried to win the election of pro-Barksdale, Farmers' Alliance legislators. Although exerting themselves with all the energy they could muster, the farmers both times had fallen well short of a majority. They believed "ring control" was responsible for their losses. By leaving the Democratic party, farmers made a dramatic statement that all was not well in the party of Jefferson. As each year went by, the Mississippi Democratic party made more and more efforts to entice the Populists back into the fold. The Democratic co-opting of the Populists' issues was bad for the Populist Party, but good for the farmers.[99]

Nationally and in Mississippi, the Populist goals were enacted, with much Democratic support. Direct election of U.S. senators came in 1913, a federal income tax amendment that same year, and prohibition for Mississippi in 1908. To secure an electoral system more responsive to the people, and to weaken "ring politics," a statewide primary election system was inaugurated in time for the 1903 election. The rising new star in 1903—and the gubernatorial victor—was James K. Vardaman. Vardaman called for a host of reforms, almost all of which had also been championed by earlier People's party platforms. Key among Vardaman's enthusiastic supporters were a number of former Populists, including Frank Burkitt. Vardaman injected an element of virulent racism that had been absent from Populist speeches, but the rhetoric appealed to a great many Missis-

sippi farmers, and there is little indication that former Populists denounced Vardaman's approach. By 1912 there were at least eight former
Populists in the legislature, including Frank Burkitt in the senate, and
former congressional candidate John H. Simpson in the house.[100]

There was, then, a new political system in Mississippi, in place by 1902
or 1903. The new system was a one-party system in which any excitement
of an election year would come during the season of the Democratic
primary. The state electorate had fallen to half its 1888 size as both blacks
and whites often failed to pay the requisite poll tax. While opposition
parties did exist in Mississippi in the first half of the twentieth century,
they would never win nearly the number of votes that had been won by the
Greenbackers, Independents, Republicans, and Populists in the late nineteenth century.

After the demise of Populism, there still were some voices in the state
that insisted the Democratic party was unlikely to bring needed reforms in
state and nation. After the 1904 presidential race, journalists across the
state raised their editorial eyebrows as they reported that in a small community named McCallum in southeast Mississippi, Socialist presidential
candidate Eugene Debs had carried the precinct. Of course, the carrying
of one rural precinct by a non-Democrat did not send shivers down the
spines of Democratic party leaders. Still, it was viewed as an interesting
curiosity and showed that even in 1904 the Democrats' one-party domination was not quite absolute.[101]

SEVEN

Conclusion

IN THE LAST QUARTER OF THE NINETEENTH CENTURY, MISSISSIPPI indisputably was a one-party state in the usual sense of the word. Yet the Magnolia State *was* home to a number of political parties and movements. These included national groups such as the Republican, Greenback, Populist, and Prohibition parties; the state also boasted a variety of state and county Independent organizations. None of these movements succeeded in electing a governor, winning electoral votes for a presidential candidate, or securing a majority in the legislature. On the other hand, some of these groups did become "locally strong," winning control of a tier of counties, a number of towns and cities, and blocs of seats in the legislature.

The Greenback party first appeared in Mississippi in 1878, attracting large numbers of farmers who favored an inflation of the money supply. The party was made up largely of white small farmers who were former Democrats and of black voters who were former Republicans. A number of the important leaders were formers Whigs who had felt politically homeless since the Civil War. The party proved strongest in certain northwestern counties in the brown loam region of the state, including Yalobusha, Tate, Panola, and Holmes counties. It won victories, too, in the central county of Hinds, also in the brown loam region, and in a few northeastern counties such as Sumner (later called Webster). In the 1879

election the party won seventeen seats in the legislature and captured control of a number of counties.

Within two years after its founding, the state Greenback party was in trouble. The greatest problem was that the former Republicans, after supplying tens of thousands of votes for the Greenbackers, began to reorganize the state GOP. After topping 40 percent of the vote in their first congressional races in 1878, the Greenback candidates proved far weaker in 1880, as the Republican party revived and ran a number of candidates. Greenback farmer W. D. Howze of DeSoto County later recalled that he had tried to convince his black neighbors to vote for congressional candidate Thomas W. Harris, but while black voters were "more favorable to us Greenbackers than to Democrats, they invariably refused." Greenbackers argued that the Republican party would never again win elections in Mississippi, because it was seen as the party of Reconstruction, high taxes, and black domination. Black Republicans countered that the Greenback party had not given them sufficient recognition.[1]

In 1881, the Greenback and Republican parties made the controversial decision to nominate a joint ticket, called the Independent People's ticket, headed by gubernatorial candidate Benjamin King. The campaign was an especially grueling one, as King traveled the state pledging relief for indebted farmers and championing free and fair elections. Conservative Democrats such as L. Q. C. Lamar were horrified by the movement of black and white small farmers and predicted that if King won, "life will be unbearable in Mississippi." After massive fraud on election day, the secretary of state declared King's opponent Robert Lowry elected, with 59.6 percent of the reported vote.[2]

Historian James S. Ferguson, in his study of Mississippi agrarianism, declared that Greenbackers "dissipated" their strength in the 1881 election by fusing with the state's Republicans.[3] Yet the Greenbackers had earlier exhibited real strength in only a dozen or so counties and, besides, they had learned in 1880 how vulnerable they were in three-way races featuring Democrats, Republicans, and Greenbackers. Fusion in 1881 offered a chance for the Greenback party to benefit from votes in the Delta, where it had previously been very weak, as well as a chance to maintain the loyalty of the party's black voters. Fraudulent counting of votes in the Delta, however, sealed the fate of the Independent People's ticket. Still, King's vote was the highest vote (as a total as well as a percentage) of any non-Democratic gubernatorial or presidential candidate on the Mississippi ballot during the years of this study.

The strongest non-Democratic congressional candidates in the period ran the following year. In 1882, Mississippi voters sent one Republican and one Greenback-Republican fusionist to the halls of Congress. In the third (Delta) district, white Republican attorney Elza Jeffords won nearly 70 percent of the vote, while in the second (north-central) district James R. Chalmers won 52 percent, with the support of the Greenback and Republican parties. By 1883 and 1884, the Republicans and Greenbackers were in decline. The national Greenback party was all but dead, as a return to relative prosperity sapped the strength of protest parties. The Republican party lost influence in the state as the White House passed into Democratic hands. Loss of the presidency meant patronage was no longer available to build up the state Republican party; it also meant that federal supervisors would not be appointed to keep an eye on congressional and presidential elections. If violations of federal election laws occurred, they would not be prosecuted. In black-majority counties like Hinds and Panola, Democrats gained control by offering black Greenbackers and Republicans places on their tickets. Once in control of the counties, including their election machinery (chancery clerks were the voting registrars), the Democrats could then drop the black candidates in future elections.

In 1885, the *Vicksburg Evening Post* reported that the Democratic state ticket was unopposed, but added, "We predict that there will not be another election in this state with only one ticket in the field—the election this year is the last of the one-sided kind." The *Post* had other virtues as a newspaper, but its powers of prognostication in this instance were not impressive. In the nineteen gubernatorial elections between 1885 and 1959, Democrats would run unopposed in all but six, and only once would the opposition candidate top 15 percent of the vote.[4]

In 1889 a Hinds County Democrat wrote a letter to the *Clarion-Ledger* arguing that the appearance of a Republican state ticket that year was "a menace to our most cherished institutions—to our liberty—to our civilization." After the Republican candidates received numerous threats they withdrew, and Democrat John M. Stone won 100 percent of the vote. Increasingly, the Mississippi Republican party became a laughingstock. Its 1892 convention was badly divided into two factions and was a shouting match from the moment the delegates assembled. Two presiding officers were elected, and in fact two conventions were held in the same room, with each group of delegates shouting so as to be heard over the din of the rival convention.[5]

Republicans regularly held county offices in one kind of case in the 1880s and 1890s. In the Delta, Democrats agreed to allow them a number of county and beat offices and a number of legislative seats. Democrats always held the key positions—a majority membership on the board of supervisors, for example—but still Republicans were allowed some voice, and violent campaigns became a thing of the past in most Delta counties.

After the decline of the Greenback party, agrarian voters worked within the Democratic fold. Their two greatest efforts, however, ended in failure. In 1885 agrarians tried to win the Democratic gubernatorial nomination for state Grange Master Putnam Darden. At the state convention Darden's supporters were outmaneuvered and outvoted, and a conservative Democrat, Robert Lowry, was nominated instead. Agrarians were disgusted at what they saw as "ring control" of the Democratic party, and a number of them wrote Darden's name on their ballots in November. Although Darden was not a candidate, he actually carried Webster County.

In 1891, Farmers' Alliance leader Frank Burkitt led an attempt to win a majority of legislative seats for the Farmers' Alliance, in hopes that the legislature would then send two new agrarian senators to Washington to support the subtreasury plan. L. Q. C. Lamar groused that farmers used to be conservative and patriotic; now, he asserted, they cared only about "their own recently awakened cupidity and lust for office." Despite almost superhuman efforts, the agrarians again fell well short of a majority. They credited their loss to machine control of the Democratic county and state conventions.[6]

The only answer for agrarians seemed to be action outside the Democratic party. In other states, too, Farmers' Alliances were evolving into People's party organizations. Several of Mississippi's county governments defected from the Democratic to the Populist party in 1892, as did twenty-two legislators hailing from every region of the state except the southeast. Yet the People's party was unable to follow up these impressive defections with many actual victorious elections. Earlier writers have given the number of Mississippi Populists actually elected to office as about twenty-five; fuller use of county newspapers has shown that actually more than 130 were elected in two dozen counties. Yet most of these victories were at the beat level.[7]

Populist voters feared that farmers were losing their independence, as tillers of the soil fell increasingly into debt, and as large numbers of landowners were involuntarily converted into renters. During a severe

depression, they were angered at what they perceived to be wasteful government spending and special favors for railroads and for the friends of
county officers. Populists in Mississippi had conservative goals, wanting to
restore an earlier golden era, when judges were elected by the people,
taxes were low, government spending low, and elections usually honest
and fair. Some of the *means* championed by the People's party were novel,
including the subtreasury and regulation or government ownership of
railroads. Even these plans, however, aimed to restore the state to an
earlier era when all money did not emanate from eastern cities, and when
government at all levels played a major role in transportation, for the good
of the many.

The People's party in Mississippi reached its peak in voter appeal in
1894, as the depression reached its nadir for cotton farmers; the various
Populist candidates carried seven counties in 1894. In 1895, in the party's
first bid for the governor's office, Populist Frank Burkitt won more votes
(18,200) than the congressional candidates of 1894 in a larger turnout, but
he won only 28 percent of the vote across the state and carried only one
county. The 1899 Populist gubernatorial candidate won only 13 percent.
Failure of the Populists was caused in part by fraud, in part by successful
Democratic appeals to party loyalty, and in part by weak Populist organizational structures. Populists had great difficulty in contending with Democratic co-opting of Populist issues, a shrinking white electorate, and
economic upturns that happened to coincide with state and county elections.[8]

Albert D. Kirwan, in his study of late-nineteenth-century Mississippi
politics, argued that the farmers' movement suffered from retardation
because of the Populist revolt.[9] He asserted that farmers would have been
more successful had they stayed within the Democratic party. It is true
that agrarians won many Democratic seats in the state house of representatives in 1887 and 1889 and won some key leadership posts in that body.
Yet the two greatest efforts of agrarian Democrats had both ended in
failure, in 1885 and in 1891. It was pointless to suggest that farmers simply
try harder next time; they had exerted themselves to the limit in these two
elections. It seemed clear to agrarians that a conservative Democratic
machine would prevent them from ever electing a governor or a subtreasury U.S. senator. The only option seemed to be to work outside the
Democratic party. In fact, the Populists did advance many of their goals
while they held twenty-two seats in the legislature, especially the reduction of state expenses.

While the Populist experiment was ultimately a failure in terms of winning elections, it did push the state Democratic party in an agrarian direction. Populists noted repeatedly that although Democrats had denounced the People's party platforms in 1892 and 1893, by 1894 the Democrats were copying Populist planks wholesale. Soon Democrats were calling loudly for free silver, taxation of U.S. bonds, genuine regulation of railroads, suppression of monopolies, and a slashing of state government expenses. To oppose Frank Burkitt in 1895, Democrats nominated Anselm J. McLaurin, who, although an attorney, was championing most of the farmers' fondest goals.

This study has focused on opposition political parties in the state of Mississippi. One important question clearly is: Was there, in fact, an opposition *movement* in the state? Or do we simply have a case of numerous discrete opposition parties and movements that had little in common? There are two ways of coming to an answer to these questions. First, we can examine the regions where the opposition parties did well, to see if, for example, the Greenback party regions later supported the Populists. Also, we can examine the various movements' political ideologies to determine whether in fact their platforms had much in common.

In his recent study of dissident movements in Georgia, Alabama, and Mississippi, Michael R. Hyman looked to the hill counties as the region where white dissenters were most numerous. In Georgia and Alabama he found flourishing Greenback and Independent movements. While he stressed that these were important in their own right, he also argued that dissident groups helped prepare the way for the later Populists, who flourished in the same region. In looking at Mississippi, Hyman examined ten counties in the state's northeast corner (Alcorn, Calhoun, Itawamba, Lee, Pontotoc, Prentiss, Sumner, Tippah, Tishomingo, and Union). In these counties, Hyman found that opposition movements did not flourish, and that agrarians tended to work within the Democratic party.[10]

As a general pattern across the Deep South, Hyman suggested that the Greenback party attracted white dissidents in the black counties, while in white counties the opposition was more likely to support Independent movements. He also argued that counties that were the home of flourishing Greenback and Independent movements also saw the rise of viable Populist parties. Once again, since his ten-county region of Mississippi did not generally support strong Greenback or Independent movements, Hyman argued that it is not surprising Populism did not arise in those

counties. Hyman's identification of the places where dissenters did and did not flourish needs some modification when applied to the various counties of Mississippi, both within and without the northeastern bloc of counties he studied.[11]

In Mississippi, Independent movements were not, as Hyman suggested, most likely to arise in white-majority hill counties. As the accompanying map shows, of the seven counties electing Independent legislators between 1877 and 1890, only two were among those in Hyman's northeastern hill region. Also, only two were white-majority counties. Other prominent Independent movements arose in Yazoo and Rankin counties, also well away from the hill counties, and also black-majority counties. Most of the Greenback strength was outside the hills; of the eight counties electing Greenback legislators, only two were in Hyman's study area. Although Hyman argued that white dissidents in white counties generally found Independentism preferable to Greenbackism, and that the reverse was true in black counties, three of the Greenback counties had white majorities, while only two of the Independent counties did.

It is also true that Populist influence was most strongly felt outside of the ten counties studied by Hyman. Map 3 shows the ten counties that gave the greatest support to People's party gubernatorial nominee Frank Burkitt in 1895; of these ten counties, only Pontotoc and Webster were in Hyman's hill country. Hyman argued in the closing pages of *The Anti-Redeemers* that Populism generally arose and flourished in the same areas that had once supported strong Independent and Greenback movements. This was not true in the Magnolia State. In Mississippi, the Greenbackers, Independents, and Populists each tended to flourish in different areas, and each of these regions was largely outside Hyman's study area.

The Republican party in this period won most of its victories in black-majority counties where a city was located, particularly Hinds, Warren, and Adams counties. In many other black-majority counties, especially in the Delta, blacks continued to vote Republican and to hold offices through cooperation with local Democrats. The very strongest counties for the Greenback party were in a north-south band just east of the Delta, in the brown loam section of the state. Here the large numbers of black voters were a key ingredient of Greenback success, while white agrarian dissidents provided many votes and most of the candidates. Meanwhile, in several white-majority counties white voters split between the Democratic and Greenback parties, while the smaller number of black voters provided the balance of power. Black voters were also important to most Indepen-

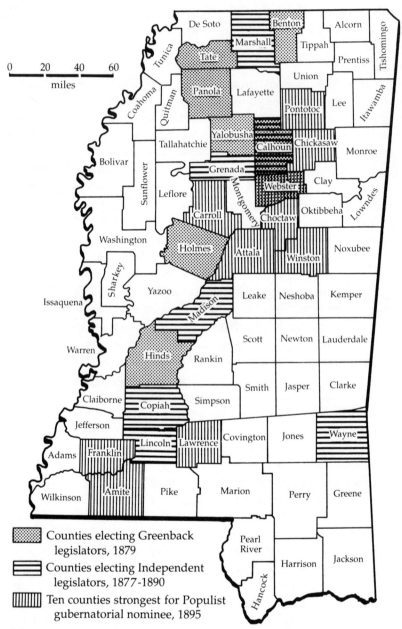

Map 3. Stronger Counties for Opposition Movements in Mississippi

Legend:

- Counties electing Greenback legislators, 1879
- Counties electing Independent legislators, 1877-1890
- Ten counties strongest for Populist gubernatorial nominee, 1895

dent movements, and most such movements arose in black-majority counties.

The ten strongest counties for the Populists in the 1895 election were in the north-central part of the state, as well as in the southwest corner. These generally were white-majority counties where the growing of corn was more important than it was elsewhere in the state. The poorer quality of the soil meant that these farmers were usually less caught up in the commercial revolution that was sweeping the Deep South; a majority of the farmers in these counties still owned their own farms. Yet as they faced the prospect of frightening change in an increasingly commercialized system of agriculture, farmers in these counties supported the conservative goals of the Populist party. In only one of these ten counties had the Greenback party showed any real strength; only one of the ten counties had ever elected an Independent to the legislature. Mississippi's political history is unlike that of many other southern states; Populists did not flourish in the same area as Greenbackers and Independents. The areas are different because the earlier movements had included black voters; the Populist party appealed almost exclusively to white voters and usually did best in white-majority counties. Like the Socialist movement that would follow in the twentieth century, Populism tended to do best in white-majority counties where appeals to white unity were less potent.[12]

In their platforms and public speeches, the various dissident groups did have one major factor in common: all called for decisive action by the federal government to achieve a number of goals. This position was in marked contrast to that of the Democratic party, which believed in states' rights and a weak national government. Republicans, Independents, Greenbackers, and Populists all called on the federal government to act to help restore free and fair elections to Mississippi. The Republicans took the strongest stand in this area, even calling for the passage of additional, more stringent voting-rights laws such as the Lodge Elections Bill. The other groups typically did not call for new laws but did seek enforcement of several federal voting laws that were already on the books. Independents, Greenbackers, and Populists all asked the U.S. district judge in Mississippi to appoint federal election supervisors with the power to witness the balloting and the count.

Greenbackers and Populists wanted the U.S. government to play a more active role in regulating the size of the money supply. Both groups wanted the government to regulate big business, including railroads and other near-monopolies. Both asked the federal government to curb the power of

the privately held national banks. The Greenbackers sought an end to the purchase of public lands by speculators; they also asked Congress to prohibit Chinese immigration in order to protect the jobs of American producers, including farm workers in the Delta. The Populists asked the federal government to act in a bold and unprecedented way, to build a subtreasury system of warehouses, in order to help restore the independence of America's farmers.

At the state level, Greenbackers, agrarian Independents, and Populists all sought decisive—though essentially negative—actions. These included repeal of the state's stringent crop lien laws and an end to the convict leasing system (which provided special economic opportunities for a tiny clique). These dissident groups also sought an end to special favors for corporations, including especially railroads but also manufacturing companies. Other goals at the state level included effective railroad regulation and, for most Populists, prohibition.

Democrats sometimes warned that the dissidents put too much emphasis on new state and federal laws. They pointed out that a key tenet of Jacksonianism was the necessity of limiting government's size and power. The Greenbackers and Populists, however, believed that bankers, investors, merchants, and lawyers had seized too much power in the United States and in Mississippi. They believed that only government had the strength to limit this power and influence and to restore some of it to the producing masses. Besides, not all of the government actions sought by the agrarian dissenters would increase the size of government. The dissidents believed that both the state and national governments spent too much money, borrowed too readily, and taxed too heavily. All three groups sought a reduction in government salaries and in government spending for institutions ranging from the state colleges to the state asylums.

The Greenbackers and Populists (but not the Republicans) developed a class-conscious vocabulary that presaged the Socialist party writing that would appear in the state in the early twentieth century. The Grange newspaper *Patron of Husbandry* supported a number of Independent and Greenback legislative candidates in 1881, complaining that conservative Democrats "will tolerate no opposition from the 'lower classes,' as they call those who gain their living in the sweat of their brows." The Grange editor looked forward to the day when "the toiling millions will cast their votes untrammeled by the dictation of scheming politicians." Thirteen years later, the *Mississippi Populist* called to the state's farmers: "Ye toiling

sons of earth, arise! Shake off the chains of night! In heaven's name, demand your own! In God's name demand the right!" Like the later Socialists, Greenbackers and Populists spoke of the working class and the plutocrats and complained of class legislation. The *People's Banner* even took an antimilitarist stand, as would the state's Socialists in the first two decades of the twentieth century. The *Banner* complained that the Democratic president Grover Cleveland wanted to keep a standing army and that the Congress "squanders millions on man-killing machines." Yet clearly the Greenbackers and Populists did not favor an end to capitalism; they only sought to prevent its worst abuses.[13]

A number of the leaders of Mississippi's opposition parties moved from one group to another over time. Greenbackers Jackson Taylor Griffin, Absalom M. West, and William H. Vasser had once been Whigs; Griffin and West came into the Greenback party through the Democratic camp, while Vasser was a former Republican. Greenbackers Reuben Davis and A. T. Wimberly became Republicans after the decline of the Greenback party, while J. H. Simpson, Rufus K. Prewitt, and John E. Gore moved from the Greenback into the Populist party. James R. Chalmers was variously a Democrat, Greenbacker-Independent, Independent, and Republican. William D. Frazee was one of few Republicans who joined the Populists; he returned to the Republican party after the Populist decline. At least three Populists later helped lead the state Socialist party: M. E. Fritz, David R. Hearn, and Sumner W. Rose. It is clear, though, that the most fertile ground for winning new recruits to any opposition movement was inside the Democratic party. The majority of new members for each opposition party were former Democrats.[14]

Overall, the various opposition groups had some ideological traits in common, shared some personnel over time, and occasionally did well in the same counties. Yet it can hardly be said that there was a unified opposition movement in the state. Even the Greenback and Populist parties, which arguably had the most in common, featured a number of differences as well. The former was a coalition that included members of both races and that championed black voting rights. Predictably, it often did well in counties with sizeable black populations. The Populist party in Mississippi did not champion black voting or black rights in general, and there were no black Populist leaders at any level. The Populist party typically did best in white-majority counties. It is clear that a majority of Mississippi Populists had had no involvement in the earlier Greenback party.[15]

Repeatedly, a large number of Mississippians devoted their energies to building or revitalizing an opposition party only to see their efforts come to naught. In 1878 two former congressmen, two sitting state senators, a number of newspaper editors, and hundreds of other citizens defected from the Democrats, risking their political careers to lead the new Greenback party. In 1880 through 1882 Republicans risked sabotaging the promising Greenback movement by devoting new energy to building up the GOP. In 1892 twenty-two Legislators, as well as several county governments, discarded their Democratic affiliation and joined wholeheartedly the new Populist organization. Despite the best efforts of these opposition party leaders, however, none of the movements was able to win a statewide election or gain and maintain control of Mississippi counties.

Two problems proved insurmountable to the Republicans, Greenbackers, Independents, Populists, and other members of opposition parties. One was white solidarity; the other, organizational weakness. White solidarity provides an answer to the question, Why were white Mississippians so incredibly intolerant of dissent?

The tendency toward white solidarity had a long history in Mississippi. Prior to the Civil War, white solidarity was seen as a virtue because slaves greatly outnumbered white citizens; public opinion held that only the diligence of all whites and their service in slave patrols and the like prevented a massive slave uprising. During Reconstruction, a majority of white Mississippians felt anger as they watched the political events; whether rightly or wrongly, they viewed Republican Reconstruction as an era of absurdly high taxes and extravagance and incompetence in government. They blamed the excesses of Reconstruction governments on black voting, black office-holding, and a small group of evil white men who were willing to use black votes to build their own political fortunes. Beginning in the mid-1870s, Democrats argued that in this black-majority state, only white unity within the Democratic party could prevent "black domination" and ruinous taxes. Radical Reconstruction gave a bad name to political insurgency. After Reconstruction, any political action outside the Democratic party was immediately suspect. Democrats' strong belief in the necessity of white solidarity made them willing to use almost any tactic to insure victory for their party.[16]

Clearly, white Democrats' threats and violence played a large role in suppressing the opposition vote in the last quarter of the nineteenth century. A classic case of intimidation came in 1883 in Copiah County, where white Independent candidates threatened both white solidarity and Dem-

ocratic hegemony. Democrats used paramilitary action to intimidate blacks into not voting, then turned their attention to whites. Copiah County Democrats argued that blacks must not hold the balance of power in the county, and they warned white Independents to return to the Democratic party. The murder of Independent leader Print Matthews seconds after he had deposited his ballot received nationwide attention.[17]

Often intimidation made actual violence unnecessary. After years of rule by a Republican county government, a number of Democrats in the river county of Warren penned letters to the 1885 Republican candidates urging them to withdraw from their candidacies in the pending election so as to "bring into more harmonious relations the two races in our midst." The letters added that the Republicans should "appreciate the force of these suggestions." The Republicans did withdraw, and Warren County was fully in white Democratic control after 1885. A number of other tickets were similarly withdrawn over the years, after a campaign of intimidation. Madison County's Independents in 1883 withdrew their slate rather than face the kind of violence suffered by their colleagues in Copiah County. The 1889 Republican ticket for statewide offices was withdrawn after gubernatorial candidate James R. Chalmers received numerous threats on his life.[18]

Independents, Greenbackers, and Populists learned from the Republican party's experiences in 1875 and 1876 and often refused to be intimidated, or themselves resorted to intimidation. Greenbackers struck the first blows in the riots at Coffeeville and Lexington after arguably minor provocation. Black supporters of the Anti-Monopoly ticket in Lauderdale County in 1881 fired the first shots during the Marion riot. Populist legislator W. P. Ratliff shot and killed his Democratic colleague from Attala County rather than let pass the latter's disparaging remark, which had been given wide publicity. By refusing to be intimidated, these opponents of the state's Democrats hoped to avoid being overawed into oblivion. Still, refusing to be intimidated could have fatal consequences. Henry M. Dixon refused to abandon his 1879 Independent bid for sheriff of Yazoo County, despite warnings, and was shot dead on the streets of Yazoo City. In Jasper County, Marsh Cook ignored warnings that he should stop making speeches in his Republican bid for constitutional convention delegate; he was shot fatally from ambush prior to election day.[19]

The clearest example of Democrats' seeking white solidarity was the campaign tactic called "drawing the color line." Democrats urged that it was the duty of every white man to vote the Democratic ticket. As the

editor of the *Walthall Warden* put it, every white voter should support the Democratic nominees "whether he likes them or not." Democrats in black-majority Hinds County were able to beat back an Independent threat in 1877 by drawing the color line. The Democratic county platform resolved that all Independent movements were "dangerous" to white unity, and that all Independent candidates "shall be treated as common enemies to the welfare of the people." When an Independent movement appeared in Noxubee County in 1881, the *Macon Beacon* declared, "Democracy and white men forever should be our battle cry." The *Beacon* added that white Independents must realize "that they are digging their political, social, and financial graves." Repeatedly, Democratic newspapers printed the names of white leaders of third parties and Independent movements and urged readers to save the names for future reference, so that they might remember the opponents of white unity and white supremacy.[20]

The color line was so effective not only because it socially ostracized whites who might wish to support the Greenback, Populist, or Republican parties. The color line could also be used to deny a dissident leader the right to make a living. Several economists writing about the post-Civil War South have stressed the importance of one's good name in the community. Even a poor farmer with little collateral could secure loans locally if his reputation in the community was a good one. Those who were known to be trouble-makers, rather than the "decent sort," either were denied credit or advanced credit on less favorable terms. Farmers who participated in commercial agriculture (and this was the great majority) knew that few things were more important than their local reputation. Becoming a political renegade carried a high cost.[21]

After 1890, Democrats' use of the color line was less strident. Had they warned that divisions among white voters could lead to a revival of "black domination," they would have been admitting that the Democrat-led disfranchisement of 1890 had been a failure. Still, Mississippi Democrats did urge voters to ignore the Populists and show loyalty to the party that had "removed the black heel from white necks" in 1875. The *Grenada Sentinel* addressed its white readers in 1892, telling them that they must vote Democratic—"unless your liver is white, your blood pale, your manhood shrunk."[22]

As the years went by, Mississippi Democrats relied less on violence, intimidation, and the color line, and more on the use of fraud to insure

white solidarity and the defeat of opposition movements they believed threatened this solidarity. Ballot box stuffing could be a heroic act if done in the name of white unity. Though sometimes tried in federal court, ballot box stuffers often received free legal counsel provided by local Democratic parties. In one instance, Clay County ballot box stuffers found themselves the subject of a heroic poem penned by a local matron.

A Mississippi Republican interviewed by the *New York Tribune* in 1880 reported that planters were tiring of violence directed toward Republicans and Independents. "If two or three negroes are killed on the plantation, the rest get dissatisfied and go off in a body, leaving the crop to take care of itself." This Mississippi Republican observed that "the era of bulldozing has gone by," since Democrats had discovered that "it is much easier to commit election frauds." U.S. Attorney Greene C. Chandler agreed. In 1880 he reported to Attorney General Charles Devens that at the recent balloting, "There was less violence and bloodshed than is usual in our elections . . . for the reason that other crimes were just as effectual in suppressing the vote, and would attract less notice." Members of the opposition parties found it very difficult to counter election fraud. Consider a case where a Democratic precinct officer in a Populist neighborhood went home for lunch on election day, taking the ballot box with him. If the Populists did not challenge him, they would likely be the victims of ballot box stuffing. If they did complain to the county election commissioners, the commissioners would "rectify" the situation by simply throwing out the results from this Populist precinct.[23]

A rich illustration of the combination of fraud and intimidation used by Democrats in many counties is provided by the 1880 congressional election in the second district. This race pitted Democrat Vannoy H. Manning against Republican George M. Buchanan and Greenbacker Thomas W. Harris. At this election the federal judge appointed U.S. supervisors of elections to serve at most polling places. These supervisors had few powers but were permitted to witness all aspects of the election, from the balloting itself to the count. One U.S. supervisor in DeSoto County, Republican Felix Davis, heard a Democratic precinct officer say that Davis "ought to have his damned stones cut out," and the officer said he would help with the cutting. As the ballots were counted, Davis later testified, four or five Democrats were "continually around the box, . . . swearing and exhibiting pistols in a threatening manner." Greenbacker M. V. Todd, another U.S. supervisor, refused to serve after a Democrat warned him to

stay away from the polls, and after he saw one precinct officer show a pair of brass knuckles to another.[24]

Deputy U.S. Marshal B. P. Scruggs was sitting in his office in Oxford on election day when out the window he saw a number of Republican voters fleeing the polling place. Before he could get to the door he heard, and felt, the report of a cannon. Looking outside, he saw to his amazement that Democrats were firing a cannon (not loaded with shell) directly into the line of waiting voters, most of whom were black. The distance from the muzzle of the cannon to the voters was about twenty feet. Observers later testified that several voters were hit with wadding, at least one was injured by flying dirt clods, and two had their pants caught on fire by the burning wadding. Inside the courthouse, where the balloting was taking place, the report of the cannon made a section of plaster ceiling fall, and a Republican precinct officer was cut badly on the face. Oxford's Democratic mayor refused to put a halt to the firing, saying it was doing no real harm. Other Democrats, too, denied that the cannon prevented anyone from voting.[25]

In other parts of the second district, threats and violence were less dramatic, but the Republican and Greenback candidacies nevertheless were beaten back. In the congressional investigation of this election, U.S. supervisors testified that ballot boxes had been left alone, unguarded, for one or more hours. They also testified that in a number of counties, hundreds of Republican voters' names had been stricken from the registration lists days before the election for no apparent reason. A few U.S. supervisors and other observers testified that they had actually observed a ballot box being stuffed with Democratic ballots. The official returns showed the Republican Buchanan winning 35 percent of the vote. He was not able to prove that he had actually received more votes than Manning; still, it was clear that a great many Buchanan voters were prevented from voting by intimidation and by having their names stricken from the poll books for no legitimate reason.[26]

In a federal election like this one, the opposition parties could hope for redress of some kind from the U.S. government. The federal judge *did* provide the U.S. supervisors of elections, without whom the Democrats' election crimes would not have come to light. After the election, U.S. marshals arrested more than ninety persons in the northern half of the state, including the sheriff of Monroe County. Yet election crimes were hard to prove. Intimidated persons often were very reluctant witnesses,

and while it was possible to prove that a ballot box had been left unguarded, it was more difficult to prove that it had actually been stuffed. The largely white juries often proved unwilling to convict white men for an action that was aimed at preserving white unity and white supremacy.[27]

Federal prosecutors were also discouraged at the very lenient sentencing handed down by federal judge Robert A. Hill. Three Panola County officers were convicted in Hill's court of refusing to register certain qualified voters in 1880; their fine was ten dollars. Democrats in Lee and Monroe counties were convicted of obstructing voters by force and threats on election day; their fines were five dollars each. Only in especially grievous crimes such as ballot box stuffing did the fine surpass one hundred dollars, and in these cases the federal attorney *had* asked the judge to impose a prison sentence. In a few cases Judge Hill imposed a fine of just one dollar, causing even the attorney general of the United States to take notice.[28]

The presence of Democrat Grover Cleveland in the White House between 1885 and 1889 helped reinforce the decline of the state's opposition parties. Not only was patronage unavailable to bolster the Republicans and Independents, but federal election crimes would no longer be prosecuted. In fact, the Democratic federal prosecutor for southern Mississippi served as one of the leaders of the campaign of intimidation that toppled Jackson's Republican government. Federal prosecutor James B. Harris told a rally that he would give his life if necessary to insure that white voters were able to choose the capital city's government. There had been 201 federal prosecutions for election crimes in Mississippi between 1881 and 1884; there were none during the four years of Cleveland's first administration.[29]

By the time the Populist party was founded, Republicans once again controlled the executive branch. Populists moved to counter potential fraud in the 1892 election by asking for the appointment of U.S. supervisors of election. The Democratic backlash, however, was furious. Democrats charged that once the federal government became increasingly involved in state elections, U.S. marshals and soldiers soon would be working to insure that black political involvement returned to the state. Soon, warned a Tupelo editor, the people of Mississippi would be living in "absolute vassalage." The *Meridian Standard* editor linked the Populist bid for U.S. supervisors with the "bayonet elections" of Reconstruction, and warned that Frank Burkitt and his followers would be held responsible for

this attack on the white people of the state. Populists lost more than they gained by securing the appointment of federal election supervisors in 1892.[30]

Organizational weaknesses were also a severe problem for the various opposition parties in Mississippi. None of the groups was able to benefit very much from a national organization. The Republicans dominated the federal government during most of the years of this study. The national Republican party was most interested in aiding Mississippi Republicans; it displayed little zeal in helping groups such as the Greenbackers and Populists. Yet Mississippi was in an unusual situation. Since the Republican party there was so weak, in most years of the late nineteenth century the state's two-party system was Democrat versus Greenbacker, Democrat versus Independents, or Democrats versus Populists. The problem here was that there was no powerful national organization backing up Mississippi's opposition. State Republicans had patronage to aid in building up their organization and received some national campaign funds. Yet because of the very negative connotations felt by white voters when they heard the word *Republican*, the state's GOP was not able to use the patronage to build a winning organization at the state level.

Republican President Chester Arthur gave some patronage and modest campaign funds to Independent James R. Chalmers, aiding Chalmers somewhat in winning a seat in Congress. Generally, however, patronage was reserved for Republicans, and the other opposition movements had to do without. The Greenback party was part of a national organization, but a loosely organized one, and one that was in precipitous decline by 1884. The Populist national organization was stronger, but could not begin to compare with the nationwide organization of Democrats and Republicans. The Populist national organization was also short-lived. The Independents lacked any national organization and usually had no state organization either. Some Independent candidates did not even have a formal county organization behind them. Independents, Greenbackers, and Populists suffered from the lack of strong organizations that could have provided aid to the local opposition press, funds for campaigns, and patronage.

At the local level, the opposition parties' greatest organizational weakness was the inadequacy of their press. The Greenback party could boast some eighteen newspapers, while the Populists founded thirty-eight. At least eight papers supported Independent movements, five backed the Palmer Democrats, and one functioned as the Prohibition party organ.

Yet the Democratic party had hundreds of statewide titles. Moreover, the figures given for the opposition press can be misleading; these are the total numbers of newspapers operating over time. At any *one* time, the number of newspapers was considerably smaller. Many of the opposition newspapers lasted only one or two years, or even less.

Populists in particular recognized the need for an opposition press. A Leake County member of the People's party wrote to a national publication, complaining that the party was in trouble in Leake County because there was no Populist paper there. "The Democratic dishrags lie on us and slap us in the face," he explained. Webster County had a well-edited People's party organ, but it did not always reach the small farmers who lived remote from the county seat. When to everyone's surprise the Populists failed to elect a single important county officer in Webster County in 1895, observers attributed the loss to the fact that so many farmers had not recently seen any Populist publications. Given the overwhelming domination of the state's Democratic press, far more citizens read about the opposition parties in the Democratic newspapers than elsewhere. Democratic editors usually gave wholly negative coverage to the opposition, as might be expected; many Mississippians never saw any other coverage.[31]

One way for the opposition parties to build up their organization was to write a state platform that would attract a large following. In an era when voters took the platforms seriously, a strong platform could lead to a fresh infusion of funds, party workers, and votes. Independent candidates, however, were often accused of having no platform at all. Indeed, a few of the Independent candidates described in these pages seem to have had little ideological basis for their try for office. Independent congressional candidate W. D. Miller in 1896 based his candidacy chiefly on the allegation that his Democratic opponent's nomination was technically flawed. Democrats accused Independents Benjamin King and James R. Chalmers of standing for nothing and of being mere political opportunists. In Chalmers's case they may have been right, as he used almost any political vehicle to fight the Democratic faction of his enemy L. Q. C. Lamar. Benjamin King was accused of being an opportunist because he had been nominated by both Republicans and Greenbackers, but refused to join either party. King's candidacy, however, was firmly based on a detailed platform, including railroad regulation, honest elections, and repeal of the lien law.

The platforms of the state Republican party were often badly out of step with the wishes of Mississippi's white voters. The party's platforms invari-

ably called for a high tariff, which was consistent with the national platform. Yet in the overwhelmingly agricultural state of Mississippi, few
farmers supported the Republican tariff. High tariffs seldom protected
U.S. agricultural products but did mean a higher cost in the marketplace
for merchandise ranging from shovels to gin machinery. Republicans as
well as the National Democrats of 1896 favored a strict gold standard,
while the great majority of Mississippi voters favored a dual monetary
standard based on gold and silver. Republicans also won few white converts as they spoke of new legislation to ensure black voting. On these
three issues—the tariff, the gold standard, and black voting—Republicans
were opposed to the ideas of a majority of white voters, making it very
unlikely that the GOP would experience any revival in the Magnolia State.

The platforms of the Greenback and Populist parties were very popular
with the voters, especially small farmers. The only problem here was that
as Democrats saw some early successes by these two parties, they quickly
moved to adopt the more popular planks in their opponents' platforms.
Greenbackers flourished when they could oppose conservative Democrats; they withered and fell away when the Democrats, too, began to
advocate inflation. The Populist platform won thousands of converts for
the new party in its first two years, but then the Democrats won back
many of the defectors by stressing the need for free silver, economical
government, and regulation of railroads. With its weaker party structure,
the People's party could do little to stem the tide of voters returning to the
Democratic fold. In 1895 many voters noted that the Populist and Democratic platforms were quite similar; the Populists had strength in some
counties, but the Democrats controlled the state government, the Congress, and the White House. Democrats controlled immense patronage
and the bulk of the state press. Many former Populists decided to return to
the stronger party once the Democrats were clearly supporting the Populists' goals.

All of these many obstacles sapped the voting strength of Mississippi's
opposition parties. They were also hurt by the shrinking of the state's
electorate. Republicans, Independents, and Greenbackers benefited from
black voting; these groups could not win statewide elections when the
black vote declined sharply between 1876 and 1880, and again after 1890.
Stronger party organizations could have aimed to lessen this decline, but
after 1875 the opposition parties' organizations were never strong enough
to sustain any serious challenge to the Democrats except at the county and

district level. Populists suffered similarly from the smaller electorate, specifically the smaller number of white yeomen farmers remaining on the registration books after 1892.

In 1890 a constitutional convention met and among other things revised the requirements for voter registration. Political historian J. Morgan Kousser has identified partisanship as a chief motive of the disfranchisers in Mississippi and elsewhere. According to Kousser, Democrats tended to work for disfranchisement, while Republicans, Independents, and members of third parties opposed it. Yet it is striking how passive the small corps of Republicans and Independents was in the disfranchisement of 1890. The Republican party was singularly inactive in the delegate elections, offering slates to oppose the Democrats in only a handful of counties.

In the convention, white Republican Horatio F. Simrall was among the most eager to secure a successful disfranchisement, while his party colleague James Lusk Alcorn enthusiastically contributed his ideas for reducing blacks' influence in politics. Black Republican Isaiah T. Montgomery, dramatically announced his support for the disfranchising section. The votes of all three men were dictated, not by party, but by the region they represented. Like other Delta members, the three Republicans supported disfranchisement and voted to protect the black county majority in the legislature. Of the opposition members, only Greenbacker John E. Gore of Webster County bitterly opposed the suffrage section and final passage of the constitution itself. The three Republicans, as well as the three other delegates who won election by defeating Democratic nominees, all voted to approve the constitution.

In 1890, the chief political division in Mississippi pitted agrarian Democrats from white counties against more conservative leaders from the Delta and from other black-majority counties. Undoubtedly a majority of white voters favored the former group, yet in the convention the agrarians could muster only thirty-six votes for the popular elective judiciary proposal. The problem for white agrarian leaders was that representation in the convention had generally the same apportionment as did the state house of representatives, where a majority of the seats were controlled by the more conservative black counties. An additional fourteen seats in the constitutional convention were elected from the state at large; only five of these delegates were from white counties. Thus, despite the popularity of agrarian politics among many white voters, the agrarian bloc in the con-

vention was never strong enough to make its influence felt. Some agrarian delegates floated voter registration proposals that they believed would result in little white disfranchisement, but they were never able to secure a sizeable number of votes to back them.

In his influential *Southern Politics in State and Nation*, V. O. Key pointed to a Southwide movement toward disfranchisement during the years from 1890 to 1908 that he called the legalization of a fait accompli. Using Texas as an example, Key pointed out that widespread black disfranchisement, suppression of Populism, and a vast dropping off of the electorate as a whole, all *preceded* passage of the state's disfranchising law. In Mississippi, however, the massive reduction of the black electorate did not occur until after 1890. The overwhelmingly black state Republican party won 26 percent of the vote for its presidential candidate two years before passage of the constitution, while it won less than 3 percent just after passage. James Hill, a black Republican congressional candidate, won 4,614 votes (or 28 percent of the total) in 1888; another black Republican running in the same district in 1892 won only 194 votes. Nor did the *white* electorate shrink prior to passage of the new constitution; in fact, it grew somewhat between 1880 and 1888. Populism had not been crushed prior to passage of Mississippi's new constitution; in fact, it had not yet appeared.

J. Morgan Kousser is undoubtedly correct in his assertion that Key's fait accompli thesis is useful only in a limited way. In Mississippi, the weakening of the Greenback, Republican, and Independent movements toward the end of the 1880s did facilitate the overwhelming Democratic control of the constitutional convention. Certainly if the Greenbackers had not fallen apart in the 1880s, and if the Republicans had been still active enough to nominate and elect delegates interested in universal suffrage, the opposition groups could have joined with certain dissident Democrats from the white counties to oppose the poll tax and literacy tests. It is not true, however, that the constitution of 1890 simply formalized an already existing situation. Immediately after passage of the constitution, black voter registration plummeted (dropping 70 percent in a four year period), while white voter participation also fell. The Populist party soon found itself hamstrung by the reduction in the white electorate, while it also faced a number of other serious obstacles to winning large numbers of offices in the state. As Kousser explained, "By lopping off the lower economic strata," white as well as black, the constitutional convention delegates created a "fairly homogenous polity—white, middle-class, and

Democratic." Protest parties like the Populists depended on struggling farmers, who faced deep indebtedness and the possibility of perpetual tenancy, for their base of mass support. Yet because of the constitution of 1890, far fewer of the struggling small farmers still voted.[32]

Soon the Jackson *Clarion-Ledger* was joking that any black Mississippian could vote, "provided he has sense enough to 'read or understand the Constitution,' translate Hebrew, parse a little Greek or Latin, square a circle and solve a few other mathematical problems." Yet it was not only black voters who were disfranchised, and it was not the literacy and understanding tests that were most effective in disfranchising voters. The requirement that voters pay a poll tax for two years in succession (at least four dollars) caused many voters to let their registration lapse in Mississippi's cash-poor economy. An initially strong People's party organization helped register so many voters that the number of voters actually rose between 1892 and 1896, especially in the party's stronger counties. But public support for the Populist organization waned as it proved itself unable to win elections, as it endorsed the Democratic presidential candidate in 1896, and as the Democratic platforms became increasingly Populist in tone.[33]

The state of Mississippi was going through a period of great change between 1877 and 1902. In 1870, the state had only two towns that could boast populations above 5,000, and only three more were home to more than 2,500 persons. Meridian was officially classed as a village, with 2,700 residents, while less than 1,000 citizens lived at Biloxi. By the turn of the century Meridian was the largest city in the state, with a population of 14,050. The number of towns above 2,500 residents had grown from five in 1870 to twenty-two in 1900. Still, "urbanizing" would be too strong a word to apply to Mississippi. In 1900 no city in the state had yet reached a population of 15,000.[34]

In agriculture, the number of acres in cultivation had grown from 4.2 million in 1870 to 7.6 million in 1900. The size of the cotton crop more than doubled in this thirty-year period, and the size of the corn crop did too. By 1900 state farmers were raising ever larger amounts of vegetables for city markets, and orchard fruits as well. The number of farmers raising cattle for commercial sale went up each year, also. Lumbering on a large scale was beginning in the piney woods in the southern part of the state. Manufacturing was increasing as well, as the number of persons employed

in manufacturing rose from 6,000 in 1870 to 26,500 in 1900. Compared with the other states of the union, however, Mississippi was still an overwhelmingly agricultural state, and cotton was still the paramount crop.[35]

In agriculture, arguably the worst news involved farmers' continuing problems with indebtedness. While writers and speakers for the Grange, the Farmers' Alliance, and the People's party all stressed the need for growing some subsistence crops, and avoiding indebtedness, farmers' debts continued to mount. Economists Roger L. Ransom and Richard Sutch have described southern merchants' "lock-in" system. Under this scheme, merchants insisted that farmers grow cotton, not only because cotton best secured a loan, but because it kept farmers buying foodstuffs on credit. It was almost impossible for an indebted farmer to break out of the cycle of indebtedness, since even if he paid his debt at the end of the year, effectively breaking even, he still would not have the food or the funds to see his family through the coming year. A new year of indebtedness for purchased food and supplies would be unavoidable.[36]

So farmers remained in debt, and over the years a number of them lost their farms to their creditors. The story is told well by U.S. government statistics reporting the number of farms that were operated by their owners (rather than by sharecroppers or cash renters). The decline over two decades was precipitous. In 1880, 56 percent of farms were operated by the owner; in 1900 the comparable number was only 38 percent. The Populist party showed its greatest strength in counties where a majority of farms were farmed by the owners. It did poorly in areas with large numbers of renters, yet the trend in Mississippi was toward more and more sharecroppers and cash tenants. No great political uprising of sharecroppers or tenants was likely, because these farmers did not pay the poll tax and were no longer a part of the state's political system.[37]

By the time of the 1900 presidential election, only an estimated 16.9 percent of Mississippi's adult males were participating in elections. This compared with 91.5 percent in Ohio, 70.2 percent in North Carolina, and 73.2 percent nationwide. Mississippi was not forever doomed to absurdly low voter participation, however. In 1902, agrarian Democrats in the legislature secured passage of a primary election bill. The law stipulated that each party hold a primary election for county and state offices. The Democratic party chose to limit participation in its primary to whites only. This then, became another tool for black disfranchisement. If a black voter passed the literacy test, paid the poll tax, and braved white community disapproval, it still made little difference because he could vote only in

the general election, when typically only one name for each office, the name of a Democrat, would be on the ballot.[38]

The primary system also hurt the weak opposition parties, because by 1902 it was generally conceded that only Democrats were likely to win elections in Mississippi. If one were to join the remnant Populists, the ragtag Republicans, or the emerging Socialists, one would have to give up the most exciting elections, the Democratic primaries. On the other hand, voter participation rates did begin to rise in these primary elections. In the closely contested 1911 primary for U.S. senator, for example, estimated turnout was over 70 percent of eligible whites. This was slightly above the national average for voter participation in general elections. So large numbers of farmers did begin to vote again.[39]

On the other hand, the new primary system did not usher in a golden era of democratic, as well as Democratic, politics. Charges of dishonest counting, the purchase of votes, use of liquor and bribes, even candidates' improper use of black voters, were all freely made after Democratic primaries. Many Democrats complained that under the primary system, only wealthy individuals could run for office, since a statewide race could cost more than twenty thousand dollars. Under the old system, a poorer candidate could convince a Democratic convention of his merits, then use party funds for the general election. Under the old system, skills of diplomacy, cooperation, and compromise were important in winning the nomination at a convention. In the primary system, candidates won the nomination by appealing to the masses. While former Populists applauded the new mass techniques, other Mississippians warned that the primary system would lead to the emergence of demagogues who would rise to power by their inflammatory rhetoric.[40]

The earliest victor in the new primary system was James K. Vardaman, a lawyer and newspaper editor and former speaker of the state house of representatives. Vardaman was considered an agrarian, and he won the warm support of Populists such as Frank Burkitt. Vardaman borrowed a page from the campaign histories of the 1870s and 1880s and used racist appeals to white solidarity to whip up voters' interest. Now, however, the racial invective was used against his Democratic opponents rather than Republicans, Independents, and third-party supporters. In one speech Vardaman denounced other Democrats for allegedly allowing black schools to receive large amounts of funding, saying that the Negro was "a lazy, lying, lustful animal which no conceivable amount of training can transform into a tolerable citizen." Some Democrats countered that Varda-

man's words were unfair to those black citizens who were honorable; Vardaman admitted that this might be true. Nevertheless, "the good are few, the bad are many, and it is impossible to tell what ones are . . . dangerous to the honor of the dominant race until the damage is done."[41]

The histories of Mississippi agrarianism have typically ended on a cheerful note, arguing that while the Greenback and Populist parties went down to defeat, the agrarians still got what they wanted when they elected men like James K. Vardaman to office. It is true that Vardaman worked for the regulation of banks, railroads, and utilities; he also pushed for the final end to convict leasing. The state was left, however, far out of the national mainstream. On a host of statistical measures, Mississippi was among the very highest—or lowest—states on the list. Mississippi had the largest percentage of the population living on farms, and the largest black majority. Ominously, the state had the lowest per capita income in the nation. Compared with other states, Mississippi had very few factories and very few towns of any size.[42]

Politically, Mississippi almost became an island unto itself. The 1908 presidential election, for example, excited great interest nationwide. The flamboyant President Theodore Roosevelt stumped hard for his hand-picked successor William Howard Taft, while farmers again got a chance to vote for their idol, William Jennings Bryan. Also adding interest was the participation of the Socialist party, which was expected to win at least half a million votes. Nationwide, an estimated 65 percent of the eligible voters turned out. In Mississippi, only 16.5 percent of eligible persons registered and voted; this was the lowest voter participation in the nation. Even if we factor out the black citizens who were theoretically eligible to register, the *white* voter turnout in Mississippi was only an estimated 37.8 percent. This was still far below the national average, and well below the average for other southern states. While it is true that Mississippi's voter turnout could be quite respectable in Democratic primaries, the state's lack of interest in presidential races helped lead to its political isolation.[43]

In the first half of the twentieth century, many observers believed that the federal government, and even the Democratic party, tended to ignore Deep South states like Mississippi. The reason was that these states were seen as "in the bag" for the Democrats. It wasn't necessary to give Mississippi federal funds for internal improvements or to appoint Mississippi politicians to cabinet or Supreme Court positions; the Magnolia State was safe for the Democratic party, no matter what. On the other hand, national leaders of both parties actively courted states like Ohio, which featured

huge voter turnout and razor-thin margins; these states were first in line to receive federal largess.

In the early twentieth century, a hardy band of dissidents continued to agitate for reforms through the agency of the Mississippi Socialist party. The Socialists regularly ran gubernatorial, congressional, and local candidates—and were the only opposition party to do so regularly. Their state platforms supported woman suffrage, city-owned utilities, a general old age pension, free textbooks, and an end to child labor. While at least two Socialists won election—one to the Forrest County Board of Supervisors and the other to Biloxi's City Council—the party won few votes statewide and offered no credible threat to the state Democratic party.[44]

The Greenback, Independent, Populist, and Socialist movements did not offer any long-term solution to Mississippi's problems. Given the nationwide two-party system, what Mississippi needed was an active Republican party, so that the state would have influence in Washington when the Republicans were in power, and so that both national parties would actively court the state with attention and favors. Four things would have to happen, however, before the Republicans could experience a revival. First, the party would have to wait until white voters' memories of Reconstruction had dimmed. This would take an amazingly long time, as lore was passed down from generation to generation. Even as late as the 1960s, Democrats cited Reconstruction as a reason for the state's voters to shun the Republican party.[45]

To help erase the stigma of Reconstruction, the Mississippi Republican party would have to be led entirely by white citizens. Any appearance of black influence within the party would only strengthen Democratic assertions that the GOP was the party of black domination. With few black voters in the state, white Republicans believed it made sense for the party to concentrate on winning mass white support. Black Republicans countered that the party of Lincoln was not going to carry Mississippi anyway, and that as longtime, loyal supporters, they should occupy many of the chief leadership positions. Not until 1960 would white Mississippians be fully in control of the Republican party.[46]

Two other things could facilitate the growth of the Mississippi Republicans. One would be an influx of citizens from outside the state. As increasing numbers of northerners began to arrive in the first decades of the twentieth century, interest in the Republican party began to increase, and the party actually began to carry some precincts, if not counties. Such an influx would have helped the GOP in the late nineteenth century as well,

but such was not to be. In 1870, 68 percent of Mississippians were native to the state. By 1900, this figure had increased to more than 94 percent. With the memories and folklore of Reconstruction lingering, and with few new state residents, the Republican party would find growth very difficult.[47]

Finally, the Mississippi Republican party was strongest in urban areas. The last strongholds of the Republican party were the city councils of Jackson and Vicksburg. After 1890, what votes the GOP did receive came in the cities; few farmers in the rural beats showed much interest in Republican voting. In the first half of the twentieth century, the GOP would be strongest (although not really strong) in Vicksburg, Laurel, Biloxi, Natchez, and Greenville. Once again, though, Mississippi Republicans would have to play a waiting game. With only three cities topping ten thousand inhabitants in 1900, and none boasting fifteen thousand, any largely urban political movement was doomed to failure.

Emotional issues such as prohibition and anti-Catholicism could lead Mississippi counties to temporarily lay aside their devotion to the Democracy and vote Republican. This happened in 1928, when Republican Herbert Hoover carried three counties as he opposed the Catholic candidate Al Smith, who was a "wet." By 1964 all the pieces were in place for a Republican victory. Reconstruction was nearly a century in the past; a large influx of persons born out of state had occurred; white Republicans had full control of the party, and Mississippi was increasingly urban. Add a galvanizing issue—integration—and you have the ingredients for a Republican victory. In 1964, for the first time since 1872, Mississippi voted for the Republican presidential candidate. Also, for the first time since 1882, the state elected a non-Democrat to Congress—Republican poultry farmer Prentiss Walker. Ironically, by 1964 the national Republican party had stood its earlier platform on its head. The party now denounced the new civil rights laws and called loudly for a less active federal government. Yet to Mississippi Republican leaders, the 1964 victories seemed like a miracle, after the decades of waiting.

The non-Democrats of the 1870s, 1880s, and 1890s believed *they* had achieved some near-miraculous victories. They had managed to elect three candidates to Congress and had controlled opposition blocs of fifteen to twenty-seven seats in several legislatures. In other instances, such as the 1881 gubernatorial race, they lost the election, with fraud playing a decisive role. For twenty-five years these groups kept a voice of opposition alive by publishing newspapers, providing speakers, and running candi-

dates. In some cases they voiced minority opinions, as the Republicans, for example, advocated a high tariff and a single gold standard. In other cases, agrarian opposition movements pushed hard for ideas that proved to be popular, including railroad regulation, prohibition, an elective judiciary, repeal of the crop lien law, and abolition of convict labor. By presenting a threat, these opposition parties forced the Democrats to move in a more agrarian direction, and these opposition goals were finally enacted into law. One goal that was never achieved, however, was the establishment of a free and fair two-party system. For that, the state of Mississippi would have to wait many decades.

Notes

1. INTRODUCTION

1. *Congressional Quarterly's Guide to U.S. Elections*, 2nd ed. (Washington, D.C., 1985), 325–61, 511, 703–1054. South Carolina was by most measures the second most Democratic state.

2. W. Dean Burnham, *Presidential Ballots: 1836–1892* (Baltimore, 1955), 434–59, 552–71.

3. *Congressional Quarterly's Guide*, 333–53, 531–32.

4. Albert D. Kirwan, *Revolt of the Rednecks: Mississippi Politics, 1876–1925* (Lexington, Ky., 1951), 122–29; *Congressional Quarterly's Guide*, 849.

5. Monticello *Lawrence County Press*, October 20, 1898 (quotations). For another description of the typical candidate, see Jackson *Clarion-Ledger*, November 10, 1898.

6. J. W. Harden, "Local or Webster County Politics," in *History of Webster County, Mississippi* (n.p., 1985), 22.

7. U.S. Bureau of the Census, *A Compendium of the Ninth Census, June 1, 1870* (Washington, D.C., 1872), 236–40.

8. Lacy K. Ford, "Rednecks and Merchants: Economic Development and Social Tensions in the South Carolina Upcountry, 1865–1900," *Journal of American History* 71 (1984): 294–318; Roger L. Ransom and Richard Sutch, *One Kind of Freedom: The Economic Consequences of Emancipation* (Cambridge, 1977).

9. Michael R. Hyman, *The Anti-Redeemers: Hill Country Political Dissenters in the Lower South from Redemption to Populism* (Baton Rouge, La., 1990); Gavin Wright, *Old South, New South: Revolutions in the Southern Economy Since the Civil War* (New York, 1986); Ford, "Rednecks and Merchants," 294–318.

10. Wright, *Old South, New South*; Ransom and Sutch, *One Kind of Freedom*; Thomas D. Clark, "The Furnishing and Supply System in Southern Agriculture Since 1865," *Journal of Southern History* 12 (1946): 24–44.

11. James S. Ferguson, "Agrarianism in Mississippi, 1871–1900: A Study in Nonconformity," (Ph.D. dissertation, University of North Carolina at Chapel Hill, 1952); James G. Revels, "Redeemers, Rednecks, and Racial Integrity," in Richard Aubrey McLemore, ed., *A History of Mississippi*, 2 vols. (Jackson, Miss., 1973), 1: 590–621.

12. The stories of Matt Brown and several other farmers are covered in some detail in Clark, "The Furnishing and Supply System," 39–43.

13. Ferguson, "Agrarianism in Mississippi," 42.

14. Wright, *Old South, New South*, 3–50 (quotation at 12).

15. Kirwan, *Revolt of the Rednecks*, 46–48, 180–87; Ferguson, "Agrarianism in Mississippi," 607–20. Some genuine success with railroad regulation came years *after* agrarians had secured passage of the 1884 regulation law.

16. Willie D. Halsell, "The Bourbon Period in Mississippi Politics, 1875–1890," *Journal of Southern History* 11 (1945): 530–31. Halsell concluded that Mississippi farmers were "neither ignored nor overridden" between 1875 and 1890, since they were supported by one of two governors, one of three U.S. senators, seven of seventeen congressmen, and a majority of members of the state house of representatives. Yet considering the huge percentage of farmers in the general population, Halsell's figures really seem to support the idea that farmers were badly underrepresented in government.

17. *Journal of the House of Representatives of the State of Mississippi* (imprint varies; 1878–1900) and *Journal of the Senate of the State of Mississippi* (imprint varies; 1878–1900); roster bound at the back of each volume. If one rejects as farmers those who listed farming as the second of their two occupations, the legislative majority for 1892 vanishes, while the 1890 legislature is perfectly balanced between farmers and non-farmers.

18. On black involvement in politics, see Neil R. McMillen, *Dark Journey: Black Mississippians in the Age of Jim Crow* (Urbana, Ill., 1989), 36–60; Vernon Lane Wharton, *The Negro in Mississippi, 1865–1890* (Chapel Hill, N.C., 1947), 157–215. On white involvement in the state GOP, see Warren A. Ellem, "Who Were the Mississippi Scalawags?" *Journal of Southern History* 38 (1972): 217–40.

19. William C. Harris, *The Day of the Carpetbagger: Republican Reconstruction in Mississippi* (Baton Rouge, La., 1979); David G. Sansing, "Congressional Reconstruction," in Richard Aubrey McLemore, ed., *A History of Mississippi*, 2 vols. (Jackson, Miss., 1973), 1: 571–89. See also John R. Lynch, *The Facts of Reconstruction* (1913; reprint, New York, 1969).

20. Sansing, "Congressional Reconstruction," 585–89 (quotation at 586); Harris, *The Day of the Carpetbagger*, 650–90.

21. Stephen Cresswell, *Mormons and Cowboys, Moonshiners and Klansmen: Federal Law Enforcement in the South and West* (Tuscaloosa, Ala., 1991), 29–32; Sansing, "Congressional Reconstruction," 587 (quotations); Harris, *The Day of the Carpetbagger*, 650–90.

22. *Congressional Quarterly's Guide*, 789; Sansing, "Congressional Reconstruction," 588–89; Harris, *The Day of the Carpetbagger*, 691–712.

23. Billy Burton Hathorn, "Challenging the Status Quo: Rubel Lex Phillips and the Mississippi Republican Party, 1963–1967," *Journal of Mississippi Histo-*

ry 47 (1985): 240–64; Sansing, "Congressional Reconstruction," 576–77; Eric Foner, *Reconstruction: America's Unfinished Revolution, 1863–1877* (New York, 1988), 346–92.

24. Harris, *The Day of the Carpetbagger,* 295–325; Sansing, "Congressional Reconstruction," 581–89.

25. U.S. Bureau of the Census, *Abstract of the Twelfth Census of the United States, 1900* (Washington, D.C., 1902), 75.

26. Howard N. Rabinowitz, ed., *Southern Black Leaders of the Reconstruction Era* (Urbana, Ill., 1982). Despite the lack of a gubernatorial candidate to oppose Democrat John M. Stone, more than one thousand write-in votes were cast for various candidates, especially former governor Albert Gallatin Brown, who won about one third of the votes in Copiah County. Brown seemed to be flirting with the early Greenback movement, which was still highly amorphous in the state. See 1877 gubernatorial election returns, Old Election Returns Book (hereinafter cited as OER), Mississippi Secretary of State Papers (hereinafter MSSP), Record Group 28, Department of Archives and History, Jackson (hereinafter DA&H).

27. W. W. Graham to Governor John M. Stone, November 15, 1877 (quotations), Official Papers of the Governor, Record Group 27, DA&H.

28. James E. Boyle, *Cotton and the New Orleans Cotton Exchange: A Century of Commercial Evolution* (Garden City, N.Y., 1934), 181; *Crystal Springs Monitor,* October 4 and 18, 1877; *Jackson Weekly Clarion,* October 24 (quotation) and 31, 1877.

29. *Jackson Weekly Clarion,* October 24 (quotations), and November 14, 1877.

30. Ferguson, "Agrarianism in Mississippi," 401.

31. Kirwan, *Revolt of the Rednecks,* 18–26; 93–102 (quotation at 18).

32. Halsell, "The Bourbon Period in Mississippi Politics," 519–37; idem, "Democratic Dissensions in Mississippi, 1878–1882," *Journal of Mississippi History* 2 (1940): 123–35; idem, "James R. Chalmers and 'Mahoneism' in Mississippi," *Journal of Southern History* 10 (1944): 37–58; idem, ed., "Republican Factionalism in Mississippi, 1882–1884," *Journal of Southern History* 7 (1941): 84–101.

33. Hyman, *The Anti-Redeemers.* Hyman's ten counties in Mississippi are contiguous, white-majority counties in the northeast hills: Alcorn, Calhoun, Itawamba, Lee, Pontotoc, Prentiss, Sumner, Tippah, Tishomingo, and Union.

34. Hyman, *The Anti-Redeemers,* 7, 11, 16, 20–22, 199–201.

35. V. O. Key, with the assistance of Alexander Heard, *Southern Politics in State and Nation* (New York, 1949), 531–643; see also pages 229–53.

36. J. Morgan Kousser, *The Shaping of Southern Politics: Suffrage Restriction and the Establishment of the One-Party South, 1880–1910* (New Haven, Conn., 1974).

2. BIRTH OF THE GREENBACK PARTY

1. *Jackson Weekly Clarion*, September 18 and October 16, 1878; John H. Ellis, *Yellow Fever and Public Health in the New South* (Lexington, Ky., 1992), 14–59; Marshall Legan, "Mississippi and the Yellow Fever Epidemics of 1878–1879," *Journal of Mississippi History* 33 (1971): 199–217.

2. *Crystal Springs Monitor*, January 2, 1879; Jackson *Weekly Clarion*, September 18 and October 9, 1878; U.S. Bureau of the Census, *Statistics of the Population of the United States at the Tenth Census* (Washington, D.C., 1883), 235; *Appleton's Annual Cyclopaedia and Register of Important Events of the Year 1878* (New York, 1879). Grenada's population was 1,914; Vicksburg's was 11,814.

3. Nathan Fine, *Labor and Farmer Parties in the United States: 1828–1928* (New York, 1928), 56–63; Michael R. Hyman, "Taxation, Public Policy, and Political Dissent: Yeoman Dissatisfaction in the Post-Reconstruction Lower South," *Journal of Southern History* 40 (1989): 49–76; Ferguson, "Agrarianism in Mississippi," 20–28, 397–405.

4. Hyman, "Taxation," 49–76; U.S. Bureau of the Census, *Report on Valuation, Taxation, and Public Indebtedness in the United States, as Returned at the Tenth Census* (Washington, D.C., 1884), 135–37.

5. Jackson *Weekly Clarion*, July 31, 1878 (first quotation); Hernando *DeSoto Press and Times*, August 29, 1878 (second quotation).

6. *Holmes County Times*, quoted in *Batesville Blade*, September 17, 1880 (first two quotations); *Aberdeen Examiner*, quoted in Jackson *Weekly Clarion*, August 28, 1878, (third quotation).

7. Jackson *Weekly Clarion*, August 7, 1878 (first quotation), October 16, 1878 (second quotation), and October 28, 1878. On West, see *New York Times*, June 16, 1884. On Wright, see *Biographical Directory of the American Congress, 1774–1971* (Washington, D.C., 1971), 1959.

8. Fine, *Labor and Farmer Parties*, 56–67; Margaret Buker Jay, "The Greenback Road: A Political History of the Greenback Party in Maine," (M.A. thesis, University of Virginia, 1977); Ralph R. Ricker, "The Greenback-Labor Movement in Pennsylvania," (Ph.D. dissertation, Pennsylvania State University, 1955); R. M. Doolen, "The Greenback Party in the Great Lakes Middlewest," (Ph.D. dissertation, University of Michigan, 1969); Paul Kleppner, "The Greenback and Prohibition Parties," in Arthur M. Schlesinger, Jr., ed., *History of U.S. Political Parties*, 4 vols. (New York, 1973), 2: 1549–81; Roscoe E. Martin, "The Greenback Party in Texas," *Southwestern Historical Quarterly* 30 (1927): 161–77.

9. *Congressional Quarterly's Guide*, 794–97.

10. Ferguson, "Agrarianism in Mississippi," 401–2; Jackson *Weekly Clarion*, November 14, 1877; *New York Times*, November 21, 1877.

11. Hazlehurst *Weekly Copiahan*, October 4 and November 8, 1879; *Congressional Quarterly's Guide*, 759. For the senate directory, see Jackson *Weekly Clarion*, special supplement, March 10, 1880. Mississippi Whigs maintained their organization longer than Whigs in any other southern state.

12. *Biographical and Historical Memoirs of Mississippi*, 2 vols. (Chicago, 1891), 2: 822–27, 828 (first quotation); *Yalobusha Standard*, quoted in Jackson *Weekly Clarion*, January 14, 1880; Jackson *Weekly Clarion*, special supplement, March 10, 1880 (second quotation).

13. U.S. Congress, Senate, "Mississippi in 1878," S. rep. 855, vol. 2, pt. 1 (45th Cong., 3rd sess.), 733 (quotation).

14. Jackson *Weekly Clarion*, September 17, 1879.

15. "Mississippi in 1878," 729 (quotation); Hyman, *The Anti-Redeemers*, 22. Tate County had only a small black majority in 1880; its black population later rose markedly relative to the white population.

16. Martin, "The Greenback Party in Texas," 162.

17. For lists of state and county Grange officers, see Columbus *Patron of Husbandry*, November 15, 1879, and November 19, 1881. Columbus *Patron of Husbandry*, September 20, 1879 (quotations).

18. Columbus *Patron of Husbandry*, September 13, 1879 (quotations).

19. Jackson *Weekly Independent*, August 29, 1879 (quotation), and August 28, 1878; *Brookhaven Ledger*, September 26, 1878.

20. Jackson *Weekly Independent*, August 28, 1878 (quotation), and August 29, 1879; *Brookhaven Ledger*, September 26, 1878.

21. *Batesville Blade*, August 27, 1880; Jackson *Weekly Independent*, August 29, 1879; *Brookhaven Ledger*, September 26, 1878; Jackson *Weekly Clarion*, August 28, 1878.

22. "Mississippi in 1878," 699–700; *Biographical Directory of the American Congress*, 835; Stewart Sifakis, *Who Was Who in the Civil War* (New York, 1988), 173.

23. "Mississippi in 1878," 699–700; Jackson *Weekly Clarion*, August 28, 1878 (quotation).

24. *Brookhaven Ledger*, September 26, 1878 (first quotation); *New York Times*, February 13, 1879; "Mississippi in 1878," 700 (middle quotations), 702 (fifth quotation), 703.

25. "Mississippi in 1878," 703–5; OER.

26. "Mississippi in 1878," 705 (quotations).

27. "Mississippi in 1878," 719–26.

28. Jackson *Weekly Clarion*, October 23 and November 13, 1878; 1878 congressional returns, OER; Hernando *DeSoto Press and Times*, August 22 and November 21, 1878; *Ashland Register*, October 2, 1879.

29. Dunbar Rowland, *History of Mississippi: Heart of the South*, 2 vols. (Chicago, 1925), 2: 217.

30. Jackson *Weekly Independent*, August 29, 1879.

31. Jackson *Weekly Clarion*, October 22, 1879 (quotations). A recording that includes good examples of fife and drum music is *Afro-American Folk Music from Tate and Panola County, Mississippi*, edited by David Evans (Washington, D.C.: Library of Congress, n.d. [1974?]).

32. *Jackson Comet*, November 15, 1879; *Raymond Gazette*, quoted in Jackson *Weekly Clarion*, October 29, 1879.

33. Jackson *Weekly Clarion*, October 29, 1879 (quotations).

34. *Brookhaven Ledger*, November 6, 1879; Jackson *Weekly Clarion*, December 3, 1879; *Jackson Comet*, November 15, 1879.

35. *Ashland Register*, September 11, October 2, 16, and 23, and November 6, 1879.

36. *Ashland Register*, October 30 and November 6, 1879; *Daily Memphis Avalanche*, October 31, 1879; Jackson *Weekly Clarion*, October 29, 1879 (quotation).

37. *Ashland Register*, October 30 and November 6, 1879; *Daily Memphis Avalanche*, October 31, 1879.

38. Sardis *Weekly Panola Star*, quoted in Jackson *Weekly Clarion*, September 17, 1879; Jackson *Weekly Clarion*, October 22, 1879 (quotation); *New York Times*, November 6, 1879. In Panola County, Greenbackers came to control the town government of Batesville, but not Sardis.

39. "Independent" tickets formed the chief opposition in several counties, including Madison, Copiah, and Yazoo. In Yazoo County the contest was marred by murder and by at least one forced resignation from the Independent ticket, and the Independents lost all races there. In Copiah County they won the two legislative seats. Hazlehurst *Weekly Copiahan*, October 4, 1879; Jackson *Weekly Clarion*, August 27 and October 29, 1879; *Appleton's Annual Cyclopaedia . . . 1879*, 638.

40. *New York Times*, November 21, 1877 and November 3, 1879. Some estimates put the number of Republican and Independent members at thirteen rather than eleven; the difference probably results from counting some of the black Democrats as Republicans.

41. *Appleton's Annual Cyclopaedia . . . 1880*, 527; Jackson *Weekly Clarion*, December 24, 1879 and January 28, 1880.

42. *Journal of the House . . . 1880*, 351, 397–98, 540; *Appleton's Annual Cyclopaedia . . . 1880*, 527–28; Jackson *Weekly Clarion*, February 25, 1880.

43. *Journal of the House . . . 1880* 284, 309, 344–45, 485, 493–501, 538; Jackson *Weekly Clarion*, January 14, February 11, 18, 25, and March 10, 1880.

44. *Journal of the House . . . 1880*, 485, 573, 578; *Appleton's Annual Cyclopaedia . . . 1880*, 527–28; Jackson *Weekly Clarion*, January 14, February 11, 18, 25, and March 10, 1880; Rowland, *History of Mississippi*, 2: 219.

45. Lee F. Anderson, Meredith W. Watts and Allen Wilcox, *Legislative Roll-Call Analysis* (Evanston, Ill., 1966). I have not calculated the index of relative cohesion for the six Republican legislators, because on some three quarters of the reported roll calls their absentee rate was 50 percent or higher, and this could easily lead to deceptive figures. I have not calculated indexes of relative cohesion for the senate, since only the Democrats had a respectable number of members in that body.

46. Legislative roster, Jackson *Weekly Clarion*, special supplement, March 10, 1880.

47. Ibid.; where legislators listed two occupations, I have taken the first listed. Columbus *Patron of Husbandry*, November 29, 1879 (first quotations), September 20, 1879 (third quotation), and October 15, 1881 (fourth quotation); *Ashland Register*, October 9 (fifth quotation), and November 6, 1879.

48. *Ashland Register*, November 6, 1879; Tenth Census of the United States, 1880, returns for Benton County, Records of the Bureau of the Census, Record Group 29, National Archives.

49. Benton County Personal Property Tax Rolls for 1879, Auditor of Public Accounts Records, Record Group 29, Microfilm 43, DA&H. The sample of citizens was made by taking the first and fifth names on each page. Arrangement of the tax rolls was by precinct, then alphabetically by name.

50. Benton County Personal Property Tax Rolls for 1877 and 1879, DA&H. The scarcity of extant tax rolls from this era makes a larger sample (including other counties) impossible.

51. "Mississippi in 1878," 721 (quotation); *Brookhaven Ledger*, November 14, 1878; Jackson *Weekly Clarion*, November 27, 1878; 1878 congressional returns, OER.

52. *New York Times*, November 6, 1879; Wharton, *The Negro in Mississippi*, 201–5; *Daily Memphis Avalanche*, November 12, 1879; 1879 district attorney returns, OER.

53. *Biographical Directory of the American Congress*, 1318; John R. Lynch, *Reminiscences of an Active Life: the Autobiography of John Roy Lynch*, edited by John Hope Franklin (Chicago, 1970).

54. Lynch, *Reminiscences*, 224 (quotation), also 219–24.

55. Lynch, *Reminiscences*, 227–28.

56. Lynch, *Reminiscences*, 232–33.

57. 1880 congressional returns, OER; Jackson *Weekly Clarion*, November 18, 1880; Lynch, *Reminiscences*, 233–34; *Appleton's Annual Cyclopaedia . . . 1880*, 528 (quotation); *Vicksburg Daily Herald*, November 16, 1880.

58. Jackson *Weekly Clarion*, November 18, 1880; 1880 congressional returns, OER.

59. *Batesville Blade*, September 17, 1880, and October 15, 1880 (quotation); *Ashland Register*, November 4, 1880; Jackson *Weekly Clarion*, November 18, 1880; 1880 congressional returns, OER; U.S. Congress, House, "Buchanan vs. Manning," H. Misc. Doc. 14 (47th Cong., 1st sess.).

60. *Macon Beacon*, October 30, 1880 (quotation); Jackson *Weekly Clarion*, November 18, 1880; 1880 congressional returns, OER.

61. *Brookhaven Ledger*, October 14, 1880 (quotations); Jackson *Weekly Clarion*, November 18, 1880; 1880 congressional returns, OER; *Congressional Quarterly's Guide*, 794–801.

62. *Batesville Blade*, August 20 (quotation), and October 15, 1880.

63. *Batesville Blade*, October 8 and 15, 1880; Jackson *Weekly Clarion*, October 13, 1880; Fine, *Labor and Farmer Parties*, 71; 1880 presidential returns, OER; Burnham, *Presidential Ballots*, 552–71; *Congressional Quarterly's Guide*, 340; Ferguson, "Agrarianism in Mississippi," 406 (quotation).

64. *Lexington Advertiser*, May 27, 1880; Jackson *Weekly Clarion*, October 22 and November 26, 1879; *Grenada Sentinel*, quoted in *Lexington Advertiser*, January 15, 1880 (quotations). The *Daily Memphis Avalanche*, November 11, 1879, reported that Greenbackers in Yalobusha won all offices except chancery and circuit clerks.

65. *Batesville Blade*, August 6, 1880.

66. *Batesville Blade*, September 10, 1880.

67. *Batesville Blade*, August 27, 1880; *Crystal Springs Monitor*, August 26, 1880; Clark Leonard Miller, "'Let Us Die to Make Men Free': Political Terrorism in Post-Reconstruction Mississippi, 1877–1896," (Ph.D. dissertation, University of Minnesota, 1983).

68. *Batesville Blade*, August 27, 1880; *Crystal Springs Monitor*, August 26, 1880.

69. *Journal of the House . . . 1880*, 89; *Lexington Advertiser*, September 25, 1879, and January 15 and October 22, 1880; *Jackson Comet*, November 15, 1879; Greenwood *Yazoo Valley Flag*, November 13, 1879; *Daily Memphis Avalanche*, November 11, 1879; Jackson *Weekly Clarion*, January 14, 1880.

70. *Lexington Advertiser*, June 24 and August 26, 1880.

71. *Lexington Advertiser*, October 22, 1880; *Batesville Blade*, October 14, 1881 (quotation), and November 12, 1880; Jackson *Weekly Clarion*, November 3, 1880; *Washington Post*, November 3, 1880.

72. Sardis *Weekly Panola Star*, November 20, 1880; U.S. Congress, House, "Buchanan vs. Manning: Report," H. rep. 1890, 47th Cong., 2nd sess. (1883), 22 (quotation).

73. *Batesville Blade*, October 1, 1880.

74. *Macon Beacon*, November 6, 1880.

75. Cresswell, *Mormons and Cowboys*, 19–78; idem, "Enforcing the Enforce-

ment Acts: The Department of Justice in Northern Mississippi, 1870–1890,"
Journal of Southern History 53 (1987): 421–40.

76. *United States v. James Evan et al.*, Docket number 1789, General Docket
Book IV: 62, and Record Book V: 152–53 (first quotation), Records of the
U.S. District Court of Northern Mississippi (hereinafter cited as RDC), Federal Records Center, East Point, Georgia. Charles Devens to G. C. Chandler,
January 25, 1881, Instruction Books, Records of the Department of Justice
(cited hereinafter as RDJ), Record Group 60, National Archives (second quotation).

77. *United States v. James Ruffin et al.*, Docket number 1796, General Docket
Book IV: 69, and Record Book V: 239–42, RDC.

78. *United States v. W. P. Conner, George Patterson, and Lewis Sanders*, Docket
number 1842, General Docket Book IV: 115, and Record Book V: 325–27,
RDC.

79. *United States v. W. P. Conner, Andrew Caradine, and William Hallum*,
Docket number 1843, General Docket Book IV: 116, and Record Book V:
327–28, RDC; Unidentified newspaper clipping in J. L. Morphis to B. H.
Brewster, August 21, 1882 (quotation), Source-Chronological file for northern Mississippi, RDJ.

80. Carthage *Carthaginian*, quoted in Hernando *DeSoto Press and Times*,
August 29, 1878; *Ashland Register*, October 2, 1879.

81. *Water Valley Central*, quoted in *Brookhaven Ledger*, October 9, 1879;
Halsell, "The Bourbon Period in Mississippi Politics," 519–37.

82. *Jackson Comet*, October 18, 1879.

83. Jackson *Weekly Clarion*, September 24, 1879.

84. *Lexington Advertiser*, September 25, 1879; Hernando *DeSoto Press and
Times*, August 8, 1878 (first quotation), and October 9, 1879 (second quota-
tion); Jackson *Weekly Clarion*, October 2, 1878; *Starkville Times*, quoted in
Jackson *Weekly Clarion*, September 17, 1879.

85. *Lexington Advertiser*, September 11 and 25, 1879; Jackson *Weekly Independent*, August 29, 1879 (quotation).

86. Jackson *Weekly Clarion*, October 29, 1879 (quotations), and August 27,
1879.

87. Jackson *Weekly Clarion*, August 27, 1879.

88. Jackson *Weekly Clarion*, October 18, 1879 (first quotations), and August
27, 1879 (fourth quotation).

89. *Ashland Register*, November 6, 1879; Jackson *Weekly Clarion*, July 31 and
October 16, 1878.

90. *Batesville Blade*, November 26, 1880 (quotations); Minute Books, Benton County Board of Supervisors, 1: 519 (1880), Benton County Courthouse,
Ashland.

3. Fusion, Confusion, Republicans, and Independents

1. *Jackson Comet*, October 15 (first quotation), and October 1, 1881 (second and third quotations); Jackson *The Crisis*, September 30, 1881 (fourth quotation); Water Valley *National Record*, quoted in Jackson *The Crisis*, September 23, 1881.

2. Lynch, *Reminiscences*, 258–60; *Daily Memphis Avalanche*, October 15, 1881.

3. *Daily Memphis Avalanche*, October 15, 1881; Jackson *The Crisis*, September 23, 1881; *Jackson Comet*, September 17, 1881.

4. *Jackson Comet*, October 8 (first quotation), and September 17, 1881 (subsequent quotations).

5. *Jackson Comet*, October 15, 1881 (quotations).

6. *Brookhaven Ledger*, September 15, 1881; *Jackson Comet*, October 15, 1881.

7. Jackson *The Crisis*, September 30, 1881; *Jackson Comet*, September 24, 1881.

8. *Jackson Comet*, October 15, 1881 (quotation); Jackson *The Crisis*, September 30, 1881; Senatobia *Tate County Record*, November 4, 1881.

9. *Brookhaven Ledger*, September 15, 1881; *Daily Memphis Avalanche*, October 15, 1881.

10. *Daily Memphis Avalanche*, October 15, 1881 (first quotations); Hernando *DeSoto Times*, November 3, 1881; *Brookhaven Ledger*, September 15, 1881; *Jackson Comet*, September 24, 1881 (third quotation).

11. Jackson *The Crisis*, September 30, 1881; Greenwood *Yazoo Valley Flag*, November 3, 1881; *Daily Memphis Avalanche*, November 2, 1881 (quotation).

12. Hernando *DeSoto Times*, October 20, 1881 (first quotations); *Jackson Comet*, October 15, 1881 (subsequent quotations).

13. Jackson *The Crisis*, September 23 and 30, 1881; Wharton, *The Negro in Mississippi*, 204 (quotation); Miller, "'Let Us Die to Make Men Free,'" 254.

14. *Jackson Comet*, October 8 (quotations) and September 17, 1881.

15. Columbus *Patron of Husbandry*, August 20, 1881 (first quotations); Jackson *The Crisis*, September 23, 1881 (third quotation).

16. Senatobia *Tate County Record*, November 28, 1881 (quotation).

17. Jackson *The Crisis*, September 30, 1881 (quotations).

18. *Jackson Comet*, September 17, 1881 (quotations).

19. *Jackson Comet*, October 1 and 8, 1881; Jackson *The Crisis*, September 23, 1881; Hyman, *The Anti-Redeemers*, 98–123.

20. Jackson *Weekly Clarion*, November 16 and 23, 1881; Hernando *DeSoto Press and Times*, November 17, 1881.

21. *Daily Memphis Avalanche*, November 13, 1881 (first quotations); Kous-

ser, *The Shaping of Southern Politics*, 153 (third quotation); Lynch, *Reminiscences*, 260 (fourth quotation, emphasis added).

22. Kousser, *The Shaping of Southern Politics*, 28. Kousser provides the ecological regression analysis figures I use here, but the interpretation is my own.

23. *Daily Memphis Avalanche*, November 13, 1881 (quotation).

24. *Daily Memphis Avalanche*, November 13, 1881 (first quotation); *Crystal Springs Monitor*, September 30, 1881 (second quotation); Hernando *DeSoto Press and Times*, December 22, 1881 (third quotation); *Brookhaven Ledger*, quoted in Hernando *DeSoto Press and Times*, December 15, 1881 (final quotations).

25. *Daily Memphis Avalanche*, November 7, 1881 (first quotation); Columbus *Patron of Husbandry*, November 26, 1881 (subsequent quotations).

26. Jackson *Weekly Clarion*, November 10, 1881; *Vicksburg Daily Herald*, quoted in *Daily Memphis Avalanche*, November 7, 1881 (quotations), and November 9, 1881.

27. *Batesville Blade*, October 7, 1881; Sardis *Weekly Panola Star*, October 15 (quotations) and November 5, 1881.

28. *Batesville Blade*, October 21 (quotations), and October 7, 1881; Sardis *Weekly Panola Star*, October 22, 1881.

29. Sardis *Weekly Panola Star*, October 29 and November 5, 1881.

30. Columbus *Patron of Husbandry*, September 17 (first quotation), October 22, and November 19 (second quotation), 1881.

31. *Macon Beacon*, November 12, 1881 (quotation); *Jackson Comet*, November 12, 1881; Miller, "'Let Us Die to Make Men Free,'" 266–70. Democratic accounts accused blacks of provocative displays of guns on election day; Republican accounts do not mention blacks carrying arms, but say that the elderly white man was intoxicated and tore up the ballot of a black voter.

32. *Macon Beacon*, November 12, 1881 (first quotations); *Daily Memphis Avalanche*, November 6, 1881; *Jackson Comet*, November 12, 1881; *Vicksburg Daily Herald*, quoted in *DeSoto Press and Times*, November 17, 1881 (third quotation).

33. *Macon Beacon*, October 29 (first quotations), November 5 (third quotation), and November 12, 1881.

34. *Jackson Comet*, November 12, 1881; *Tate County Herald*, November 18, 1881; Jackson *Weekly Clarion*, November 10, 1881; Ferguson, "Agrarianism in Mississippi," 408–9; *Journal of the House . . . 1881*, 722–27; *Appleton's Annual Cyclopaedia . . . 1881*, 596–600.

35. Wharton, *The Negro in Mississippi*, 201–3; *Jackson Comet*, October 15, 1881. The Republicans were strongest in Warren County, but even in Warren the races were not simple Democrat-versus-Republican races, and Democrats won a number of offices and legislative seats there. I use the word "fusion" to

refer to two parties allying against a third, while "office-sharing" involved two parties cooperating and typically eliminating the need for a general election campaign.

36. *American Newspaper Directory* (New York: Rowell, 1881), 194–98; Columbus *Patron of Husbandry*, quoted in Jackson *The Crisis*, September 23, 1881.

37. *Jackson Comet*, October 8 and 15, 1881; *Macon Beacon*, October 29, 1881; *Crystal Springs Monitor*, October 15, 1881; *Walthall Pioneer*, October 7, 1881; and *Brookhaven Ledger*, September 15, 1881.

38. *Biographical Directory of the American Congress*, 1184–85; Greenwood *Yazoo Valley Flag*, October 26, 1882 (quotation). A third candidate also made this race; he was variously described as an Independent Republican and as a Democrat.

39. Halsell, "James R. Chalmers," 37–58; *Biographical Dictionary of the American Congress*, 721.

40. Halsell, "James R. Chalmers," 44 (quotation); Vincent P. DeSantis, "President Arthur and the Independent Movements in the South in 1882," *Journal of Southern History* 19 (1953): 346–63.

41. William Charles Sallis, "The Color Line in Mississippi Politics, 1865–1915," (Ph.D. dissertation, University of Kentucky, 1967), 248 (first quotation); Halsell, "James R. Chalmers," 43–46; *Batesville Blade*, November 3, 1882 (second quotation); *Ashland Register*, November 2, 1882.

42. *Batesville Blade*, October 20 and November 3, 1882.

43. Senatobia *Tate County Record*, October 27, 1882; *Batesville Blade*, October 20, 1882.

44. *Batesville Blade*, October 20 (quotations), and November 3, 1882; *Ashland Register*, November 9, 1882.

45. *Ripley Advertiser*, October 4, 1882 (first quotation); *Ashland Register*, October 26, 1882 (second quotation); *DeSoto Times*, October 26, 1882 (final quotations).

46. *Oxford Falcon*, November 2, 1882 (first quotation); *Batesville Blade*, November 3, 1882 (final quotations).

47. *Batesville Blade*, November 3, 1882 (first quotation). J. R. Chalmers to B. H. Brewster, telegram, November 7, 1882 (subsequent quotations), Source-Chronological File for Northern Mississippi, RDJ, Record Group 60, National Archives; J. L. Morphis to B. H. Brewster, telegram, November 8, 1882, Source-Chronological file, ibid.

48. 1882 congressional election returns, OER; *Ripley Advertiser*, November 11, 1882 (first quotations); *DeSoto Times*, November 16, 1882; *Batesville Blade*, November 10, 1882 (subsequent quotations).

49. *Macon Beacon*, November 25, 1882 (quotation); Miller, "'Let Us Die to Make Men Free,'" 286–331. Actually, the official certificate from Tate County

gave the votes to Chalmers, but the tally sheet listed the votes as being cast for Chambless.

50. U.S. Congress, House, "Chalmers vs. Manning," H. Misc. Doc. 15, 48th Cong., 1st sess. (1884), 35, 73–74, 98.

51. "Chalmers vs. Manning," 74, 100; *Biographical Dictionary of the American Congress*, 721.

52. *Macon Beacon*, November 4, 1882, November 25 (first quotation), and October 14, 1882 (second quotation). Earlier in the fourth district race, Greenbacker S. M. Roane announced himself a candidate, then withdrew in favor of Griffin.

53. 1882 congressional election returns, OER; *Congressional Quarterly's Guide*, 803.

54. Lynch, *Reminiscences*, 265–276.

55. *Jackson Tribune*, September 8, 1883. Note that the more famous People's party would not appear in the state until nine years later.

56. *Jackson Tribune*, September 15, 1883.

57. Jackson *Clarion*, October 24, 1883 (quotations). See also *Jackson Tribune*, September 22, 1883.

58. *Jackson Tribune*, September 8, 1883 (quotation), and September 15, 1883.

59. *Biennial Report of the Secretary of State to the Legislature of Mississippi* (Jackson, 1884), 68–78; *Aberdeen Examiner*, October 12, 1883; *Macon Beacon*, November 10, 1883.

60. Jackson *Clarion*, October 31, 1883; *Jackson Tribune*, September 29, 1883.

61. *Batesville Blade*, November 2 (first quotation), and November 9 (second quotation), 1883; *Jackson Tribune*, September 29, 1883.

62. U.S. Congress, Senate, "Mississippi in 1883," S. Rept. 512, 48th Cong., 1st sess. (1884), xviii–xix, xx (quotation); *Batesville Blade*, November 9, 1883; *Crystal Springs Meteor*, November 10, 1883; Miller, "'Let Us Die to Make Men Free,'" 370–79.

63. *Crystal Springs Meteor*, quoted in *Jackson Tribune*, September 8, 1883 (first quotations); *Copiah Signal*, quoted in *Batesville Blade*, November 9, 1883 (second quotation); "Mississippi in 1883," xxiii–xxiv.

64. *Jackson Tribune*, September 8, 1883; "Mississippi in 1883," xxv, xxvi (first quotation), xxviii (middle quotations), xxx–xxxii; *Crystal Springs Meteor*, November 10, 1883 (fourth quotation); Jackson *State Ledger*, quoted in *Batesville Blade*, November 16, 1883; *Macon Beacon*, November 10, 1883. The Independent legislative candidates won about 23 percent of the votes cast; this is not, of course, necessarily a reasonable indication of their popularity. Manuscript returns for 1883 Copiah County general election, MSSP.

65. "Mississippi in 1883," i–v, lxi–lxix; 21–25; 189–93; John Sherman, *Rec-*

ollections of Forty Years in the House, Senate, and Cabinet, 2 vols. (Chicago, 1895), 2: 869–75; *Jackson Weekly Clarion,* November 14, 1883; Miller, "'Let Us Die to Make Men Free,'" 370–79.

66. *Journal of the House . . . 1884,* tabular matter bound at back.

67. 1884 congressional election returns, OER; *Batesville Blade,* October 31, 1884; *Ashland Register,* October 30, 1884.

68. Jackson *Clarion,* November 19, 1884; Greene C. Chandler, *Journal and Speeches of Greene Callier Chandler* (n.p., 1953), 156–57 (quotation).

69. Jackson *Clarion,* November 5, 1884; *Macon Beacon,* November 1, 1884.

70. Alwyn Barr, "B. J. Chambers and the Greenback Party Split," *Mid-America* 49 (1967), 281–82.

71. 1885 gubernatorial election returns, OER; Ferguson, "Agrarianism in Mississippi," 422.

72. Jackson *Clarion,* November 4 and 11, 1885; *Aberdeen Examiner,* November 4, 1885; *Walthall Warden,* October 29, 1885.

73. Jackson *Clarion,* October 28, 1885 (quotations).

74. Senatobia *Tate County Record,* October 16, 1885; *Macon Beacon,* October 10, 1885 (quotations).

75. Jackson *Clarion,* October 28, 1885 (quotation); *Aberdeen Examiner,* November 11, 1885; *Journal of the House . . . 1886,* tabular matter at back. The Independent representative from Wayne, J. R. S. Pitts, had a strong history of Republican involvement before and after 1885. One source gives the number of non-Democratic legislators as twelve, instead of eleven—see *Appleton's Annual Cyclopaedia . . . 1885,* 604.

76. Senatobia *Tate County Record,* October 30, 1886; Jackson *Clarion,* October 13, 1886 (quotation), and October 20, 1886; 1886 congressional election returns, OER.

77. *Batesville Blade,* May 22, 1885; Jackson *Clarion,* November 14, 1883.

78. Sallis, "The Color Line in Mississippi Politics," 252 (quotation); Halsell, "James R. Chalmers," 41–47.

79. My statement that six in one hundred whites in Mississippi considered themselves Republicans is based loosely on the estimate made by J. Morgan Kousser that six percent of the state's white adult males went to the polls in 1888 and voted Republican. Kousser, *The Shaping of Southern Politics,* 144.

80. Burnham, *Presidential Ballots,* 570–71; A. T. Morgan, *Yazoo, or On the Picket Line of Freedom in the South* (1884; reprint, New York, 1968), 208 (first quotation) and 494–95 (second quotation); Bettye J. Gardner, "William H. Foote and Yazoo County Politics, 1866–1883," *Southern Studies,* Winter 1982, 398–407.

81. Morgan, *Yazoo,* 497–501, quotation at 501; Gardner, "William H. Foote," 404–5; Miller, "'Let Us Die to Make Men Free,'" 379–89. Morgan's

account of Foote's death is from a long article in the *St. Louis Globe-Democrat*, which he quotes verbatim.

82. *Biographical and Historical Memoirs of Mississippi*, 1: 1204–5; U.S. Congress, Senate, "Municipal Election at Jackson, Mississippi," S. Misc. Doc. 166, 50th Cong., 1st sess., 1888, 4, 13 (first and second quotations); Walter McCluskey Hurns, "Post-Reconstruction Municipal Politics in Jackson, Mississippi," (Ph.D. dissertation, Kansas State University, 1989); Jackson *Daily Mississippian*, November 30, 1887 (subsequent quotations). In 1886 Democrats had won control of the Board of Aldermen, but McGill retained the mayor's office.

83. "Municipal Election," 4 (quotation), 13–30.

84. "Municipal Election," 4, 30–65; Jackson *Clarion-Ledger*, November 20, 1890.

85. *Aberdeen Examiner*, November 11, 1887; Jackson *Clarion*, November 9 and 16, 1887; *Journal of the House . . . 1888*, tabular matter bound at back, 2–8. The two independent legislators were John B. Deason of Lincoln County and J. R. S. Pitts of Wayne County, both of whom had a history of Republicanism.

86. State senate election returns, 1879–1887, OER. Note that these total numbers of candidates include Democrats, Independent Democrats, Independents, and members of third parties.

87. Congressional election returns, 1882–1888, OER; *Congressional Quarterly's Guide*, 815.

88. Jackson *Clarion-Ledger*, October 24 (quotation), and October 3, 1889; Lynch, *Reminiscences*, 294–98.

89. Lynch, *Reminiscences*, 294 (first quotation), 295 (second quotation); Jackson *Clarion-Ledger*, October 10, 1889 (third quotation), and November 6, 1889. One source gives seven as the number of Republican legislators elected in 1889: See *Appleton's Annual Cyclopaedia . . . 1889*, 565.

90. On the decline of Greenbackism, see Martin, "The Greenback Party in Texas," 161–77, and Jay, "The Greenback Road."

91. *Walthall Warden*, November 2 and 16, 1887; Ferguson, "Agrarianism in Mississippi," 396–440; Hyman, *The Anti-Redeemers*, 54–74.

92. Docket Book Four, Records of the U.S. District Court for the Northern District of Mississippi, Federal Records Center, East Point, Georgia. The cases from the 1882 election were docket numbers 1902 and 1908–24. For the J. J. Brooks case, see docket numbers 1776–77. See also Cresswell, *Mormons and Cowboys*, 19–78; Senatobia *Tate County Record*, July 7, 1882; Hernando *DeSoto Press and Times*, January 12, 1882.

93. *Jackson Comet*, October 15, 1881; *Macon Beacon*, October 25, 1881 (first quotations); *Aberdeen Examiner*, November 4, 1885 (final quotation).

94. *Aberdeen Examiner*, November 12, 1883; Kirwan, *Revolt of the Rednecks*;

Ferguson, "Agrarianism in Mississippi," 339, 396–440. The list of counties where Democrats made no nominations is not intended to be exhaustive.

4. A New Constitution
and New Directions for Agrarians

1. Carthage *Carthaginian*, August 8, 1890; *Tupelo Journal*, August 1, 1890 (quotation). Cook was a forty-three-year-old farmer; he was married and had a number of children. A number of modern writers have erroneously reported that Cook was black. See returns from Census of Population, Tenth Census of the United States, 1880 (Jasper County, enumeration district 158, page 30, line 2), Record Group 29, National Archives.

2. Jackson *Clarion-Ledger*, May 1, 1890 (first quotation); *Meridian News*, quoted in Carthage *Carthaginian*, August 1, 1890 (second quotation); *Tupelo Journal*, August 1, 1890.

3. *Walthall Warden*, August 6, 1890; Carthage *Carthaginian*, August 8, 1890; Henry Clay Niles to William H. H. Miller, August 20, 1890, Year Files, RDJ, Record Group 60, National Archives.

4. Jackson *Clarion*, October 27, 1886 (first quotation); Ferguson, "Agrarianism in Mississippi," 411, quoting Jackson *New Mississippian*, June 12, 1889 (second quotation).

5. Ferguson, "Agrarianism in Mississippi," 444–45; James P. Coleman, "The Mississippi Constitution of 1890 and the Final Decade of the Nineteenth Century," in Richard Aubrey McLemore, ed., *A History of Mississippi*, 2 vols. (Jackson, Miss., 1973), 2: 3–28. Of course, a chief unstated question in debates over apportionment was whether representation should reflect the number of citizens in a county, the number of taxpayers, or the number of voters.

6. Ferguson, "Agrarianism in Mississippi," 444–45; Coleman, "The Mississippi Constitution," 3–28.

7. Wharton, *The Negro in Mississippi*, 208; Coleman, "The Mississippi Constitution," 5–10.

8. Kousser, *The Shaping of Southern Politics*, 140–41; Ferguson, "Agrarianism in Mississippi," 453–56; Coleman, "The Mississippi Constitution," 7 (quotation).

9. Jackson *Clarion-Ledger*, July 3, 1890 (quotations).

10. *Tupelo Journal*, August 8, 1890; Jackson *Clarion-Ledger*, July 17, 1890.

11. *Brookhaven Leader*, July 31, 1890; Columbia *Pearl River News*, July 17 (quotations), and August 7, 1890.

12. *Walthall Warden*, July 16, 23, and 30, 1890.

13. Jackson *Clarion-Ledger*, August 14, 1890; Kirwan, *Revolt of the Rednecks*, 65; Ferguson, "Agrarianism in Mississippi," 462; *Journal of the Proceedings of the*

Constitutional Convention of the State of Mississippi (Jackson, 1890), 704–8; Kousser, *The Shaping of Southern Politics*, 142. Among other occupations represented in the convention were planters (eleven), merchants (nine), and a number of commercial occupations. Many of the merchants listed a second occupation, often planter.

14. *Journal of the Proceedings*, 704–8; *Walthall Warden*, August 13, 1890. Melchoir, Rotenberry, and Holland called themselves Democrats in the convention roster; Simrall used the label "National Republican," while Alcorn called himself a "Conservative." Over his political career Melchoir had moved back and forth between the Republican and Democratic parties. Alcorn was an active supporter of national Republican politics; in the 1880s he had been elected as a Republican to the Coahoma Board of Supervisors.

15. Wharton, *The Negro in Mississippi*, quoting Jackson *Clarion-Ledger*, (quotation) 206–7; Jackson *Clarion-Ledger*, November 27, 1890; Kirwan, *Revolt of the Rednecks*, 67. Some sources say that Alcorn advocated allowing blacks to control the state house of representatives; others say Alcorn had in mind a third, all-black house of the legislature.

16. Kirwan, *Revolt of the Rednecks*, 68; Coleman, "The Mississippi Constitution," 11–14.

17. Wharton, *The Negro in Mississippi*, 212; Jackson *Clarion-Ledger*, November 27, 1890 (quotations).

18. Jackson *Clarion-Ledger*, October 30, 1890; Coleman, "The Mississippi Constitution," 17–19; Ferguson, "Agrarianism in Mississippi," 478–82. Ten delegates voted against ratification; two of them changed their votes to aye. On apportionment, note that delegates had access only to the 1880 population figures, which showed the white counties gaining a majority in the house of representatives. See Eric C. Clark, "Legislative Apportionment in the 1890 Constitutional Convention," *Journal of Mississippi History* 42 (1980): 298–315.

19. *Port Gibson Reveille*, quoted in Wharton, *The Negro in Mississippi*, 214 (first quotation); Kirwan, *Revolt of the Rednecks*, 68–71; Jackson *Clarion-Ledger*, October 30 and November 6, 1890 (second quotation).

20. Coleman, "The Mississippi Constitution," 16.

21. James H. Stone, "A Note on Voter Registration Under the Mississippi Understanding Clause, 1892," *Journal of Southern History* 38 (1972), 293–96; Burnham, *Presidential Ballots*, 564–65.

22. Wharton, *The Negro in Mississippi*, 215; Kousser, *The Shaping of Southern Politics*, 3.

23. Key, *Southern Politics in State and Nation*, 531–33; Kousser, *The Shaping of Southern Politics*, 3–5, 243.

24. Burnham, *Presidential Ballots*, 552–71; Kousser, *The Shaping of Southern Politics*, 144–45, 241.

25. *Congressional Quarterly's Guide*, 342–43; Kousser, *The Shaping of Southern Politics*, 241.

26. "The Ocala Demands, December 7, 1890," reproduced in Arthur M. Schlesinger, Jr., ed., *A History of U.S. Political Parties*, 4 vols., 2: 1758–59; Ferguson, "Agrarianism in Mississippi," 490–94.

27. *Walthall Warden*, October 14, 1891; Kirwan, *Revolt of the Rednecks*, 87–90; Ferguson, "Agrarianism in Mississippi," 496.

28. *Grenada Sentinel*, October 17 and 24, and November 14, 1891 (quotations); Ferguson, "Agrarianism in Mississippi," 505–9.

29. *Grenada Sentinel*, October 3, 1891 (first quotations); Columbia *Pearl River News*, October 29, 1891 (third quotation); *Pontotoc Democrat*, September 10, 1891 (fourth quotation).

30. *Grenada Sentinel*, November 14, 1891; *Tupelo Journal*, October 16, 1891 (first quotations); *Natchez Democrat*, quoted in *Tupelo Journal*, October 30, 1891 (third quotation); Kirwan, *Revolt of the Rednecks*, 88; Ferguson, "Agrarianism in Mississippi," 421.

31. *Grenada Sentinel*, November 21, 1891 (first quotation); Robert C. Latham, "The Dirt Farmer in Politics: A Study of Webster County, Mississippi During the Rise of Democratic Factionalism, 1880–1910," (M. A. thesis, Mississippi College, 1951); *Walthall Warden*, November 4, 1891 (second quotation); *Winona Times*, November 13, 1891.

32. Ferguson, "Agrarianism in Mississippi," 421, 522–25.

33. Ackerman *Choctaw Plaindealer*, June 10, 1892; Ferguson, "Agrarianism in Mississippi," 534–36, 551. The *Plaindealer* returned to the Democratic fold prior to the 1892 election. On Populism nationally, see Norman Pollack, *The Populist Response to Industrial America* (Cambridge, Mass., 1962); Richard Hofstadter, *The Age of Reform* (New York, 1955); Lawrence Goodwyn, *The Populist Moment: A Short History of the Agrarian Revolt in America* (New York, 1978).

34. William David McCain, "The Populist Party in Mississippi" (M.A. thesis, University of Mississippi, 1931), 1–22; George W. Tindall, "The People's Party," in Arthur M. Schlesinger, Jr., ed., *History of U.S. Political Parties*, 4 vols., (New York, 1973), 2: 1701–31, 1766–68 (quotation at 1714); Steven Hahn, *The Roots of Southern Populism: Yeoman Farmers and the Transformation of the Georgia Upcountry, 1850–1890* (New York, 1983); William Warren Rogers, *One-Gallused Rebellion: Agrarianism in Alabama, 1865–1896* (Baton Rouge, La., 1970); Sheldon Hackney, *Populism to Progressivism in Alabama* (Princeton, N.J., 1969).

35. Lilibel Broadway, "Frank Burkitt: The Man in the Wool Hat," (M.A. thesis, Mississippi State College, 1948), 15 (quotation); Ferguson, "Agrarianism in Mississippi," 334–40; Edward L. Ayers, *The Promise of the New South: Life After Reconstruction* (New York, 1992), 228–29.

36. Frank Burkitt, "Our State Finances and Our School System, Illustrated and Exposed by 'Wool Hat' . . . " (Okolona, Miss., 1886), pamphlet, copy in Special Collections, Mitchell Memorial Library, Mississippi State University; Broadway, "Frank Burkitt," 21–36.

37. *Biographical Dictionary of the American Congress,* 1018–19; Monroe Lee Billington, *Thomas P. Gore: The Blind Senator from Oklahoma* (Lawrence, Kans., 1967), 6–9.

38. *Walthall Warden,* August 6, 1890.

39. *Grenada Sentinel,* October 8, 1892 (first and second quotations); Jackson *Daily Clarion-Ledger,* quoted in *Eupora Sun,* August 3, 1895 (subsequent quotations); McCain, "The Populist Party in Mississippi," 558.

40. Ackerman *Choctaw Plaindealer,* October 7, 1892; *Grenada Sentinel,* September 24, 1892.

41. *Tupelo Journal,* October 7, 1892 (first quotation); Jackson *Daily Clarion,* September 13, 1892 (second quotation); *Grenada Sentinel,* October 8, 1892 (subsequent quotations); McCain, "The Populist Party in Mississippi," 13.

42. *Grenada Sentinel,* September 17, 1892; *McComb City Enterprise,* September 17, 1892; Jackson *Daily Clarion,* September 13, 1892; *Winona Times,* October 14, 1892; McCain, "The Populist Party in Mississippi," 13.

43. *Grenada Sentinel,* November 5, 1892 (quotation).

44. *Tupelo Journal,* October 7, 1892 (quotation); Columbia *Pearl River News,* September 23, 1892; *McComb City Enterprise,* October 15, 1892; *Tupelo Journal,* September 23, 1892.

45. Columbia *Pearl River News,* October 21, 1892 (quotation).

46. Ackerman *Choctaw Plaindealer,* August 12 and 19, 1892.

47. *McComb City Enterprise,* October 1 and 15, 1892.

48. Ackerman *Choctaw Plaindealer,* October 7, 1892 (quotations).

49. *Winona Times,* October 14, 1892; *Grenada Sentinel,* October 15, 1892.

50. *Grenada Sentinel,* November 5, 1892 (first quotation), and September 3, 1892 (second quotation).

51. *Grenada Journal,* October 22, 1892 (quotation); *Tupelo Journal,* October 28, 1892.

52. Jackson *Daily Clarion,* September 15 (first quotation) and 20 (second quotation), 1892; Carthage *Carthaginian,* October 21, 1892; *Tupelo Journal,* October 21, 1892.

53. Carthage *Carthaginian,* October 7 (quotation) and 14, 1892; *Kosciusko Star,* November 1, 1892; Jackson *Daily Clarion,* October 21, 1892.

54. *Tupelo Journal,* October 14, 1892 (first quotation); Jackson *Daily Clarion,* September 13, 1892 (second quotation); Monticello *Lawrence County Press,* November 10, 1892 (third and sixth quotations), and November 3, 1892 (fifth quotation); *Grenada Sentinel,* October 8, 1892 (fourth quotation); *Winona Times,* July 15, 1892 (seventh quotation).

55. *Tupelo Journal,* October 7, 1892 (quotations).

56. *Grenada Sentinel,* September 17, 1892 (first quotation); *Tupelo Journal,* September 23, 1892 (second quotation); Columbia *Pearl River News,* September 23, 1892; Ackerman *Choctaw Plaindealer,* October 21, 1892; Broadway, 38.

57. Jackson *Daily Clarion,* November 11, 1892 (first quotation); Ferguson, "Agrarianism in Mississippi," 549 n. 79 (second quotation).

58. *McComb City Enterprise,* October 15, 1892 (first quotation); *Grenada Sentinel,* November 5, 1892 (second quotation); *Tupelo Journal,* November 4, 1892 (third quotation); Jackson *Daily Clarion,* November 15, 1892 (fourth quotation).

59. Jackson *Daily Clarion,* November 5, 1892; Henry Ware to B. T. Hobbs, November 13, 1892, B. T. Hobbs Papers, Special Collections, Mitchell Memorial Library, Mississippi State University (quotation).

60. Cumberland *Mississippi Populist,* May 17, 1894; Henry Ware to B. T. Hobbs, November 13, 1892, Hobbs Papers (quotation).

61. *Congressional Quarterly's Guide,* 343; Burnham, *Presidential Ballots,* 552–71.

62. Jackson *Daily Clarion,* November 25, 1892.

5. HEYDAY FOR POPULISTS

1. *Grenada Sentinel,* November 12 and 19, 1892; Ackerman *Choctaw Plaindealer,* November 11 and 18, 1892.

2. *Rocky Mountain News,* quoted in Pontotoc *People's Banner,* February 1, 1894. Several additional members were considered Populists during the early part of the session only—these included W. P. Reeves of Itawamba County, Jesse D. Wade of Union County, and Senator W. W. Heidelberg of Jasper and Clarke counties.

3. *Liberty Southern Herald,* October 18, 1895; Pontotoc *People's Banner,* December 14, 1893, and January 11 and February 1, 1894.

4. *Journal of the House . . . 1894; Journal of the Senate . . . 1894.* Bound at the back of each journal is the official roster, which includes occupation, age, and nativity. Where lawmakers listed two occupations, I have taken the first named.

5. *Journal of the House . . . 1894,* 376; Jackson *Clarion-Ledger,* February 15, 1894.

6. These statements are based on simple calculations based on all roll calls in the 1894 house journal on which at least three members voted on the losing side. The number of such roll calls was 104. For a discussion of the index of relative cohesion, see Anderson, Watts, and Wilcox, *Legislative Roll-Call Analysis.*

7. *Journal of the House . . . 1894,* 167–68 (veterans' home), 181 (pensions),

155–56 (prohibition), 373 (Industrial Institute), 162–63 (penitentiary farm), 357–58 (insurance companies). I say that Populist efforts were "decisive" or "crucial" when a change of their votes would have led to the vote going the other way; in most cases, if the Populists had simply abstained, results of the vote would also have been reversed.

8. *Journal of the House* . . . *1894*, 92–94 (nepotism), 448–49 (privilege tax), 328–29, 354 (judiciary).

9. Jackson *Clarion-Ledger*, March 8, 1894 (first quotation); *Kosciusko Star*, quoted in Jackson *Clarion-Ledger*, March 8, 1894 (second quotation).

10. Jackson *Clarion-Ledger*, March 15 and 22, 1894.

11. Boyle, *Cotton and the New Orleans Cotton Exchange*, 178–83; Cumberland *Mississippi Populist*, May 10, 1894; Monticello *Lawrence County Press*, November 29, 1894.

12. Cumberland *Mississippi Populist*, June 28, 1894 (first and second quotations); *Kosciusko Star*, July 13, 1894 (subsequent quotations).

13. Monticello *Lawrence County Press*, September 13 and 27, 1894; Columbia *Pearl River News*, September 14 and 28, 1894. Denny's devotion to the gold standard led him to join the Republican party in 1896.

14. Columbia *Pearl River News*, September 21, 1894 (first quotation); Liberty *Southern Herald*, October 19, 1894 (second quotation).

15. Columbia *Pearl River News*, September 21 (first quotation) and November 2 (second quotation), 1894; Jackson *Weekly Clarion-Ledger*, November 1, 1894.

16. Liberty *Southern Herald*, October 26, 1894 (first, second, third, and fifth quotations); Monticello *Lawrence County Press*, November 1, 1894 (fourth quotation); Columbia *Pearl River News*, November 9, 1894 (sixth quotation).

17. Carthage *Carthaginian*, November 2 (first quotation) and September 27, 1894; *Kosciusko Star*, July 13, 1894 (second quotation).

18. Pontotoc *People's Banner*, August 2, 1894 (quotations).

19. Pontotoc *People's Banner*, October 4 (first quotation) and 11 (second quotation), and November 1, 1894.

20. In the third district Populists ran no candidate in 1892; in 1894 their nominee G. W. Wise managed to get his name on the ballot only in Bolivar County. See Greenwood *Delta Flag*, November 2, 1894.

21. Pontotoc *People's Banner*, November 15, 1894 (quotations).

22. For treatments of the party nationally, see Jack S. Blocker, *Retreat from Reform: The Prohibition Movement in the United States, 1890–1913* (Westport, Conn., 1976); Roger C. Storms, *Partisan Prophets: A History of the Prohibition Party* (Denver, 1972). *Winona Times*, July 15, 1892 (first quotation); *New York Times*, July 30, 1892 (subsequent quotations), and July 19, 1888; *Congressional Quarterly's Guide*, 342.

23. Thomas Jefferson Bailey, *Prohibition in Mississippi, Or, Anti-Liquor Legis-*

lation from the Territorial Days, with Its Results in the Counties (Jackson, 1917), 83 (first quotation), 90–96; J. B. Gambrell to Henry Ware, August 6, 1892, Hobbs Papers (subsequent quotations).

24. Henry Ware to B. T. Hobbs, August 8, 1892, Hobbs Papers; *McComb City Enterprise*, September 17, 1892; *Grenada Sentinel*, September 17, 1892 (quotation).

25. Henry Ware to B. T. Hobbs, November 13, 1892, Hobbs Papers (first quotations); L. D. Posey to B. T. Hobbs, September 30, 1892, Hobbs Papers (third quotation); Henry Ware to B. T. Hobbs, December 5, 1892, Hobbs Papers; Burnham, *Presidential Ballots*, 552–71.

26. New York *The Voice*, September 13 and October 4, 1894; Monticello *Lawrence County Press*, October 11, 1894 (quotation).

27. Vicksburg *Commercial Herald*, quoted in Jackson *Weekly Clarion-Ledger*, November 8, 1894 (quotations).

28. Vicksburg *Commercial Herald*, quoted in Jackson *Weekly Clarion-Ledger*, November 8, 1894 (quotations).

29. New York *The Voice*, December 6, 1894; Returns of 1894 congressional election, OER; *Congressional Quarterly's Guide*, 830.

30. *New York Times*, January 11, 1895; New York *The Voice*, January 17, 1895; *Brookhaven Leader*, August 13 and October 10, 1895.

31. *Brookhaven Leader*, September 3 and 10, and October 29 (quotation), 1895.

32. *Brookhaven Leader*, October 29, 1895 (quotations).

33. New York *The Voice*, October 29, 1896; *Brookhaven Leader*, November 5, 1895; *Congressional Quarterly's Guide*, 344; Bailey, 97–99.

34. *Standard Encyclopedia of the Alcohol Problem*, 6 vols., s.v. "Mississippi," (Westerville, Ohio, 1925), 4: 1784–88 (quotation at 1785); W. H. Patton, "History of the Prohibition Movement in Mississippi," *Publications of the Mississippi Historical Society* 10 (1909): 181–201; J. K. Vardaman to B. T. Hobbs, July 1, 1907, Hobbs Papers.

35. U.S. Congress, House, "Hill vs. Catchings," H. rept. 4005, 51st cong., 2nd sess. (1891); Jackson *Clarion-Ledger*, November 6, 1890; Jackson *Daily Clarion*, November 26, 1892.

36. *Grenada Sentinel*, October 22, 1892; *Brookhaven Leader*, September 10, 1895 (first quotation); Jackson *Clarion-Ledger*, July 3, 1890 (subsequent quotations).

37. *Summit Sentinel*, September 26 (quotations), October 17, and November 7, 1895; Ripley *Southern Sentinel*, October 10, 1895.

38. Thomas N. Boschert, "Politics of Expediency: Fusion in the Mississippi Delta, Late Nineteenth Century," (M.A. thesis, University of Mississippi, 1985); *Brookhaven Leader*, November 12, 1896.

39. Columbia *Pearl River News*, October 18, 1895 (quotation); *Grenada Sentinel*, October 5, 1895.

40. Boyle, *Cotton and the New Orleans Cotton Exchange*, 184; Monticello *Lawrence County Press*, September 12, 1895; *Tupelo Journal*, November 15, 1895; *Grenada Sentinel*, October 12, 1895; Liberty *Southern Herald*, October 18, 1895 (quotation).

41. *Eupora Sun*, November 29, 1895 (quotation).

42. Broadway, "Frank Burkitt," 45–46; McCain, "The Populist Party in Mississippi," 45 (quotation).

43. Monticello *Lawrence County Press*, September 26, 1895 (quotation); Ferguson, "Agrarianism in Mississippi," 325.

44. Columbia *Pearl River News*, August 23, 1895; *Grenada Sentinel*, October 5, 1895 (quotation); McCain, "The Populist Party in Mississippi," 50–59.

45. Pontotoc *People's Banner*, October 3, 1895; *Eupora Sun*, July 20, 1895; Latham, "The Dirt Farmer in Politics," 66 (quotation).

46. Jackson *Weekly Clarion-Ledger*, October 10, 1895 (quotations); Pontotoc *People's Banner*, August 15, 1895.

47. Jackson *Weekly Clarion-Ledger*, October 10, 1895.

48. Jackson *Weekly Clarion-Ledger*, October 10, 1895.

49. Batesville *Weekly Panolian*, October 25, 1895 (first quotation); Meridian *Daily Herald*, October 23 (middle quotations) and November 4 (fourth quotation), 1895.

50. Ackerman *Choctaw Plaindealer*, October 4, 1895; Ackerman *Phagocyte*, quoted in *Choctaw Plaindealer*, October 4, 1895 (quotation); *Kosciusko Star*, October 11, 1895.

51. *Eupora Sun*, July 13 and 20, and September 7, 1895; Pontotoc *People's Banner*, May 9, 1895.

52. Monticello *Lawrence County Press*, July 25, 1895; *Pearl River News*, October 4 (quotation), September 13, and November 1, 1895. For material on Mississippi agrarianism, particularly in Marion County before and after 1895, see William F. Holmes, "Whitecapping: Agrarian Violence in Mississippi, 1902–1906," *Journal of Southern History* 35 (1969): 165–85.

53. Returns of elections for statewide offices, 1895, OER. McCain's thesis on the Mississippi People's party credits the Populists with only about twenty victories in 1895. Wider use of county newspapers has revealed the additional Populist victors. The author knows of 102 Populists who won in 1895; other People's party wins undoubtedly occurred in counties from which no 1895 newspapers are extant. This count does not include Carroll County, where Populists won control of the county, but for which no 1895 newspapers have survived. See Stephen Cresswell, "Who Was Who in Mississippi's Opposition Political Parties, 1878–1963," 1994 typescript, copy at DA&H. *Choctaw Plain-*

dealer, November 15 and 22, 1895; *Eupora Sun*, November 8, 1895; on Carroll County, see Memphis *Commercial-Appeal*, November 11, 1899.

54. Okolona *People's Messenger*, November 20, 1895; *Eupora Sun*, November 15, 1895; Batesville *Weekly Panolian*, October 25, 1895; Ackerman *Choctaw Plaindealer*, October 11, 1895. Democrats, for their part, charged that Populists who were examining the registration books had "stolen" them.

55. *Kosciusko Star*, November 29, 1895; *DeKalb Press*, November 7, 1895; *Eupora Sun*, November 15, 1895; Pontotoc *People's Banner*, October 24, 1895 (quotation); *Tupelo Journal*, November 1, 1895.

56. *Memphis Commercial-Appeal*, September 26, 1895 (quotation). The number of white voters disfranchised between the elections of 1888 and 1892 was 52,000. See *Appleton's Annual Cyclopaedia . . . 1892*, 472.

57. Carthage *Carthaginian*, October 28, 1892 (first quotation); Ackerman *Choctaw Plaindealer*, October 4, 1895; *Tupelo Journal* (subsequent quotations), September 23, 1892.

58. Pontotoc *People's Banner*, December 20, 1894 (quotation).

59. *Advertisers' Handy Guide, 1895* (New York, 1895), 248–54; *Advertisers' Handy Guide, 1896* (New York, 1896), 249–55.

60. Cumberland *Mississippi Populist*, April 26 (first quotation), May 10 (second quotation), and June 7, 1894; *McComb City Enterprise*, October 1, 1892.

61. Monticello *Lawrence County Press*, October 6, 1892; Pontotoc *People's Banner*, August 15 and September 27, 1894.

62. Pontotoc *People's Banner*, August 24 (first quotation), December 7 (subsequent quotations), 1895.

63. *Tupelo Journal*, October 7, 1892 (first quotations); *Meridian Standard*, quoted in *Tupelo Journal*, October 7, 1892 (third and fourth quotations); *Choctaw Plaindealer*, October 26, 1894 (fifth quotation); *Grenada Sentinel*, September 3, 1892 (sixth quotation).

64. Kousser, *The Shaping of Southern Politics*, 7, 247–59.

65. *Journal of the Proceedings*, 697–700.

66. Cumberland *Mississippi Populist*, June 7, 1894. Democrats did, on rare occasions, allege that Populists wanted to use black votes; Populists in rare instances accused Democrats of the same thing. Columbia *Pearl River News*, September 6, 1895; *Kosciusko Star*, October 11, 1895.

67. Kousser, *The Shaping of Southern Politics*, 28, 145.

68. Ibid.

69. U.S. Congress, House, "A. M. Newman vs. J. G. Spencer," H. rept. 1536, 54th Cong., 1st sess. (1896); idem, "W. P. Ratliff vs. J. S. Williams," H. rept. 1537, 54th Cong., 1st sess. (1896); idem, "John A. Brown vs. John M. Allen," H. rept. 1538, 54th Cong., 1st sess. (1896). *Williams v. Mississippi*, 170 U.S. 213 (1898).

70. Jackson *Weekly Clarion-Ledger*, November 21, 1895 (first quotation); *Eupora Sun*, December 6, 1895 (subsequent quotations).

6. THE DECLINE OF ALL OPPOSITION

1. *Yazoo Herald*, quoted in Columbia *Pearl River News*, October 30, 1896 (first quotation); *Pearl River News*, October 30, 1896 (second quotation); *Gulf Coast Progress*, quoted in *Pearl River News*, October 30, 1896 (third quotation).

2. Jackson *Clarion-Ledger*, November 12, 1896; *Grenada Sentinel*, November 7, 1896; *Vicksburg Evening Post*, November 2, 1896.

3. Jackson *Clarion-Ledger*, November 12, 1896.

4. *Kosciusko Star*, October 11, 1895 (first quotation); Tindall, "The People's Party," 1720–21; Robert F. Durden, *The Climax of Populism: The Election of 1896* (Lexington, Ky., 1965).

5. *New York Times*, February 20, 1896; Jackson *Daily Clarion-Ledger*, February 19, 1896 (first quotation); Pontotoc *People's Banner*, July 10 (second quotation), and February 14, 1896.

6. McCain, "The Populist Party in Mississippi," 76 (quotation); *Grenada Sentinel*, August 1, 1896; Tindall, "The People's Party," 1722–24.

7. *Grenada Sentinel*, August 1 and September 12, 1896; Tindall, "The People's Party," 1721–23; McCain, "The Populist Party in Mississippi," 78.

8. Pontotoc *People's Banner*, July 31 (first quotation), and July 17, 1896 (subsequent quotations).

9. Kosciusko *Alliance Vindicator*, August 28, 1896 (first quotation); Pontotoc *People's Banner*, August 14, 1896 (second quotation); Ackerman *Choctaw Plaindealer*, August 21, 1896.

10. Tindall, "The People's Party," 1723–25.

11. *Grenada Sentinel*, September 19, 1896; *Magnolia Gazette*, October 21, 1896.

12. *Tupelo Journal*, October 16 and 23, 1896; Jackson *Clarion-Ledger*, October 29, 1896; *Magnolia Gazette*, October 28 and 31, 1896; *Vicksburg Evening Post*, October 24, 1896; McCain, "The Populist Party in Mississippi," 81.

13. *Greenwood Enterprise*, October 23, 1896 (first quotation); *Magnolia Gazette*, October 28, 1896 (second quotation); Ackerman *Choctaw Plaindealer*, October 16 and 23, 1896.

14. *Biloxi Herald*, October 31, 1896; Okolona *People's Messenger*, quoted in Memphis *Commercial-Appeal*, October 23, 1896 (first quotation); Ferguson, "Agrarianism in Mississippi," 575 (second quotation); Kosciusko *Alliance Vindicator*, August 14, 1896 (third quotation); Kosciusko *Attala Ledger*, October 9, 1896; Okolona *People's Messenger*, quoted in *Vicksburg Evening Post*, October 31, 1896.

15. Ackerman *Choctaw Plaindealer*, September 4, 1896 (quotation); Mead-

ville *Franklin Advocate*, September 24, 1896; *Biloxi Herald*, October 3, 1896; *Jackson Clarion-Ledger*, October 22, 1896.

16. *Biloxi Herald*, October 17, 1896. Statements about the gold Democrat defectors are based on the list of delegates to their state convention, printed in the *Vicksburg Evening Post*, October 8, 1896. See also *Vicksburg City Directory* (Vicksburg, Miss., 1895).

17. *Biloxi Herald*, October 3, 1896 (first quotation); the *Herald* was one of a number of state newspapers that favored sound money but remained loyal to the main body of the Democratic party. *Grenada Sentinel*, October 3, 1896 (second quotation); *Newton County Progress*, quoted in Poplarville *Free Press*, October 22, 1896 (third quotation); Columbia *Pearl River News*, October 23, 1896 (fourth quotation); Monticello *Lawrence County Press*, October 8, 1896; *Port Gibson Reveille*, excerpted in Vicksburg *Evening Post*, October 9, 1896.

18. *Vicksburg Evening Post*, October 8 (quotations) and October 6, 1896; Jackson *Clarion-Ledger*, October 15, 1896; *Magnolia Gazette*, October 14, 1896.

19. *Vicksburg Evening Post*, October 14 (first quotation), 26, and 31, 1896; *Vicksburg Evening Post*, November 2, 1896 (second quotation).

20. *Biloxi Herald*, October 17, 1896; Jackson *Clarion-Ledger*, October 22, 1896; *Vicksburg Evening Post*, November 2, 1896 (quotation).

21. *Magnolia Gazette*, October 7, 1896 (first quotation); *Jackson News*, quoted in *Vicksburg Evening Post*, October 9, 1896 (second and third quotations); Jackson *Clarion-Ledger*, October 15, 1896 (fourth and fifth quotations); *Eupora Progress*, quoted in *Vicksburg Evening Post*, October 6, 1896 (sixth quotation).

22. Jackson *Clarion-Ledger*, October 29, 1896; *Magnolia Gazette*, October 31, 1896.

23. Handsboro *Grander Age*, September 1896; Biloxi *Grander Age*, August 1903; Co-opolis file, Local History collection, Biloxi-Gulfport Library, Biloxi; Pontotoc *People's Banner*, November 5, 1897. Rose had once edited a Prohibition party organ in Indiana.

24. *New York Times*, November 15, 1896; *Vicksburg Evening Post*, November 28, 1896; Jackson *Clarion-Ledger*, November 19, 1896.

25. Jackson *Clarion-Ledger*, November 19, 1896; *New York Times*, November 15, 1896.

26. Kosciusko *Alliance Vindicator*, August 28, 1896 (quotations).

27. *Vicksburg Evening Post*, October 26, 1896; Ackerman *Choctaw Plaindealer*, August 21, 1896.

28. Monticello *Lawrence County Press*, October 15, 1896; *Magnolia Gazette*, October 21, 1896; Columbia *Pearl River News*, October 16, 1896.

29. *Ripley Advertiser*, September 4 and October 15, 1896; Holly Springs *South*, October 1 and 8, 1896; Senatobia *North Mississippi Democrat*, October 16 and 30, 1896.

30. Friar's Point *Coahomian*, quoted in *Vicksburg Evening Post*, October 12, 1896 (quotation).

31. *Greenwood Enterprise*, October 16, 1896; Ackerman *Choctaw Plaindealer*, October 2, 1896 (quotations); *Vicksburg Evening Post*, October 22, 1896; *Grenada Sentinel*, September 26, 1896.

32. *Tupelo Journal*, October 30, 1896; *Vicksburg Evening Post*, October 9, 20, 21, and 24, 1896; Jackson *Clarion-Ledger*, October 15, 1896; *Greenwood Enterprise*, October 30, 1896 (quotation). Chalmers apparently admitted he was not a resident of the third district, but the U.S. Constitution requires only that members of Congress be *state* residents.

33. *Vicksburg Evening Post*, October 21 (first quotation), 20 (second quotation), and 23, 1896.

34. 1896 election returns, OER; Jackson *Clarion-Ledger*, November 19, 1896.

35. Holly Springs *South*, April 14, 1898; *New York Times*, April 24, 1898; *Franklin Advocate*, April 14, June 23, and December 1, 1898; Jackson *Clarion-Ledger*, September 14, 1899 (quotation).

36. Meadville *Franklin Advocate*, October 1, 1896; also July 28 and August 5, 12, 19, 1897.

37. Meadville *Franklin Advocate*, September 9 and 16, November 25, and December 2, 1897; also March 10 and 17, 1898.

38. Pontotoc *People's Banner*, December 3 and 10, 1897.

39. Boyle, *Cotton and the New Orleans Cotton Exchange*, 183–84; Meadville *Franklin Advocate*, September 8 (first quotation), and March 3, 1898 (subsequent quotations).

40. *Pontotoc Sentinel*, October 27, 1898; Jackson *Clarion-Ledger*, November 3, 1898.

41. Columbia *Pearl River News*, October 21 (first quotation), November 4 (second quotation) and 18, 1898; Meadville *Franklin Advocate*, November 10, 1898; Jackson *Clarion-Ledger*, November 24, 1898; 1898 Congressional Election Returns, OER.

42. Jackson *Clarion-Ledger*, November 17, 1898; Columbia *Pearl River News*, November 18, 1898.

43. Jackson *Clarion-Ledger*, August 24, 1899 (quotation); Ackerman *Choctaw Plaindealer*, September 1, 1899; Columbia *Pearl River News*, February 21, 1896; Pontotoc *People's Banner*, March 27, 1896; McCain, "The Populist Party in Mississippi," 106, 132–35.

44. Jackson *Clarion-Ledger*, September 21, 1899 (first quotation); *Sardis Reporter*, quoted in Jackson *Clarion-Ledger*, September 21, 1899 (second quotation); Senatobia *North Mississippi Democrat*, October 13, 1899 (third quotation); Kosciusko *Attala Democrat*, November 14, 1899.

45. Jackson *Clarion-Ledger*, September 21, 1899; Pontotoc *People's Banner*,

February 28, 1896; John R. Skates, *Mississippi's Old Capitol: Biography of a Building* (Jackson, 1990), 100–112.

46. Meadville *Franklin Advocate*, October 12, 1899.

47. *Magnolia Gazette*, October 21, 1899; Meadville *Franklin Advocate*, September 28, 1899.

48. *Magnolia Gazette*, October 18 and 21, 1899.

49. Ackerman *Choctaw Plaindealer*, November 3 (first quotation) and October 20, 1899; *Walthall Warden*, quoted in Jackson *Clarion-Ledger*, November 23, 1899 (second quotation); *Walthall Warden*, November 3, 1899.

50. Belen *Quitman Quill*, September 16, 1898 (quotations); Ackerman *Choctaw Plaindealer*, September 28, 1900.

51. *Magnolia Gazette*, July 22, 1899; *Pontotoc Sentinel*, June 29, 1899; *Walthall Warden*, October 20, 1899 (quotation).

52. Holmes, "Whitecapping," 165–85.

53. Meadville *Franklin Advocate*, September 8 and October 26, 1899.

54. Meadville *Franklin Advocate*, November 17 and December 28, 1898, and July 27, August 17, and October 12, 1899.

55. Meadville *Franklin Advocate*, November 9, 1899.

56. Pontotoc *People's Banner*, October 6 (quotation) and 13, 1899.

57. Pontotoc *People's Banner*, October 13, 1899 (quotations).

58. Pontotoc *People's Banner*, November 10, 1899.

59. Pontotoc *People's Banner*, November 10, 1899 (quotations).

60. *Brookhaven Leader*, November 15, 1899 (quotation); Meadville *Franklin Advocate*, November 16, 1899; *Pontotoc Sentinel*, November 23, 1899; Monticello *Lawrence County Press*, November 23, 1899. Prewitt was not a good loser; see Louisville *Winston County Journal*, November 10, 1899.

61. Ripley *Southern Sentinel*, November 9, 1899; Monticello *Lawrence County Press*, November 23, 1899; *Magnolia Gazette*, April 5, 1899. It is impossible to know precisely how many counties featured Populist opposition, since many 1899 newspaper titles are not extant.

62. Jackson *Clarion-Ledger*, August 23, 1900; *Appleton's Annual Cyclopaedia . . . 1900*, 338.

63. Ackerman *Choctaw Plaindealer*, October 26, 1900 (quotation).

64. Jackson *Clarion-Ledger*, October 11, 1900; *Vicksburg Herald*, extracted in Jackson *Clarion-Ledger*, October 18, 1900; Ackerman *Choctaw Plaindealer*, September 21, 1900; *Congressional Quarterly's Guide*, 342–46.

65. 1900 election returns, OER; *Congressional Quarterly's Guide*, 844.

66. Tindall, "The People's Party," 1725; McCain, "The Populist Party in Mississippi," 122–24; *Congressional Quarterly's Guide*, 345–47.

67. *Journal of the House . . . 1903*, 77, 482. Official returns, 1903 general election, volume 106, MSSP, DA&H. George Sheldon, former Republican

governor of Nebraska, was elected to the legislature in 1919, but was not a Republican nominee and was supported by the Democrats.

68. Jackson *Clarion-Ledger*, October 25, 1900; Meadville *Franklin Advocate*, September 10, 1903.

69. Natchez *Evening Bulletin*, November 8, 1899 (first quotation); Biloxi City Council Minutes, Biloxi City Hall, 10: 56–57; Belen *Quitman Quill*, November 11, 1898 (second quotation).

70. *Terry Headlight*, quoted in Columbia *Pearl River News*, November 18, 1898 (first quotations); Meadville *Franklin Advocate*, September 9, 1897 (fourth quotation).

71. *Vicksburg Evening Post*, October 20, 1896 (first quotations); E. F. Brennan, "An Address to the Republican Voters of the Seventh Congressional District of Mississippi," pamphlet, Hobbs Papers (third quotation); Jackson *Clarion-Ledger*, December 1, 1898 (fourth quotation).

72. Pontotoc *People's Banner*, March 6, 1896; *New York Times*, March 5, 1896.

73. Jackson *Clarion-Ledger*, August 24 (first quotations), and September 7, 1899; Ackerman *Choctaw Plaindealer*, November 23, 1900 (third quotation); *Greenwood Enterprise*, October 23, 1896 (fourth quotation).

74. Meadville *Franklin Advocate*, October 28, 1897 (quotations); Kosciusko *Attala Democrat*, September 24, 1899; *Magnolia Gazette*, September 30, 1899.

75. *Magnolia Gazette*, October 21, 1899; *Greenville Spirit*, quoted in *Vicksburg Evening Post*, November 2, 1898 (quotation); Kirwan, *Revolt of the Rednecks*, 116–17.

76. *Biennial Report of the Secretary of State* (1897), 45–51; Natchez *Evening Bulletin*, November 7, 1899; Jackson *Clarion-Ledger*, November 5, 1896, and November 17, 1898.

77. Hackney, *Populism to Progressivism in Alabama*, 27–29; 1894 congressional returns, OER.

78. Kirwan, *Revolt of the Rednecks*, 93–102; Ferguson, "Agrarianism in Mississippi," 325–32.

79. Louisville *Winston County Journal*, October 20, 1899 (quotation).

80. Boyle, *Cotton and the New Orleans Cotton Exchange*, 183–84.

81. Pontotoc *People's Banner*, February 14 (first quotation), and July 17 (second quotation), 1896; *Vicksburg Evening Post*, October 26, 1896.

82. *Remington Brothers' Newspaper Manual, Ninth (1896) Issue* (Pittsburgh and New York: Remington, 1896), 149–52; *Advertisers' Handy Guide, 1896*, 249–55; see also Cresswell, "Who Was Who."

83. *Neshoba Democrat*, November 14, 1895 (first quotation); Pontotoc *People's Banner*, January 1 (second quotation) and February 28, 1896; Jackson *Clarion-Ledger*, October 5, 1899.

84. Pontotoc *People's Banner*, February 28, 1895, and July 17, 1896.

85. *Grenada Sentinel*, September 12, 1896; Meadville *Franklin Advocate*, October 26, 1899; Kosciusko *Attala Democrat*, October 31, 1899; Jackson *Clarion-Ledger*, September 15, 1898.

86. Pontotoc *People's Banner*, January 10 and March 27, 1896; Meadville *Franklin Advocate*, October 14, 1897 (quotations).

87. While a few Mississippi newspapers did occasionally allege that the state's Populists were seeking black votes, Populist editors sometimes made the same charge about Democratic candidates.

88. Kousser, *The Shaping of Southern Politics*, 145.

89. Ackerman *Choctaw Plaindealer*, November 15, 1895, and March 8, 1901.

90. Several excellent studies of various states' People's parties have addressed the question of who the Populists were. A number of these monographs are listed in the Bibliography; for a thorough bibliographic overview of them, see William F. Holmes, "Populism: In Search of Context," *Agricultural History* 64 (1990): 26–58.

91. Personal Property Tax Assessment Books, 1895, for Amite, Attala, Choctaw, Lauderdale, and Webster counties, in Auditor of Public Accounts Records, Record Group 29, DA&H. The sample was made up of the first and fifth names listed on each page of each book. Arrangement in the books was by precinct, then alphabetical by name.

92. Personal property tax data indicates that both the Populist and the Democratic candidates were experiencing declining fortunes over the two or three years before 1895; the decline was at about the same rate for the two parties.

93. The best overview of regional trends in Populist strength is in Holmes, "Populism: In Search of Context," 26, 35–51.

94. Admittedly, a remaining mystery is why some nearby white counties that also featured high rates of farm ownership and extensive farming of corn were weaker in their support of the Populists. It is hoped that future studies of individual counties will shed further light.

95. Hahn, *The Roots of Southern Populism*; Barton Shaw, *The Wool-Hat Boys: Georgia's Populist Party* (Baton Rouge, La., 1984); Holmes, "Populism: In Search of Context," 35.

96. Jackson *Clarion-Ledger*, February 19, 1896 (quotation); McCain, "The Populist Party in Mississippi," 74. My discussion is based largely on Populist platforms; see Pontotoc *People's Banner*, January 3, 1896, and Jackson *Clarion-Ledger*, August 24, 1899. For other discussions of Populism's conservative or progressive nature, see Holmes, "Populism: In Search of Context," 55–58, and Tindall, "The People's Party," 1727–29.

97. On claims of various groups to Jacksonianism, see Ford, "Rednecks and

Merchants," 294, 316–18; also Hyman, *The Anti-Redeemers*, 143–66, 196–97.

98. Holmes, "Populism: In Search of Context," 43, 58. One of several authors portraying the Populists in an anticapitalist light is Bruce Palmer, *"Man Over Money": The Southern Populist Critique of American Capitalism* (Chapel Hill, N.C., 1980).

99. Ferguson, "Agrarianism in Mississippi," 525 (quotation), 542; Kirwan, *Revolt of the Rednecks*, 91.

100. Kirwan, *Revolt of the Rednecks*, 101–2, 146; McCain, "The Populist Party in Mississippi," 145–46; Mississippi, Secretary of State, *Official and Statistical Register of the State of Mississippi, 1912* (Nashville, 1912), 369–461. A number of southern former Populists turned to racist rhetoric around the turn of the century, most notably Tom Watson of Georgia.

101. *Walthall Warden*, November 4, 1904.

7. CONCLUSION

1. "Buchanan vs. Manning," 21 (quotation).

2. Edward Mayes, *Lucius Q. C. Lamar: His Life, Times, and Speeches, 1825–1893* (Nashville, 1896), 435 (quotations); *Congressional Quarterly's Guide*, 511.

3. Ferguson, "Agrarianism in Mississippi," 407 (quotation).

4. *Vicksburg Evening Post*, November 4, 1885 (quotation); *Congressional Quarterly's Guide*, 511, 803.

5. Jackson *Clarion-Ledger*, October 10, 1889 (first quotation); *New York Times*, February 24, 1892.

6. Mayes, *Lucius Q. C. Lamar*, 553 (quotation).

7. McCain, "The Populist Party in Mississippi," 70, 115; Kirwan, *Revolt of the Rednecks*, 101. For information about Populist candidates at each election, see Cresswell, "Who Was Who."

8. 1894 Congressional Returns, 1895 and 1899 Gubernatorial Returns, OER; *Congressional Quarterly's Guide*, 511, 830, 345–47; Boyle, *Cotton and the New Orleans Cotton Exchange*, 183–84.

9. Kirwan, *Revolt of the Rednecks*, 91; Ferguson, "Agrarianism in Mississippi," 525, 542, 612.

10. Hyman, *The Anti-Redeemers*, 11, 22–23.

11. Hyman, *The Anti-Redeemers*, 22.

12. Stephen Cresswell, "Red Mississippi: The State's Socialist Party, 1904–1922," *Journal of Mississippi History* 50 (1988): 153–71; idem, "Grassroots Radicalism in the Magnolia State: Mississippi's Socialist Movement at the State and Local Level, 1910–1919," *Labor History* 33 (1992): 81–101.

13. Columbus *Patron of Husbandry*, November 26, 1881 (first quotations);

Cumberland *Mississippi Populist*, April 26, 1894 (third quotation); Pontotoc *People's Banner*, September 27, 1894 (fourth quotation); Cresswell, "Red Mississippi," 153–71.

14. For information about these individuals and others, see Cresswell, "Who Was Who."

15. For movement between parties over time, see ibid.

16. Robert F. Durden, *The Self-Inflicted Wound: Southern Politics in the Nineteenth Century* (Lexington, Ky., 1985).

17. "Mississippi in 1883," xx.

18. *Vicksburg Evening Post*, November 2, 1885 (quotations). The quoted letter was addressed to black Republican Cyrus J. Marshall; a similar letter led white sheriff candidate R. F. Beck to withdraw; see *Vicksburg Evening Post*, November 3 and 4, 1885.

19. *Tupelo Journal*, August 1, 1890 (quotation).

20. *Walthall Warden*, October 18, 1907 (first quotation); Jackson *Weekly Clarion*, October 24, 1877 (second and third quotations); *Macon Beacon*, October 28 (fourth quotation) and November 5 (fifth quotation), 1881.

21. Wright, *Old South, New South*, 97–99; Ransom and Sutch, *One Kind of Freedom*, 109–37.

22. Memphis *Commercial-Appeal*, September 26, 1895 (first quotation); *Grenada Sentinel*, September 3, 1892 (second quotation).

23. *New York Tribune*, July 30, 1880 (first quotations); Greene C. Chandler to Charles Devens, December 13, 1880 (fourth quotation), Source-Chronological file, RDJ, Record Group 60, National Archives.

24. "Buchanan vs. Manning," 32 (quotations), 37–38.

25. Ibid. 51–57, 304–5.

26. "Buchanan vs. Manning"; *Congressional Quarterly's Guide*, 799. For the investigating committee's recommendations, see "Buchanan vs. Manning: Report."

27. Cresswell, *Mormons and Cowboys*, 19–78; idem, "Enforcing the Enforcement Acts," 421–40; "Chalmers vs. Manning," 5–9.

28. *United States v. James Ruffin et al.* (1881), Docket number 1796, Docket Book IV: 69, and Record Book V: 239–42, RDC, Federal Records Center, East Point, Georgia; *United States v. James Evans et al.* (1880), Docket number 1789, Docket Book IV: 62, and Record Book V: 152–53, RDC; *United States v. Alfonzo Garmon* (1881), Docket number 1802, Docket Book IV: 75, and Record Book V: 163–65, RDC. These are the cases from Panola, Monroe, and Lee counties, respectively. "Buchanan vs. Manning," 5–9.

29. Cresswell, *Mormons and Cowboys*, 19–78; Miller, "'Let Us Die to Make Men Free,'" 460. Note that the 201 prosecutions often involved multiple defendants. U.S. Department of Justice, *Annual Report of the Attorney General of the United States*, 1881–1888 (Washington, D.C., 1881–88), table B1 for

each year. Two cases were tried in the early part of *fiscal* year 1885, before the Democratic administration took office.

30. *Tupelo Journal*, October 7, 1892 (first quotation); *Meridian Standard*, quoted in *Tupelo Journal*, October 7, 1892 (subsequent quotations).

31. Carthage *Carthaginian*, October 28, 1892 (quotation).

32. Kousser, *The Shaping of Southern Politics*, 72 (quotations).

33. Jackson *Clarion-Ledger*, October 29, 1896 (quotation).

34. *A Compendium of the Ninth Census*, 236–40; *Abstract of the Twelfth Census*, 142.

35. U.S. Bureau of the Census, *Statistics of the Wealth and Industry of the United States* (Washington, D.C., 1872), 184–87; *Abstract of the Twelfth Census*, 258–87, 332; *A Compendium of the Ninth Census*, 796–97.

36. Ransom and Sutch, *One Kind of Freedom*, 163–65.

37. *Abstract of the Twelfth Census*, 295.

38. The estimates of voter participation were prepared by Walter Dean Burnham and published in *Historical Statistics of the United States, Colonial Times to 1970*, 2 vols. (Washington, D.C., 1975), 2: 1067–69, 1071–72. Note that in this and the following paragraphs, "eligible voters" refers to persons who were legally eligible to register, and not to persons who had actually registered. Kousser, *The Shaping of Southern Politics*, 72–80; Kirwan, *Revolt of the Rednecks*, 114–29.

39. *Official and Statistical Register*, 124. My figures on white voter participation are based on the figures cited above from *Historical Statistics*, 2: 1071–72; I have made calculations based on the percentage of the population that was black at the time of the different censuses. The estimates of turnout by race must be regarded as mere approximations; strict accuracy is not possible.

40. Kirwan, *Revolt of the Rednecks*, 125–26, 185–90, 230.

41. Ibid., 146 (first quotation), 147 (second quotation), 143–45.

42. Ferguson, "Agrarianism in Mississippi," 615–16; Kirwan, *Revolt of the Rednecks*, 101–2; Charles Granville Hamilton, "Mississippi Politics in the Progressive Era, 1904–1920" (Ph.D. dissertation, Vanderbilt University, 1958), 1–12.

43. *Historical Statistics*, 2: 1071–72. Once again, I have calculated estimates of white participation using on the percentage of the state's population that was white in 1910. This white participation figure must be regarded as an approximation.

44. Cresswell, "Red Mississippi"; idem, "Grassroots Radicalism."

45. Guy Paul Land, "Mississippi Republicanism and the 1960 Presidential Election," *Journal of Mississippi History* 40 (1978): 33–48; Hathorn, "Challenging the Status Quo," 240–64.

46. James Edward Cliatt, "The Republican Party in Mississippi, 1952–1960," (M.A. thesis, Mississippi State University, 1964); Martha Huddleston

Wilkins, "The Development of the Mississippi Republican Party," (M.A. thesis, Mississippi College, 1965).

47. *Statistics of the Wealth and Industry*, 376–79; *Abstract of the Twelfth Census*, 51.

Bibliography

BOOKS

Abney, F. Glenn. *Mississippi Election Statistics: 1900–1967*. University, Miss.: Bureau of Governmental Research, 1968.

Anderson, Lee F., Meredith W. Watts, and Allen Wilcox, *Legislative Roll-Call Analysis*. Evanston, Ill.: Northwestern University Press, 1966.

Ayers, Edward L. *The Promise of the New South: Life After Reconstruction*. New York: Oxford University Press, 1992.

Bailey, Thomas Jefferson. *Prohibition in Mississippi, Or, Anti-Liquor Legislation from Territorial Days, with Its Results in the Counties*. Jackson, Miss.: n.p., 1917.

Billington, Monroe Lee. *Thomas P. Gore: The Blind Senator from Oklahoma*. Lawrence: University of Kansas Press, 1967.

Biographical and Historical Memoirs of Mississippi. 2 vols. Chicago: Goodspeed, 1891.

Blocker, Jack S. *Retreat from Reform: The Prohibition Movement in the United States, 1890–1913*. Westport, Conn.: Greenwood Press, 1976.

Boyle, James E. *Cotton and the New Orleans Cotton Exchange: A Century of Commercial Evolution*. Garden City, N.Y.: Dutton, 1934.

Brandfon, Robert L. *Cotton Kingdom of the New South: A History of the Yazoo Mississippi Delta from Reconstruction to the Twentieth Century*. Cambridge: Harvard University Press, 1967.

Burnham, W. Dean. *Presidential Ballots: 1836–1892*. Baltimore: Johns Hopkins University Press, 1955.

Chandler, Greene C. *Journal and Speeches of Greene Callier Chandler*. N.p.: Privately printed, 1953.

Colvin, D. Leigh. *Prohibition in the United States: A History of the Prohibition Party and of the Prohibition Movement*. New York: Doran, 1926.

Congressional Quarterly's Guide to U.S. Elections. 2nd ed. Washington: Congressional Quarterly, 1985.

Cresswell, Stephen. *Mormons and Cowboys, Moonshiners and Klansmen: Federal Law Enforcement in the South and West, 1870–1893*. Tuscaloosa: University of Alabama Press, 1991.

Degler, Carl N. *The Other South: Southern Dissenters in the Nineteenth Century.* New York: Harper and Row, 1974.

DeSantis, Vincent P. *Republicans Face the Southern Question: The New Departure Years, 1877–1897.* Baltimore: Johns Hopkins University Press, 1959.

Durden, Robert F. *The Climax of Populism: The Election of 1896.* Lexington: University Press of Kentucky, 1965.

———. *The Self-inflicted Wound: Southern Politics in the Nineteenth Century.* Lexington: University Press of Kentucky, 1985.

Ellis, John H. *Yellow Fever and Public Health in the New South.* Lexington: University of Kentucky Press, 1992.

Fine, Nathan. *Labor and Farmer Parties in the United States: 1828–1928.* New York: Rand School of the Social Sciences, 1928.

Foner, Eric. *Reconstruction: America's Unfinished Revolution, 1863–1877.* New York: Harper and Row, 1988.

Garner, James W. *Reconstruction in Mississippi.* 1901. Reprint. Baton Rouge: Louisiana State University Press, 1968.

Gillette, William. *Retreat from Reconstruction, 1869–1879.* Baton Rouge: Louisiana State University Press, 1979.

Goldman, Robert M. *"A Free Ballot and a Fair Count": The Department of Justice and the Enforcement of Voting Rights in the South, 1877–1893.* New York: Garland Publishing, 1990.

Goodwyn, Lawrence. *The Populist Moment: A Short History of the Agrarian Revolt in America.* New York: Oxford University Press, 1978.

Grantham, Dewey. *Life and Death of the Solid South.* Lexington: University Press of Kentucky, 1988.

Hackney, Sheldon. *Populism to Progressivism in Alabama.* Princeton, N.J.: Princeton University Press, 1969.

Hahn, Steven. *The Roots of Southern Populism: The Transformation of the Georgia Upcountry, 1850–1890.* New York: Oxford University Press, 1983.

Hair, William I. *Bourbonism and Agrarian Protest: Louisiana Politics, 1877–1900.* Baton Rouge: Louisiana State University Press, 1969.

Harris, William C. *The Day of the Carpetbagger: Republican Reconstruction in Mississippi.* Baton Rouge: Louisiana State University Press, 1979.

———. *Presidential Reconstruction in Mississippi.* Baton Rouge: Louisiana State University Press, 1967.

Hirshson, Stanley P. *Farewell to the Bloody Shirt: Northern Republicans and the Southern Negro, 1877–1893.* Bloomington: Indiana University Press, 1962.

History of Webster County, Mississippi. N.p.: Curtis Media and Webster County Historical Association, 1985.

Hofstadter, Richard. *The Age of Reform: From Bryan to F.D.R.* New York: Alfred A. Knopf, 1955.

Hyman, Michael R. *The Anti-Redeemers: Hill-Country Political Dissenters in the*

Lower South from Redemption to Populism. Baton Rouge: Louisiana State University Press, 1990.

Key, V. O., with Alexander Heard. *Southern Politics in State and Nation.* New York: Alfred A. Knopf, 1949.

Kirwan, Albert D. *Revolt of the Rednecks: Mississippi Politics, 1876–1925.* Lexington: University of Kentucky Press, 1951.

Kousser, J. Morgan. *The Shaping of Southern Politics: Suffrage Restriction and the Establishment of the One-Party South, 1880–1910.* New Haven, Conn.: Yale University Press, 1974.

Lynch, John Roy. *The Facts of Reconstruction.* 1913. Reprint. New York: Arno Press, 1968.

———. *Reminiscences of an Active Life: the Autobiography of John Roy Lynch,* edited and with an introduction by John Hope Franklin. Chicago: University of Chicago Press, 1970.

McLemore, Richard Aubrey, ed. *A History of Mississippi.* 2 vols. Jackson: University and College Press of Mississippi, 1973.

McMillen, Neil R. *Dark Journey: Black Mississippians in the Age of Jim Crow.* Urbana: University of Illinois Press, 1989.

Mayes, Edward. *Lucius Q. C. Lamar: His Life, Times, and Speeches, 1825–1893.* Nashville: Publishing House of the Methodist Episcopal Church, South, 1896.

Morgan, A. T. *Yazoo, or On the Picket Line of Freedom in the South.* 1884. Reprint. New York: Russell and Russell, 1968.

Palmer, Bruce. *"Man Over Money": The Southern Populist Critique of American Capitalism.* Chapel Hill: University of North Carolina Press, 1980.

Pereyra, Lillian A. *James Lusk Alcorn: Persistent Whig.* Baton Rouge: Louisiana State University Press, 1966.

Perman, Michael. *The Road to Redemption: Southern Politics, 1869–1879.* Chapel Hill: University of North Carolina Press, 1984.

Pollock, Norman. *The Populist Response to Industrial America.* Cambridge: Harvard University Press, 1962.

Rabinowitz, Howard N., ed. *Southern Black Leaders of the Reconstruction Era.* Urbana: University of Illinois Press, 1982.

Ransom, Roger L., and Richard Sutch. *One Kind of Freedom: The Economic Consequences of Emancipation.* Cambridge: Cambridge University Press, 1977.

Rogers, William Warren. *The One-Gallused Rebellion: Agrarianism in Alabama, 1865–1896.* Baton Rouge: Louisiana State University Press, 1970.

Rowland, Dunbar. *History of Mississippi: Heart of the South.* Chicago: S. J. Clarke, 1925.

Schlesinger, Arthur M., Jr., ed. *History of U.S. Political Parties.* 4 vols. New York: Chelsea House, 1973.

Shaw, Barton. *The Wool-Hat Boys: Georgia's Populist Party*. Baton Rouge: Louisiana State University Press, 1984.

Sherman, John. *Recollections of Forty Years in the House, Senate, and Cabinet*. 2 vols. Chicago: Werner, 1895.

Sherman, Richard B. *The Republican Party and Black America from McKinley to Hoover, 1896–1933*. Charlottesville: University Press of Virginia, 1973.

Sifakis, Stewart. *Who Was Who in the Civil War*. New York: Facts on File, 1988.

Skates, John R. *Mississippi's Old Capitol: Biography of a Building*. Jackson: Mississippi Department of Archives and History, 1990.

Standard Encyclopedia of the Alcohol Problem. 6 vols. Westerville, Ohio: American Issue Publishing, 1925.

Storms, Roger C. *Partisan Prophets: A History of the Prohibition Party*. Denver: National Prohibition Foundation, 1972.

Tindall, George Brown. *The Disruption of the Solid South*. New York: Norton, 1972.

———. *The Emergence of the New South, 1913–1945*. Baton Rouge: Louisiana State University Press, 1967.

———. *The Persistant Tradition in New South Politics*. Baton Rouge: Louisiana State University Press, 1975.

Unger, Irwin. *The Greenback Era: A Social and Political History of American Finance, 1865–1879*. Princeton, N.J.: Princeton University Press, 1964.

Wells, James M. *The Chisholm Massacre: A Picture of "Home Rule" in Mississippi*. 3rd ed. Washington, D.C.: Chisholm Monument Association, 1878.

Wharton, Vernon Lane. *The Negro in Mississippi, 1865–1890*. Chapel Hill: University of North Carolina Press, 1947.

Woodward, C. Vann. *Origins of the New South, 1877–1913*. Rev. ed. Baton Rouge: Louisiana State University Press, 1971.

———. *Reunion and Reaction: The Compromise of 1877 and the End of Reconstruction*. Rev. ed. New York: Oxford University Press, 1991.

———. *The Strange Career of Jim Crow*. 3rd rev. ed. New York: Oxford University Press, 1974.

Wright, Gavin. *Old South, New South: Revolutions in the Southern Economy Since the Civil War*. New York: Basic Books, 1986.

Articles, Chapters, Theses, Dissertations, and Unpublished Manuscripts

Barjenbruch, Judith. "The Greenback Political Movement: An Arkansas View." *Arkansas Historical Quarterly* 36 (1977): 107–22.

Barr, Alwyn. "B. J. Chambers and the Greenback Party Split." *Mid-America* 49 (1967): 276–84.

Bond, Bradley G. "Edward C. Walthall and the 1880 Senatorial Nomination: Politics of Balance in the Redeemer Era." *Journal of Mississippi History* 50 (1988): 1–20.

Boschert, Thomas N. "The Politics of Expediency: Fusion in the Mississippi Delta, Late Nineteenth-Century." M.A. thesis, University of Mississippi, 1985.

Broadway, Lilibel. "Frank Burkitt: the Man in the Wool Hat." M.A. thesis, Mississippi State University, 1948.

Clark, Eric C. "Legislative Reapportionment in the 1890 Constitutional Convention." *Journal of Mississippi History* 42 (1980): 298–315.

Clark, Thomas D. "The Furnishing and Supply System in Southern Agriculture Since 1865." *Journal of Southern History* 12 (1946): 24–44.

Cliatt, James Edward. "The Republican Party in Mississippi, 1952–1960." M.A. thesis, Mississippi State University, 1964.

Coleman, James P. "The Mississippi Constitution of 1890 and the Final Decade of the Nineteenth Century." In *A History of Mississippi*, vol. 2, edited by Richard Aubrey McLemore, 3–28. Jackson: University Press of Mississippi, 1973.

Cresswell, Stephen. "Enforcing the Enforcement Acts: The Department of Justice in Northern Mississippi, 1870–1890." *Journal of Southern History* 53 (1987): 421–40.

———. "Grassroots Radicalism in the Magnolia State: Mississippi's Socialist Movement at the Local Level, 1910–1919." *Labor History* 33 (1992): 81–101.

———. "Red Mississippi: The State's Socialist Party, 1904–1922." *Journal of Mississippi History* 50 (1988): 153–71.

———. "Who Was Who in Mississippi's Opposition Political Parties, 1878–1963." Unpublished typescript, 1994. Copy at Mississippi Department of Archives and History, Jackson.

DeSantis, Vincent P. "President Arthur and the Independent Movements in the South in 1882." *Journal of Southern History* 19 (1952): 346–63.

Doolen, Richard M. "The Greenback Party in the Great Lakes Middlewest." Ph.D. dissertation, University of Michigan, 1969.

———. "The National Greenback Party in Michigan Politics, 1876–1888." *Michigan History* 47 (1963): 161–83.

Edwards, Thomas S. "'Reconstructing' Reconstruction: Changing Historical Paradigms in Mississippi." *Journal of Mississippi History* 51 (1989): 165–80.

Ellem, Warren A. "The Overthrow of Reconstruction in Mississippi." *Journal of Mississippi History* 54 (1992): 175–201.

———. "Who Were the Mississippi Scalawags?" *Journal of Southern History* 38 (1972): 217–40.

Ferguson, James S. "Agarianism in Mississippi, 1871–1900: A Study in Non-conformity." Ph.D. dissertation, University of North Carolina at Chapel Hill, 1952.

Ford, Lacy K. "Rednecks and Merchants: Economic Development and Social Tensions in the South Carolina Upcountry, 1865–1900." *Journal of American History* 71 (1984): 294–318.

Gardner, Bettye J. "William H. Foote and Yazoo County Politics, 1866–1883." *Southern Studies*, Winter 1982, 398–407.

Halsell, Willie D. "The Bourbon Period in Mississippi Politics, 1875–1890." *Journal of Southern History* 11 (1945): 519–37.

———. "Democratic Dissentions in Mississippi, 1878–1882." *Journal of Mississippi History* 2 (1940): 123–35.

———. "James R. Chalmers and 'Mahoneism' in Mississippi." *Journal of Southern History* 10 (1944): 37–58.

Halsell, Willie D., ed. "Republican Factionalism in Mississippi, 1882–1884." *Journal of Southern History* 7 (1941): 84–101.

Hamilton, Charles Granville. "Mississippi Politics in the Progressive Era, 1904–1920." Ph.D. dissertation, Vanderbilt University, 1958.

Harris, Carl V. "Right Fork or Left Fork? The Section-Party Alignments of Southern Democrats in Congress, 1873–1897." *Journal of Southern History* 42 (1976): 471–506.

Hathorn, Billy Burton. "Challenging the Status Quo: Rubel Lex Phillips and the Mississippi Republican Party, 1963–1967." *Journal of Mississippi History* 47 (1985): 240–64.

Henningson, Berton E., Jr. "Root Hog or Die: The Brothers of Freedom and the 1884 Arkansas Election." *Arkansas Historical Quarterly* 45 (1986): 197–216.

Holmes, William F. "Populism: In Search of Context." *Agricultural History* 64 (1990): 26–58.

———. "Whitecapping: Agrarian Violence in Mississippi, 1902–1906." *Journal of Southern History* 35 (1969): 165–85.

Horton, Paul. "The Culture, Social Structure, and Political Economy of Antebellum Lawrence County, Alabama." *Alabama Review* 41 (1988): 243–70.

———. "Testing the Limits of Class Politics in Postbellum Alabama: Agrarian Radicalism in Lawrence County." *Journal of Southern History* 57 (1991): 63–84.

Hurns, Walter McClusky. "Post-Reconstruction Municipal Politics in Jackson, Mississippi." Ph.D. dissertation, Kansas State University, 1989.

Hyman, Michael R. "Taxation, Public Policy, and Political Dissent: Yeoman Disaffection in the Post-Reconstruction Lower South." *Journal of Southern History* 55 (1989): 49–76.

Jackson, Harvey H. "Middle-Class Democracy Victorious: The Mitcham War of Clarke County, Alabama." *Journal of Southern History* 57 (1991): 453–78.

Jay, Margaret Buker. "The Greenback Road: A Political History of the Greenback Party in Maine." M.A. thesis, University of Virginia, 1977.

Kleppner, Paul. "The Greenback and Prohibition Parties." In *History of U.S. Political Parties*, vol. 2, edited by Arthur M. Schlesinger, Jr., 1549–81. New York: Chelsea House, 1973.

Land, Guy Paul. "Mississippi Republicanism and the 1960 Presidential Election." *Journal of Mississippi History* 40 (1978): 33–48.

Latham, Robert C. "The Dirt Farmer in Politics: A Study of Webster County, Mississippi During the Rise of Democratic Factionalism, 1880–1910." M.A. thesis, Mississippi State College, 1951.

Legan, Marshall Scott. "Mississippi and the Yellow Fever Epidemics of 1878–1879." *Journal of Mississippi History* 33 (1971): 199–217.

Luebke, Frederick C. "Main Street and the Countryside: Patterns of Voting in Nebraska During the Populist Era." *Nebraska History* 50 (1969): 257–75.

McCain, William David. "The Populist Party in Mississippi." M.A. thesis, University of Mississippi, 1931.

McMillen, Neil R. "Black Journalism in Mississippi: The Jim Crow Years." *Journal of Mississippi History* 49 (1987): 129–38.

Martin, Roscoe E. "The Greenback Party in Texas." *Southwestern Historical Quarterly* 30 (1927): 161–77.

Mauldin, Douglas L. "Whig and Republican Voting Trends in Mississippi." M.A. thesis, Mississippi State University, 1963.

Miller, Clark Leonard. "'Let Us Die to Make Men Free': Political Terrorism in Post-Reconstruction Mississippi, 1877–1896." Ph.D. dissertation, University of Minnesota, 1983.

Patton, W. H. "History of the Prohibition Movement in Mississippi," *Publications of the Mississippi Historical Society* 10 (1909): 181–201.

Revels, James G. "Redeemers, Rednecks, and Racial Integrity." In *A History of Mississippi*, vol. 1, edited by Richard Aubrey McLemore, 590–621. Jackson: University Press of Mississippi, 1973.

Ricker, Ralph R. "The Greenback-Labor Movement in Pennsylvania." Ph.D. dissertation, Pennsylvania State University, 1955.

Sallis, William Charles. "The Color Line in Mississippi Politics: 1865–1915." Ph.D. dissertation, University of Kentucky, 1967.

Sansing, David G. "Congressional Reconstruction." In *A History of Mississippi*, vol. 1, edited by Richard Aubrey McLemore, 571–89. Jackson: University Press of Mississippi, 1973.

Stone, James H. "A Note on Voter Registration Under the Mississippi Understanding Clause, 1892." *Journal of Southern History* 38 (1972): 293–96.

———. "General Absalom Madden West and the Civil War in Mississippi." *Journal of Mississippi History* 42 (1980): 135–44.

Tindall, George W. "The People's Party." In *History of U.S. Political Parties*, vol. 2, edited by Arthur M. Schlesinger, Jr., 1701–68. New York: Chelsea House, 1973.

Webb, Samuel L. "From Independents to Populists to Progressive Republicans: The Case of Chilton County, Alabama, 1880–1920." *Journal of Southern History* 59 (1993): 707–36.

Wilkins, Martha Huddleston. "The Development of the Mississippi Republican Party." M.A. thesis, Mississippi College, 1965.

MANUSCRIPT GOVERNMENT RECORDS

National

United States Bureau of the Census. Census of Population, Record Group 29, National Archives, Washington, D.C. Returns examined for the tenth and twelfth censuses, 1880 and 1900. (Most returns for the 1890 census, including all those for Mississippi, were destroyed by fire.)

United States Department of Justice. Records of the Department of Justice, Record Group 60, National Archives, Washington, D.C.

United States District Court for Northern Mississippi. Record Books, Docket Books, and Minute Books. Federal Records Center, East Point, Georgia.

State

Mississippi. Auditor of Public Accounts. Official records, Record Group 29. Personal Property Tax Rolls. Mississippi Department of Archives and History, Jackson.

Mississippi. Governor. Official Records, Record Group 27. Mississippi Department of Archives and History, Jackson.

Mississippi. Secretary of State. Official Records, Record Group 28. Department of Archives and History, Jackson.

County

Benton County. Board of Supervisors. Minute Books, 1879–1882. Benton County Courthouse, Ashland.

Yalobusha County. Board of Supervisors. Minute Books, 1879–1881. Mississippi Department of Archives and History, Jackson.

PUBLISHED GOVERNMENT DOCUMENTS

National

Biographical Directory of the American Congress, 1774–1971. Washington, D.C.: G.P.O., 1971.

United States Bureau of the Census. *Abstract of the Twelfth Census of the United States, 1900.* Washington, D.C.: G.P.O., 1902.

United States Bureau of the Census. *A Compendium of the Ninth Census, June 1, 1870.* Washington, D.C.: G.P.O., 1872.

United States Bureau of the Census. *Historical Statistics of the United States, from Colonial Times to 1970.* 2 vols. Washington, D.C.: G.P.O., 1975.

United States Bureau of the Census. *Report on Cotton Production in the United States.* Washington, D.C.: G.P.O., 1884.

United States Bureau of the Census. *Report on the Productions of Agriculture as Returned at the Tenth Census, June 1, 1880, Embracing General Statistics.* Washington, D.C.: G.P.O., 1883.

United States Bureau of the Census. *Report on the Statistics of Agriculture in the United States at the Eleventh Census, 1890.* Washington, D.C.: G.P.O., 1896.

United States Bureau of the Census. *Report on Valuation, Taxation, and Public Indebtedness in the United States, as Returned at the Tenth Census.* Washington, D.C.: G.P.O., 1884.

United States Bureau of the Census. *Statistics of the Population of the United States at the Tenth Census.* Washington, D.C.: G.P.O., 1883.

United States Bureau of the Census. *Statistics of the Wealth and Industry of the United States.* Washington, D.C.: G.P.O., 1872.

United States Bureau of the Census. *Twelfth Census of the United States, Taken in the Year 1900: Population.* 2 vols. Washington, D.C.: G.P.O., 1901.

United States Congress. House. "Brown vs. Allen." H. Rept. 1538, 54th Cong., 1st sess. (1894).

United States Congress. House. "Buchanan vs. Manning." H. Misc. Doc. 14, 47th Cong., 1st sess. (1881).

United States Congress. House. "Buchanan vs. Manning: Report." H. Repts. 1890 and 1891, 47th Cong., 2nd sess. (1883).

United States Congress. House. "Chalmers vs. Manning." H. Misc. Doc. 15, 48th Cong., 1st sess. (1884).

United States Congress. House. "Chalmers vs. Morgan." H. Rept. 2503, 51st Cong., 1st sess. (1890).

United States Congress. House. "Hill vs. Catchings." H. Rept. 4005, 51st Cong., 2nd sess. (1891).

United States Congress. House. "Newman vs. Spencer." H. Rept. 1536, 54th Cong., 1st sess. (1894).

United States Congress. House. "Ratliff vs. Williams." H. Rept. 1537, 54th Cong., 1st sess. (1894).

United States Congress. House. "Records of the Chief Supervisors of Elections for the Northern District of Mississippi." H. Misc. Doc. 48, 48th Cong., 1st sess. (1884).

United States Congress. Senate. "Mississippi in 1878." S. Rept. 855, 45th Cong., 3rd sess. (1879).

United States Congress. Senate. "Mississippi in 1883." S. Rept. 512, 48th Cong., 1st sess. (1884).

United States Department of Justice. *Annual Report of the Attorney General of the United States.* Washington, D.C.: G.P.O., 1878–88.

State

Mississippi. Auditor of Public Accounts. *Biennial Report of the Auditor of Public Accounts [1899–1901].* Jackson: Clarion-Ledger, 1901.

Mississippi. Constitutional Convention [1890]. *Journal of the Proceedings of the Constitutional Convention of the State of Mississippi.* Jackson: E. L. Martin, 1890.

Mississippi Legislature. House of Representatives. *Journal of the House of Representatives of the State of Mississippi.* Imprint varies. 1878–1904.

Mississippi Legislature. Senate. *Journal of the Senate of the State of Mississippi.* Imprint varies. 1878–1904.

Mississippi Secretary of State. *Biennial Report of the Secretary of State to the Legislature of Mississippi.* Imprint varies. 1878–1904.

Mississippi. Secretary of State. *Official and Statistical Register of the State of Mississippi, 1912.* Nashville: Brandon, 1912.

CONTEMPORARY PAMPHLETS

Brennan, E. F. "An Address to the Republican Voters of the Seventh Congressional District of Mississippi." N.p., 1898. Pamphlet in the Benjamin T. Hobbs Papers, Special Collections, Mitchell Memorial Library, Mississippi State University, Starkville.

Burkitt, Frank. "Our State Finances and Our School System, Illustrated and Exposed by 'Wool Hat.' . . ." Okolona, Miss.: Messenger Power Print, 1886. Copy in Special Collections, Mitchell Memorial Library, Mississippi State University, Starkville.

Randall, J. H. "The Political Catechism and Greenback Song-Book." Washington, D.C.: Rufus H. Darby, 1880. Copy at United States Senate Library, Washington.

MANUSCRIPT AND SPECIAL COLLECTIONS

Arthur, Chester A. Papers. Manuscripts Division, Library of Congress, Washington, D.C.

Burkitt, Frank. Papers. Special Collections, Mitchell Memorial Library, Mississippi State University, Starkville.

Butler, Marion. Papers. Southern Historical Collection, University of North Carolina at Chapel Hill.

Co-opolis File. Local History Collection, Biloxi Public Library, Biloxi.

Hobbs, Benjamin T. Papers. Special Collections, Mitchell Memorial Library, Mississippi State University, Starkville.

McKinley, William. Papers. Manuscripts Division, Library of Congress, Washington, D.C.

Roosevelt, Theodore. Papers. Manuscripts Division, Library of Congress, Washington, D.C.

CONTEMPORARY ANNUAL REFERENCE BOOKS

Advertiser's Handy Guide. New York: Morse, 1895, 1896.

American Newspaper Directory. New York: Printer's Ink Publishing Company, 1903, 1908.

Appleton's Annual Cyclopaedia and Register of Important Events of the Year. New York: Appleton, 1876–1902.

Remington Brother's Newspaper Manual, Ninth (1896) Issue. Pittsburgh and New York: Remington, 1896.

Rowell's American Newspaper Directory. New York: Rowell, 1879–1883.

Vicksburg City Directory. Vicksburg, Miss.: Vicksburg Printing and Publishing, 1895.

Index